Lives of Promise

Lives of Promise

What Becomes of High School Valedictorians

A Fourteen-Year Study of Achievement and Life Choices

Karen D. Arnold

Jossey-Bass Publishers • San Francisco

· Substantial discounts on bulk quantities of Jossey-Bass books are available to corporations, professional associations, and other organizations. For details and discount information, contact the special sales department at Jossey-Bass Inc., Publishers.
(415) 433–1740; Fax (800) 605–2665.

For sales outside the United States, please contact your local Paramount Publishing International Office.

 Manufactured in the United States of America on Lyons Falls Pathfinder Tradebook. This paper is acid-free and 100 percent totally chlorine-free.

The quotation in Chapter One by Colin Powell is reprinted by permission of *The Black Collegian* Copyright © 1994.

The quotation in Chapter Four by Herant A. Katchadourian and John Boli in *Careerism and Intellectualism Among College Students: Patterns of Academic and Career Choice in the Undergraduate Years* is reprinted by permission of Jossey-Bass Inc., Publishers Copyright © 1985.

Remaining credits are on p. 330.

Library of Congress Cataloging-in-Publication Data

Arnold, Karen D.
     Lives of promise : what becomes of high school valedictorians : a fourteen-year study of achievement and life choices / Karen D. Arnold.
        p.   cm. — (The Jossey-Bass social and behavioral science series) (The Jossey-Bass higher and adult education series)
     Includes bibliographical references and index.
     ISBN 0-7879-0146-6 (alk. paper)
     1. High school graduates—United States—Longitudinal studies. 2. Talented students—United States—Longitudinal studies. 3. Success—United States—Longitudinal studies. 4. Life skills—United States—Longitudinal studies. 5. Educational surveys—United States. I. Title. II. Series. III. Series: The Jossey-Bass higher and adult education series.
LB1695.6.A75 1995   95-17927
373.12'912'0973—dc20   CIP

HB Printing 10 9 8 7 6 5 4 3 2 1   FIRST EDITION

Contents

Tables

To Terry Denny and the members of the Illinois Valedictorian Project and in memory of project member Kelly Ann Albright

Preface

Who succeeds in contemporary America? Which young people reach the top of occupations and creative endeavors? Why does one high school standout "make it" in adulthood while an equally promising peer does not? And what does it take to become eminent, changing a domain for all who follow? As citizens, parents, educators, and students, we all have a strong stake in understanding how to encourage achievement and promote the fulfillment of human potential.

Americans believe in success. We do not always agree about what success is, though, much less how to get it, what price to pay for it, and what to do with it. One way to begin deciphering the puzzle of success is to trace the lives of those people whom we consider the best and the brightest. Following talented men and women from high school graduation to their early thirties reveals both optimal paths of achievement and the conditions that determine adult excellence. The life outcomes of highly able individuals also reveal the consequences of differing personal definitions of success. What happens to "the best," therefore, carries important lessons about how we can encourage and assist all young people to fulfill their potential.

The value of investigating lives over time has long been recognized as a uniquely suitable way to understand the development of human talent. Yet an examination of studies of those who were high scorers on tests, elite-college attenders, and talented musicians, mathematicians, and such, shows that no one has ever before followed the lives of American youths who win the prize for the major enterprise of childhood and youth—school itself. Lewis Terman pioneered the long-term study of gifted and talented individuals with his study of high-IQ children that began in the 1920s (Terman, 1925; Terman and Oden, 1947, 1959). The Grant Study followed high-achieving Harvard men of the 1940s, emphasizing mechanisms of psychological functioning (Vaillant, 1977). More recently, Katchadourian and Boli (1985, 1994) studied 1981 Stanford University entrants from ages eighteen to thirty-two. Other large-scale contemporary studies of gifted populations over time include the projected fifty-year Study of Mathematically Precocious Youth (see, for example, Lubinski and Benbow, 1994) and the Munich Longitudinal Study of Giftedness and Talent (Perleth and Heller, 1994). (For a review of recent and ongoing longitudinal studies in this tradition, see Subotnik and Arnold, 1994.)

However, beyond these gifted groups, there is a much larger population of top prize achievers in our schools. At the end of the high school years, U.S. schools publicly proclaim their most successful grade earner as valedictorian. Having ranked and graded students on nearly everything they do, teachers believe that grades measure real knowledge and accomplishment. Schools assume their top students are the best at something that matters outside the classroom. The public expects valedictorians to succeed beyond high school. Until now, however, the fate of America's best high school students has been communicated only by gossip and the popular media.

Lives of Promise chronicles the first systematic, longitudinal investigation of the life paths of high school valedictorians: the Illinois Valedictorian Project. The project is currently following the academic and nonacademic lives of eighty-one valedictorians and salutatorians of the high school class of 1981 in order to understand academic success—its antecedents, its prices, its rewards, and its relationship to career and personal life adaptation. This book traces the first fourteen years of that project, studying these individuals' experiences from age eighteen to the early thirties and analyzing how school success is (or is not) translated into life attainment.

As the first systematic research on high school valedictorians, a rare longitudinal study of talent development, and a rich qualitative look at the development of individual lives, the Illinois Valedictorian Project contributes a unique perspective on the pressing national issue of academic achievement. In the context of urgent national debates on the failures of U.S. education and the need to cultivate future leaders from an increasingly diverse youth population, it is necessary for us to identify the conditions under which able students sustain or discontinue their achievement, especially if we are to fulfill the potential of talented females, students of color, and economically disadvantaged students.

Formal education is the major achievement arena of childhood and youth. What does doing well in school actually mean? Do academically talented high school students become top college students? Will they reach the top of their career fields? Can we expect them to contribute creative intellectual, artistic, or leadership accomplishments as adults? If graduation day clichés hold true and high school achievers are the leaders of tomorrow, then recognizing and nurturing our best students becomes a top priority. If, however, high school valedictorians do not reach the front ranks of adult achievers, we need to investigate the obstacles that hinder their continued attainment and question our fundamental assumptions about what grades measure and what schools reward.

A knowledge of the ways we can nurture academic success can also inform our national response to widespread student underachievement. If schools are about academic achievement, we need to understand far more about achievers. How do the families of superb students get across the message to excel? What habits and skills, beliefs and abilities lift a student to become the top of the class? Which lessons about striving and succeeding can teachers and parents impart to underachieving students?

Beyond the antecedents and consequences of academic success lies a broader story about coming of age in the United States today. Although theirs is largely a best-case scenario, the high school valedictorians are part of the larger generation that began adult lives in America during the 1980s and 1990s. This book covers the life stage psychologist Daniel Levinson (1978) named the "novice phase of early adulthood," in which young people are leaving adolescence, exploring life choices, making tentative commitments, and reassessing decisions in order to commit fully to occupations and relationships. The transitions of early adulthood are as dramatic as any during the life span—carrying youths from family and high school to college, from high school or college to work and their own families. Such transition points define a person's life and determine what he or she will become. The psychological tasks of this life stage, according to life-span psychologist

Erik Erikson (1959, 1968), require young people to forge an identity and to develop the capacity for intimate relationships. The touchstones of a life—work and love—are, therefore, put into place over the decade and a half following high school.

Valedictorians undertake this journey like any other young persons. And like their age-mates, their development occurs within a specific social and historical era that shapes their lives. Born on the cusp between the end of the baby boom and the rise of the so-called Generation X, the members of the cohort under study attended college and formed their vocational aspirations during the Reagan presidency. They faced steeply rising college tuitions and looked ahead to professional paths choked with baby boomers. Like most of their college-bound classmates, 1981 valedictorians left high school preoccupied with financial success and business careers and largely uninterested in developing a meaningful philosophy of life or working for social change (Astin, Green, and Korn, 1987). Midwestern valedictorians were also exposed to a detectable wave of religious fundamentalism (Hastings and Hoge, 1981), increasing career involvement of women, and a national turn toward conservatism. The story of the valedictorians' early adult years has much to tell about the life paths of their generation.

Overview of the Illinois Valedictorian Project

By the end of June 1981, Terry Denny had attended three dozen high school commencement exercises. He had swatted mosquitoes at outdoor ceremonies and fanned himself with pleated graduation programs in sweltering gymnasiums. He had listened to string quartets, choirs, guitar folk masses, brass bands, and solo organs. He had learned that "Pomp and Circumstance" has words. He had heard one hundred speeches reminding seniors that they were the leaders of tomorrow. His body had become form-fitted to the Krueger school metal folding chair.

Denny, now professor emeritus at the University of Illinois at Urbana-Champaign, began the Illinois Valedictorian Project after a professional lifetime of studying educational success. He envisioned a ten-year study with annual interviews of the group of nearly one hundred top high school students he identified from a wide variety of Illinois high schools and communities. The study cohort included valedictorians and salutatorians and a few top honor students. (For the sake of conciseness, in this book, all project participants are referred to as *valedictorians*.)

Discovering the magnitude of following for a decade the eighty-two individuals who agreed to participate, Denny invited me to join the project soon after its inception. Over the first fourteen years of the study, I was to move from research assistant to co-researcher to director of the Illinois Valedictorian Project.

Denny's invitation to me was also partly triggered by a specific event that spurred him to ensure the survival of the valedictorian study and to make the massive commitment to annual interviews more practical. In September 1982, fifteen months after she graduated as high school salutatorian, study member Kelly Albright died. Kelly (her real name) had been an athletic and academic standout in her small rural school. Determined to make her life in a larger arena, Kelly had gone on to a Chicago university to major in business. She was killed in an automobile accident during the first month of her sophomore year.

Denny and I talked to each valedictorian for an hour or more during each of the four years after the student's graduation. The tape-recorded interviews covered all parts of the students' lives, from academics to personal and family relationships, leisure activities, and careers. We have interviewed most participants two to four more times since 1985—most recently between 1992 and 1995— and collected questionnaires and updates on their activities.

The full account of valedictorians' lives does not appear in these pages, of course, or even in the seven thousand pages of typed interview transcripts from the five hundred conversations held since 1981. We did, however, give project participants the opportunity to define for themselves the pressing issues and commitments of their lives. We asked them to help us understand what it means to be a successful student, not to confirm our hypotheses. Our goal was to understand how women and men made meaning of their achievement within the unique complexity of their individual lives.

We came to know the valedictorians very, very well. They shared with us their fears and failures as well as their dreams and successes. We sometimes knew things about them that their parents did not. We almost always knew things about them that their teachers never imagined. The men and women of the study have been remarkably generous and open in sharing their lives with us for the past fourteen years. I tell their stories, including the tough parts, with respect, trying hard not to sensationalize their foibles or their flops. In addition to the personal connections I have developed with many of the valedictorians, my own experiences and beliefs undoubtedly affect the way I interpret their words and the questions I pose about their lives. Terry Denny has provided another, different eye on the valedictorians' stories. In addition to his perspective, the study has been enriched by the valedictorians' periodic responses to portions of their own previous interviews and to reported group results. Each of the men and women whose stories are told at length in this book has seen the text that describes him or her. When my portrayal of a person's experience differed from his or hers in important ways, I have occasionally changed my text or, more often, included both interpretations.

Audience

Everyone in a society has a stake in promoting the gifts of its young people. This book is therefore written for several groups. As a study of college experiences and outcomes, it provides higher education scholars and administrators with directions for the design of achievement-oriented campus climates and the provision of career development programs for women and underrepresented groups. Educators of the gifted, testing professionals, and college admissions officers will find in the valedictorians' stories an investigation of the usefulness of high school grades in identifying future high achievers. As a unique study of achievement, the project relates to the work of social scientists interested in women and minorities, life-span development, career psychology, and social stratification. As a longitudinal view of career development, the study can inform the recruitment efforts of science and business audiences by deepening their understanding of the barriers to entrance and retention in high-level professions.

The stories of high school valedictorians provide rich case material about the unfolding lives of young Americans at the end of the twentieth century. Psychologists will find the extended profiles in the book useful in their research and teaching on human development and achievement motivation. Most importantly, parents, teachers, educational administrators, and students themselves can approach *Lives of Promise* as a guide to the conditions for talent development among all young people. How to succeed, how to grasp opportunities, how to overcome setbacks: these are only some of the lessons of the Illinois Valedictorian Project. How valedictorians make meaning of their achievements and how they choose to use their talents are equally valuable lessons not restricted to the top of the class. In the end, this text will be a catalyst for all readers, encouraging them to pose questions about what it means to "succeed" in school and in adult life.

Overview of the Contents

The chapters follow a chronological sequence, moving from the students' backgrounds and high school achievement routes, through their college experiences and career planning, and on to their early adult careers and family lives. Information from each of the surviving eighty-one valedictorians is included in the group analyses, brief individual examples, and quotations. A smaller number of men and women are profiled in detail, their stories providing a frame for trends and patterns among the larger study cohort. Table 1 in the Resources is a guide to these featured cases. Interested readers will find a detailed account of the methodology and instrumentation of the study in the concluding Note to Researchers and further supporting tables in the Resources.

I have changed participants' names—most picked their own pseudonyms—and the names of their schools. As few details as possible have been changed; in every case where such changes were made, the goal was simply to ensure study members' anonymity. All quotations are exact renditions of valedictorians' audiotaped words.

The first three chapters set the context. Chapter One describes the 1981 high school commencement exercises of the valedictorians and begins to trace the story of the Illinois Valedictorian Project through the diverging life paths of two top working-class students. Chapter Two plots the road to the top of the high school class, including motivations to excel, perceptions of academic achievement, and characteristics of valedictorians and their families. Chapter Three explores the meaning of success in the lives of talented students by investigating adult outcomes for valedictorians in light of their education, careers, life satisfaction, and personally held goals.

The next seven chapters are the heart of the book, detailing the major post–high school themes that influence the fulfillment of academic promise. Chapter Four describes the college years of high school valedictorians, utilizing a typology in which student backgrounds and academic orientations interact with college experiences to determine career aspirations and outcomes. Chapter Five focuses on the female valedictorians, reporting both gender differences and career variations between women, differences that were among the most important findings of the project. Chapter Six considers the college and career paths of African American and Hispanic men and women, including the influence of race, ethnicity, and class on their adult aspirations and achievements.

Chapter Seven evaluates the effects of various trajectories of career choice and professional socialization on valedictorians' satisfaction and adult attainment. Chapter Eight deals with the personal and intimate relationships of the valedictorians, describing the career effects of the differing configurations through which women and men balance their adult roles. Chapter Nine describes the joys and sorrows of the valedictorians over time, focusing on the sources of their deepest delights and the ways they cope with routine and serious setbacks. Chapter Ten considers potentially eminent valedictorians, those whose values infuse their adult career attainment with a sense of vocation.

Chapter Eleven reviews project findings and synthesizes the overarching themes of the longitudinal study of academic achievement, focusing on the nature of academic talent; the effects of gender, race, and class on the realization of scholastic promise; and the limitations of narrow definitions of life success.

Lives of Promise is based on the unique particular lives and words of high school valedictorians. The richness of individual lives permeates the valedictorian story and provides a continuous interplay between individual and group findings. Moreover, with valedictorians' voices at its center, this book has been written to be read, enjoyed, and—I hope—acted upon for the benefit of talented young people.

Now in their early thirties, the men and women of the Illinois

Valedictorian Project are beginning relationships, leaving relationships, finishing graduate school, buying homes, and starting
families. They are progressing in their vocations, questioning
career paths, switching jobs, making geographic moves, and temporarily leaving paid employment for full-time childrearing. The
first decade and a half after high school is only the first chapter in
the adult lives of these academically talented students. Their story
and the Illinois Valedictorian Project will continue beyond this
book to enrich our knowledge of our schools' best students and to
guide our efforts to help all students fulfill their promise.

Acknowledgments

During the past fourteen years of the Illinois Valedictorian Project, Terry Denny and I have had cause to be grateful to many organizations for funding and to a number of special individuals for
other vital forms of support.

Funding for the study was initially provided partly from the
Bureau of Educational Research of the University of Illinois at
Urbana-Champaign (and partly from Denny's own pocket). Carol
Bruene Rockhill, an undergraduate research assistant who was
herself a high school valedictorian, contributed significantly to
the study during the middle 1980s. Denny's retirement in 1986
and my departure from the University of Illinois the following year
left the project without external funding, so between 1986 and
1990 we conducted few interviews, relying instead on biannual
questionnaires.

The year 1990 was a crucial turning point for the study. Our
most recent questionnaire had shown the twenty-eight-year-old
valedictorians far from settled in their work and personal paths.
We decided to continue the Illinois Valedictorian Project beyond
the original projected decade and to seek funding for a fifth wave
of interviews. Boston College provided the research seed money
that allowed us to embark on a new round of interviewing in 1990
and 1991, in which Terry Denny and I interviewed seventy-six of
the eighty-one surviving valedictorians. We managed to discover
the whereabouts and the educational and career status of even the
few valedictorians we could not interview.

In 1992, the Office of Educational Research and Improvement

of the U.S. Department of Education, through the North Central Regional Educational Laboratory, supplied me with funds for another complete wave of interviewing and the resources for three years of travel, interview transcriptions, and related project expenses (Contract Number RP91002007). Partial research expenses were also provided by Boston College. In addition, a faculty fellowship from Boston College was vital to the completion of this book, enabling me to write full time in the spring semester of 1994. The book was also made possible by a term as a visiting scholar at the Henry A. Murray Research Center of Radcliffe College in 1994–95. The Murray Research Center is a repository for longitudinal data sets and a scholarly community for the study of lives. The original project data are currently being transferred to the center, where they will be made available for other scholars to conduct secondary analysis or replication.

As the story of the study makes clear, the first fourteen years of the Illinois Valedictorian Project have relied first and foremost on the generosity and openness of the valedictorians and salutatorians. This book is truly theirs. I am equally indebted to Terry Denny, who has been both guide and collaborator in the research process.

Among the many other individuals who contributed to the Illinois Valedictorian Project and to this book, I would like to thank Jeffrey Arnold, Carol Bruene Rockhill, Rebecca McGovern, Mela Dutka, Rena Subotnik, JoAnn Fley, Kathleen Hulbert, Ann Colby, Jacqueline James, Linda Wilson, Patricia Murphy, Kelli Armstrong, Lynette Robinson-Weening, Larry Friedman, Stafford Hood, Gordon Hoke, Jane Kroeger, Susan Wolin, Sandra Nett McPherson, Liz Abernethy, Geraldine Swift, Joan Neff, Carma Diehl, Colleen Bell, Ted I. K. Youn, Philip Huckins, Pam Saamon, and Andrea Lynn.

Chestnut Hill, Massachusetts   KAREN D. ARNOLD
June 1995

The Author

Karen Arnold is assistant professor of higher education at Boston College and director of the Illinois Valedictorian Project. She earned A.B. (French literature) and Bachelor of Music (piano performance) degrees at Oberlin College and Conservatory of Music. She also holds M.A. and Ph.D. degrees in higher education from the University of Illinois at Urbana-Champaign. Before joining the faculty at Boston College, she was a dean of students at Reed College in Portland, Oregon.

Arnold's main research activities have focused on the higher education of women and students of color, talent development in early adulthood, and longitudinal methodology. In addition to publishing articles and book chapters on these topics, she has coedited two recent books: *Beyond Terman: Contemporary Longitudinal Studies of Giftedness and Talent* (with Rena Subotnik, 1994), and *Remarkable Women: Perspectives on Female Talent Development* (with Kate Noble and Rena Subotnik, 1995).

Arnold was a visiting scholar at the Henry A. Murray Center of Radcliffe College in 1994–95. She has served as chair of the Committee on the Role and Status of Women in Educational Research and Development of the American Educational Research Association and on the Editorial Advisory Board of the *Roeper Review,* a journal on gifted education. Her Illinois Valedictorian Project research has been featured in the media, including the *New York Times, Chicago Tribune, Washington Post,* and National Public Radio.

Lives of Promise

Chapter One

Pomp and Circumstance

> *Thirty-five years ago today my mother graduated as*
> *valedictorian from Central High School. My father*
> *graduated from State College at a time when blacks*
> *encountered various racial difficulties in attending college*
> *in the South. My father died August 10, 1977, one month*
> *before I entered City High School. On June 16, 1978, the*
> *last day of my freshman year, my mother also died. On that*
> *day I made a commitment that I would be the number one*
> *student in my class. I thank God and my family for the*
> *strength and guidance that enabled me to fulfill my promise.*
> JONAS, VALEDICTORY COMMENCEMENT ADDRESS (1981)

Five thousand people rose to their feet at a city convention center as Jonas, the high school valedictorian, placed his hands on the podium and spoke these words. After a moment of silence, applause softly began, swelling within a few seconds to a resounding, dignified ovation. It subsided after many, many seconds. Men and women dabbed their faces with Kleenexes and handkerchiefs. In the balcony, a white researcher took his seat again, along with the stylishly dressed African American parents, grandparents, brothers, and sisters of the 1981 graduating class of City High. On the stage, Jonas turned to his notes. "Faculty, administrators, parents, friends, and distinguished guests," he began. Hearing that standard opening, the researcher settled back for the familiar valedictory speech in which the top graduate evokes fond memories of high school, praises teachers and parents, and exhorts classmates to continue striving. Again, something extraordinary happened.

Jonas did not begin with self-congratulations and clichés about the leaders of tomorrow. He reminded the six hundred graduates that five hundred of the students who had begun high school with them four years before were absent from the auditorium. He called on the class to reach back into their urban communities as role models and helpers. He told seniors to continue relying on the wisdom of their parents. He titled his speech "Persistence."

As graduation ceremonies go, City High's was standard fare. Uniformed junior class honor students showed guests to their seats, the school band's brass section performed notably, and an all-girl chorus sang with an organist. "Pomp and Circumstance" and flashing camera bulbs ushered the graduates to reserved seats at the front of the auditorium. Caps and gowns, special sashes, color-coded tassels, and honor insignia told initiates which graduates were academically meritorious. Principals and visiting dignitaries spoke unmemorable words and quelled outbreaks of excitement among the seniors with alert vigilance. The salutatorian (number two in the class) struggled over every sentence in a brief speech thanking his mother.

City High School's commencement was the thirtieth in three weeks that Illinois Valedictorian Project founder Terry Denny had attended. The band was better than usual, it seemed to him; the crowd more dressed up; and the graduates enthusiastic but dignified. But if the ceremony was standard, Jonas's speech was extraordinary. Struck by the quiet confidence and strong presence of the handsome young African American man, Denny was even more impressed when he met Jonas to interview him for the project. Articulate and personable, Jonas was involved in athletics, music, martial arts, and calligraphy. Trophies and certificates lined the walls of his room, representing achievements in academics, public speaking, industrial arts, and athletics. A small plaque in the shape of a torch announced that his graduating elementary school class had voted Jonas "Most Likely to Succeed." After that first meeting, Denny wrote, "Jonas is going to be somebody."

Following Success Over Time

Radiant with talent and promise and fortified by accomplishment, Jonas left high school at the top. The Illinois Valedictorian Project, which I joined six months after its inception, has followed the lives of Jonas and eighty other top-ranked men and women for the past fourteen years to learn how people succeed. Americans care about winning. To be number one is to be publicly labeled a winner in the system that counts—a system of advancement through personal merit and effort in rugged competition. Labels of success—Rhodes scholar, Nobel laureate, Heisman Trophy winner—follow a person through life and define him or her to the public. One such label, valedictorian, marks academic winners. Schools in the United States have at least one common belief: high academic achievement is a good thing. From kindergarten to the valedictory address, schools grade, rank, and label their best performers. The top high school student wins the first major life contest, a competition in which most members of society participate. Following high school, victors enter subsequent contests at an advantage. The race is never restarted.

Having marked them publicly as the best and the brightest, society expects high school valedictorians to continue succeeding. After all, they have outperformed every other classmate. They have sustained their excellence for years. They face unlimited prospects for the future and are expected to move on to academic laurels in college and to occupational success in careers. A university administrator recently told me about her family's disappointment in her brilliant valedictorian brother-in-law: "He's not doing anything with his life. We're careful to avoid talking about it." Stories of valedictorians—including perversely gleeful tales of woe and misfortune—are easily come by. The subtext is clear: valedictorians should succeed.

Do the most honored high school students go on to realize extraordinary college and career achievement? How does someone reach the top of the class? What are the consequences of being labeled the best? Does outstanding academic performance as a high school student translate into high achievement in postsecondary education? Whether doing well in school relates to life accomplishment is a more vital question. What do exceptional grades have to do with success outside academics? What makes a difference to continuing achievement? How can parents and teachers affect the fulfillment of promise among academically talented young people? What can the head of the class teach all students about optimal achievement?

After nearly a decade and half of research, the Illinois Valedictorian Project has shown that stellar academic achievement in high school generally means superb academic futures for all but a few top-ranked students. Valedictorians go on to postsecondary education, make excellent grades, finish four-year degrees, and enter graduate study much more often than lower grade earners. The world remains open to high school academic stars; they leave college as they entered it—the top academic performers.

A far more tenuous connection links academic honors to life success. Some high school valedictorians reach top professional ranks, others do not. Who succeeds as an adult? Answering this question brought us to examine valedictorians' motives, visions, and negotiations of adult achievement paths. Valedictorians' life stories form patterns that trace routes to success. What they want, how they see themselves, and how they reach desired goals depends on who valedictorians are and what happens to them during the years immediately after high school. That is, ability, values, opportunities, gender, culture, and social class all affect the aspirations and achievements of academically talented students. So does chance.

Success is a loaded term. Americans generally share some popular visions of attainment. Perfect grades, school prizes, and top rankings signify success in academics. High-level professional status, social contributions, prestige, fame, and wealth commonly flag adult success. Such popular markers of success have two things in common—they can be quantified and they occur in the public sphere. But being the happiest person, the best parent, or the most engrossed learner cannot be measured, and these successes take place in the privacy of personal lives.

The very question of who succeeds and how assumes an ideal attainment that is public and vocational. After all, high school valedictorian is a public honor. The "best and brightest" are better than others only in the framework of a competitive hierarchy and the belief that school grades measure something worthwhile. And the high social values of professional leadership and public contributions argue for retaining traditional notions of success. Such terms as *lower-level* occupation or *high-aspiring* individual reflect current popular ranking of professions. In no way do they connote people's intrinsic worth in the overall society. Yet the definition quandary persists. Valedictorians themselves struggle with what they believe it means to succeed. Their answers determine their view of themselves as achievers, their aspirations, and ultimately, the nature and level of their life accomplishments. Beyond school, men and women themselves choose the marks that count.

Learning from the Best

Snapshots isolate one point in time but cannot capture the trajectory of lives. The Illinois Valedictorian Project has followed eighty-one valedictorians (forty-six women and thirty-five men) from their 1981 high school commencement ceremonies to the present in order to record the pathways of their achievement. Denny and I met the valedictorians soon after graduation for the first of a half dozen extended interviews spaced over the next decade and a half. Their reflections and experiences also came to us in letters, questionnaires, résumés, wedding invitations, and birth announcements. Our ideas about the antecedents and consequences of academic success are embedded in the richness of the individual lives of these eighty-one women and men.

We began tracing the lives of these valedictorians at the moment of their public recognition. Elaborate ritual commemorates the finish of secondary school (graduation) and the transition to adult life (commencement). Valediction means literally "to say farewell." For centuries, British and later U.S. students demonstrated their erudition by delivering a graduation farewell address in Latin. As the highest ranked student in the school, the modern valedictorian gives a speech during the graduation ceremony to acknowledge the academic honor, to demonstrate the abilities that earned the reward, to mark a group transition, and to bask in the glow of public recognition before making the great shift to college or work.

The eighty-one valedictorians reached the top of very different high schools. Glory came in varied settings. Project field notes provide vivid commencement snapshots:

The local Mercedes dealer is busy in a posh suburb where the public high school plant looks like a small liberal arts college. Five of the top ten students in the auditorium are National Merit Scholarship winners or finalists, including the valedictorian and salutatorian. As they wait for the ceremony to begin, parents of the 310 graduating students talk quietly, pull out crossword puzzles or books, or fiddle with video camcorders.

The windows are barred at street level and the entrance to a Catholic girls school in the city is covered with graffiti in English and Spanish. Yellow chalk on the limestone proclaims "Prison walls." The salutatorian from the class of 70 gives her speech in Spanish after students enter to taped music. The black, white, and Latina graduates hear a guitar mass and most take communion.

At 4:30 on a Friday afternoon in Central Illinois, the grocery, post office, farm equipment store, and bar are open. The American Legion Post and town hall are closed. That is the town. At the high school gymnasium, 800 people have gathered as the 32 seniors from the rural consolidated school district step-together-step to "Pomp and Circumstance." Well-wishers in Wrangler jeans, three-piece suits, polyester pantsuits, and a sprinkling of feed grain hats greet the graduates in a postrecessional receiving line.

The private school campus flanks an upper-middle-class white neighborhood and a lower-middle-class African American neighborhood; the white-black ratio in the graduation crowd is three to one. Lots of everyday Detroit in the parking lot but also two Mercedes, two Lincolns, and an Alpha Romeo. On the lawn inside the gates, 600 chairs fill up in the muggy morning heat as graduates and teachers greet each other warmly. An Eastern Orthodox bishop delivers the invocation; the parents of the valedictorian and salutatorian are Greek and Armenian.

Like their settings, the valedictorians differ in everything but grades. Most of them are white, nine are African American, Latina, or Asian American. Several are sons or daughters of Asian or Eastern European immigrants. Three immigrated from Mexico as children. Some of their fathers and mothers never finished high school; one valedictorian introduced himself as third-generation Yale. Their parents are scientists, teachers, businesspeople, skilled and semiskilled laborers.

The students grew up in vastly different circumstances, even with parents in the same profession. One valedictorian's father is a tenant farmer who has no desire for his son to continue working someone else's land. Another valedictorian grew up in the farmhouse where her grandfather was born, but her father drives a Trailways bus at night to supplement the crop income. Still another valedictorian comes from a prosperous farm where her father and his brothers, local sports legends, head the leading family in town. Meritocracy means that talent and motivation alone determine destiny. Still, where you come from makes a difference in where you go.

Since 1981, we have talked to the valedictorians in offices, diners, airports, dorm rooms, and parents' homes. We have seen their first apartments or houses and met most of their parents. We have talked with these students about dreams of the future, relationships with parents, and life at college after the first B. We have followed them to graduate school, to work, to marriage, and sometimes, to divorce.

What became of the high school valedictorians of 1981? In their early thirties, they are well-educated, responsible, contributing adults. The fulfillment of promise for some has been smooth, and particularly for women and people of color, more complicated. In each of the first ten chapters, in addition to many short vignettes of the project members, I provide detailed case material for selected valedictorians, eighteen in all (see Table 1). Jonas's story, the first of these cases, previews some of the twists and turns of life after high school for the best and the brightest.

Becoming Somebody: Jonas

What Jonas became is a tale of talent, family, social class, and chance. The youngest of five children, Jonas was born when his college graduate father, a sheet metal worker, was sixty-eight years old. His high school valedictorian mother worked as a maid and then in community social services. Jonas grew up in public housing projects but traveled with his mother to plays and museums around the city. Working on cars with his father led Jonas to an early ambition to become an auto mechanic. His father was ill for most of Jonas's childhood, though. It was his mother who "demanded excellence," praised him for getting good grades, and enrolled him in a city vocational high school rather than the violence-plagued neighborhood school. Attracted by the school's championship football team and excellent band, and accepted readily on the basis of high test scores, Jonas moved in with an older sister and began attending City High. Jonas had already lost his father at this point, and his mother would pass away before he finished his first year.

During high school, Jonas decided to become an engineer. His sister's boyfriend precipitated the change, telling him, "You want to be an auto mechanic, auto mechanic is fine, but you ought to look for something more. Why don't you think about mechanical engineering?" Jonas began learning about the field, choosing to go to the local college where his sister's friend worked. The college offered him scholarship money and recruited him aggressively, Jonas said. Besides, he wanted to remain in his home city.

In college, Jonas missed the personal attention and academic help he had come to expect from his high school teachers. He remained in touch with some City High teachers, who expressed concern that he might get discouraged after "being valedictorian here and then going to college where everybody's valedictorian." At college, "the teachers are not as concerned as far as are you going to make it out of the class or not, you know. You're just a social security number as far as they're concerned." Unconnected to any faculty member and earning B's and C's, Jonas felt distant from his mechanical engineering major: "I like to get into things and I just couldn't picture myself sitting behind a desk with a white shirt and tie on." Unable to envision himself as a practicing engineer, Jonas kept up his grades because "it was expected," but felt, "it was like I was going to school for everyone else except for myself." He felt disconnected from college academics but still aspired to be "a top-line individual . . . not just an average person."

Exposure to backstage technicians at a concert and a job as a broadcast television camera operator introduced Jonas to "a whole new world" of mass media technology. "That's what I could do. That's what would make me happy for the rest of my life." After two years as an engineering major, Jonas transferred to another urban college where he could study television production.

Now twenty-one, Jonas discovered that his longtime girlfriend was pregnant. He asked her to marry him: "I don't love anybody else, and I can't see anybody else who I would want to spend the rest of my days with. . . . I would have married her if she wasn't pregnant." With new financial responsibilities and the ending of his television network job, Jonas began driving a city bus to earn enough money so the couple could have their own apartment.

"High school was a high point at a particular stage," he explained. "Now I have a new high point and that's that I'm going to be a father. . . . And when I graduate from college that's going to be another high point. So the high points will continue to come. It just takes some time."

Jonas withdrew from his new college after two months. "Came to find my interest really wasn't there, though there always seemed to be an interest to grab you. At [the college] it seemed like I was just floating." With a newborn son, financial pressures and family concerns moved other ambitions aside. Jonas took a permanent job as a delivery truck driver for a large company where he moved into a supervisory position a few years later. At age thirty-one, he has two children and a marriage that has survived some rocky times. He is no longer involved in most of his early adult interests but does remain physically active and has become much more deeply religious. He plans "to continue to mature spiritually so that my priorities stay God, family, health, job in that order." He wants to continue progressing at his company but has no plans to return to college.

Where Jonas came from made a big difference in the route he followed but so did the experiences and the people he encountered in the years just after high school. For a second valedictorian, the interplay of family background, social class, and post–high school experiences led to a dramatically different life path.

Leaving the Farm: Marilyn

In 1991, ten years after high school, Marilyn was completing a doctorate in animal science and preparing to begin a postdoctoral research fellowship. Interviewed in her rural home, the end unit of a single row of house trailers outside a Southern university town, Marilyn, thin and pale, was nearing the end of her dissertation in animal immunology and nutrition. Far from her Midwest farm town, Marilyn's accent and grammar were still country. Money had been too tight to visit home over the summer, Marilyn said, although she had indulged herself in buying the red Toyota pickup truck in the driveway. She was eagerly awaiting her first paycheck, which she planned to use to buy some furniture.

The valedictorian at Marilyn's high school had finished a business administration degree with high honors and returned home with his wife to raise their four children and work on the family farm. One B made Marilyn salutatorian of the class of thirty-six seniors in the rural school where Marilyn, too, was drawn to a farm life. Her family tilled a small part of its eighty-acre farm and raised sheep and cattle on the rest of the land. As a teenager, Marilyn was deeply involved in raising sheep, hoping to go on to "build up our flock and show in the different fairs." As she graduated from high school, she said she hoped one day to have her own farm and sheep. A career as a veterinarian, she thought, would allow her to work with farm livestock.

Marilyn's parents praised her for good grades. Her mother was a big influence on Marilyn "because she went part way through college. . . . She was always kind of pushing me, you could say. You know, telling me to do well and I would make it someday." Her mother worked at home and on the farm. Her father, a farmer and construction electrician, "is kind of pushing my brother and me, wanting us to go to college because he didn't get to go. We have the chance and he wants us to go." Marilyn's involvement in 4-H was also influential. "I think that helped. They always tell you to do well and work on your projects and do really well in that and then you'll eventually grow up to be something or somebody."

The valedictorian was a brain, Marilyn said, but she credits her own achievement to hard work. It was in junior high school that she realized she could continue to do exceptionally well academically if she worked hard. By the time she graduated from high school, Marilyn knew that she could succeed. Being salutatorian taught her that she was responsible for her own achievement and that she could only blame herself if she did not work hard enough to succeed. At college, "I'm going to pick out what I want to do and I'm going to work for it."

Marilyn was counseled that it would be "too competitive" for her to earn top grades at the state research university where the valedictorian went. Instead, she went to a regional university as a prevet major. She found college much more difficult than high school. "I sit in my classes and think I'm not as smart as I thought I was. Because I've seen a lot of kids that are really smart." But her first semester grades motivated her to work harder. "I got a B [in chemistry] this semester, and I didn't have that much chemistry in high school, and I thought, 'I'm going to try for an A next semester,' because I think it just kind of motivated me more."

After a summer of detasseling corn, showing sheep, and observing a country veterinarian, Marilyn returned to school for her sophomore year. Her father wanted her to finish college, but she reported that "Dad doesn't think I can be a vet. . . . He was raised up that a woman should be in the house and have kids and that's just what he thinks." Her mother continued to support her daughter's career plans, although Marilyn was beginning to have doubts about veterinary medicine. "I've really thought about it down here at school. Being a vet takes up all your time and then doing the sheep like I want to do takes up a lot of time, too. And so you really wouldn't be able to do both of them half and half. So I thought I like my sheep more, and I want to do more research, I think."

Marilyn switched her major to animal science and, along with a classmate, transferred as a junior to the state research university she had been told was so difficult. Her grades were superb at the new school, which she chose because of its strong program in her field. Although she was not yet sure what she would do within animal science, she continued to be interested in research. "There are so many things to learn yet. Oh, about different diseases, stuff that can help other people, whatever." Marilyn's professors were impressed by her performance. An animal nutritionist invited her to work in his research laboratory, and she got to know department professors and graduate students. Marilyn still wanted to own a farm and show quality sheep, but was not sure what direction her career might take or whether to go to graduate school. She did know that she wanted to postpone a family for "a while"—"so I can have the opportunity to do things with my career."

After two years of strong academic performance and undergraduate research, Marilyn applied to veterinary school and was rejected. She was not deeply disappointed by the decision, she said, because she still thought she would prefer a research career. "I don't want to take care of people's Fifis and Fidos for the rest of my life. . . . The area I grew up in is very small, and if you wanted to work with animals, [I thought] you had to be a vet. That wasn't true. Once I started college I realized that, and I found out that I could do more in graduate school and after graduate school than

I could being a vet." The excitement of scientific discovery and the potential to help livestock and humans through nutritional research continued to motivate Marilyn. She was surprised, she said, to be recruited by her professors for a Ph.D. in animal science. The best part of her senior year, she said, was "finding out from my advisor and other professors that I do have what it takes to make it as a woman in this field. For a while I was doubting my abilities and this helped to boost my confidence. Pleasant surprise when they actually come out and say it."

Marilyn chose a master's program in ruminant nutrition on the basis of advice from her undergraduate professors, who were part of the national research network in animal science. She worked on her own and faculty research and as a teaching assistant during the program. The degree was a "roller coaster," with thesis work taking far longer than she had expected. As she completed the program and published her thesis, she was again urged by colleagues and faculty to continue directly to the Ph.D. "I had thought in my master's that I was going to take a year off and work to figure out for sure if I wanted to go on. . . . When I was an undergraduate, I worked in a lab and one of the graduate students that was there at that time had finished and had gotten a job [as a professor]. Well, he knew I was finishing up on my master's and so he started calling me, bugging me about a Ph.D. program, and he was putting the pressure on because he knew the graduate students. He knew what I was like and the work I could do, so that started me thinking maybe I should just go ahead and go on."

The uneven progress of scientific research, including an initial dissertation project that had to be abandoned, continued the roller coaster into Marilyn's doctoral work on sheep nutrition and immunology: "If experiments don't work that you've spent four months doing, then you've just lost four months." After experiencing strong ties with her undergraduate and master's program faculty, it took some time for Marilyn to connect to her Ph.D. adviser, "one of the leading people in his field. It was kind of rough at first because I got down here and was left a little bit more on my own than I thought I would be, which I guess you need for a Ph.D. It was kind of a shock but I got through that." Marilyn continued to be deeply engaged in her research, motivated by "seeing the results that we're getting and finding out that it's really not what people think. I think that's a lot of it. Just finding out some new things. Knowing your work can go down the road." By the last few years of her Ph.D., Marilyn's adviser had worked with her on a publication and a grant. "I feel like just in the last year or so I've done pretty well with my program, and my advisor has told me that too, which helps a lot. . . . I've had to adapt everything to our labs, which means going and digging in literature and figuring out how to do things and that's what I guess he's been pretty impressed with. It's like, 'Well, I don't know how to do this, but I'm going to try it anyway.'" Marilyn's research had generated "more questions than answers," but she was excited about following the questions through her research career.

Marilyn still attributes her achievements to effort rather than ability. "I have to work hard to get grades. . . . I wouldn't say I'm real talented." She works so hard, she says, "because the only way I'm going to get [what I want] is to work hard. I don't think people can go to graduate school and not work hard. I mean you've got to want to do it. I just want to do the best I can." As for confidence:

> That's a roller coaster too. I think I've gained more self-confidence since I've been here in my Ph.D. program than I've had before, so I'm getting there. . . . I moved to go to school, which a lot of people couldn't or wouldn't do, so that's one thing. I've had to leave friends behind and I've made new friends—that helps. I think what I've been able to do [helps too], . . . like presenting [research] at meetings, talking to people, having them accept it. Maybe that's why I need the feedback, because that just kind of indicates that yes, I can do this. . . . [Sometimes] I really start to question myself. Can I really do this? Do I really have what it takes to do this? . . . I think I'm a lot closer than I used to be. I have a lot more confidence in myself than I used to, but the thought of getting out there and doing this scares me—having my own lab, having my own graduate students, having them go through the same thing I'm going through right now and I'm supposed to help them.

Marilyn's mother, who had returned to college after her children left home, continued to support Marilyn's career. "She said if you want to go on, good, then do what you want to do. She's always there and gives encouragement." Marilyn was pleased and a little surprised to find herself sought after for postdoctoral positions. Recognition by her advisor and potential postdoctoral supervisors was important: "I guess I need that a little bit."

Marilyn is now a postdoctoral fellow, preparing for an academic career in research and teaching. The ultimate, for Marilyn, will be "to get the recognition that I see a lot of people in our field get today. They're invited to give talks all around the country and even out of the country. The recognition by your peers, the people you work with [is important]." As for marriage, "it seems to me if you push it, it's not going to get you anywhere. I mean, if it's going to happen, it's going to happen." At this point, "I don't think I want kids. Maybe it would change if and when I ever get married." Marilyn does value a full life outside of her work, including the farm and sheep she has wanted since high school. Successful people, for her, have "got to be more than their job. . . . You know, the world of science and that's it, nothing else. I don't like that. I just don't think that's good. . . . I look at it [this way]: are people doing well at their job, but then outside of that, do they have a lot of friends and do other things as well? Because to me that shows that they can handle things. If you can juggle friends and career and family, you must be doing something right."

In late 1994, Marilyn sent me a fragment of the poem "Success" by Emerson. "This is what I've always felt," she wrote. "To leave the world a bit better, whether by a healthy child, a garden patch, or a redeemed social condition. To know that even one life has breathed easier because you have lived. This is to have succeeded."

Jonas, Marilyn, and Success

Jonas's city is more than just a few hours' drive away from Marilyn's farm. They do have some things in common though. Neither Jonas nor Marilyn came from upper-middle-class families or top-ranked high schools. The strong influence of a mother and a home community shaped each one's commitments and early experiences. Both Jonas and Marilyn were recognized in high school as academically talented, both changed an original career plan, and both transferred after two years of college.

In their thirties, Jonas and Marilyn have radically different lives.

From the vantage point of educational and career achievement, Marilyn is far more successful than Jonas. Their professional outcomes dramatically illustrate conditions needed for the realization of talent. Marilyn came to college with a narrow idea of how her interest in raising sheep could be made a career. In college, she was exposed to realistic alternative careers in animal science. She came to know professionals in her future field and conducted research as an undergraduate that helped crystallize her professional direction and socialize her into the field. Increasingly sophisticated about the content and career management of her specialty, Marilyn nevertheless consistently doubted her ability. Mentorship and recognition by professors, along with her unflagging belief in the efficacy of hard work, kept Marilyn on the fast track as a scientist. Postponing marriage and leaving childrearing out of her planning allowed Marilyn to focus on her professional training and to move around the country for educational and job opportunities.

Jonas relied on the advice of an acquaintance in assuming that his technical interests would be fulfilled in mechanical engineering. Unlike Marilyn, he was not exposed in college to academic fields that clearly incorporated his interests. Although he did find a vocational passion in his television job, it was never clear to Jonas how college related to this occupation. Instead of becoming close to faculty who mentored him and helped connect him to socializing professional experiences, Jonas earned good grades in courses that seemed irrelevant with professors whom he knew only as instructors. Instead of following an increasingly defined career path with the help of faculty or professional sponsors, Jonas became increasingly disconnected to his academic major and institution. After his early marriage and son's birth, he was unable to focus on career. Instead, his attention necessarily turned to the support of his family and has remained there. His values now focus on family and religion, and it is on these factors that he judges himself as successful.

Lives of Promise is about the journeys of talented young people like Jonas and Marilyn as they pursue their own visions of a successful life. The complex individual tapestries of Jonas's and Marilyn's lives show many of the patterns that determine the fulfillment of promise in academically talented men and women.

Achievement drive and consistent hard work are core qualities of professionally successful adults. Envisioning achievement goals clearly and knowing how to negotiate the paths to those goals affect motivation and work commitment, however. The confidence to continue comes partly from reinforcement by professional supporters. The vision of where to aim and how to get there depends on connections to sponsors and guides. The fulfillment of academic promise, in short, is an interpersonal endeavor.

Chapter Two

School Smart
Becoming High School Valedictorian

> *There are no secrets to success. It is the result of preparation, hard work, learning from failure.*
> GENERAL COLIN L. POWELL, QUOTED IN "THE
> SECRETS OF SUCCESS," *THE BLACK COLLEGIAN* (1988,
> P. 100)

> *The way to rise is to obey and please.*
> BEN JONSON, *SEJANUS, HIS FALL* (1603)

> *I was brought up to do my best in everything, always.*
> DAVID

"I'm not the smartest person in the school. I just know how to get good grades." Over and over, star students told us they rose to the top partly because they were intelligent, partly because they were schoolwise, and mostly because they worked hard, persisted, and drove to achieve. Grades came easily to some valedictorians and painfully for others, but all the top achievers cared about their performance and worked for their laurels. Talented musicians or athletes or chess players pursue their gifts outside of the classroom. In contrast, school was at the center of academic performers' lives. Responsible, focused, and hard-working, valedictorians found comfortable social niches for themselves among high school leaders and serious students.

Families, teachers, rewards, and pressures drove academic performers in high school. Allie and Kate graduated at the top of the same Catholic high school in a small industrial city. Both were from working-class families. Beginning in high school, however, Allie and Kate took different roads leading to different notions of success. Allie was salutatorian of her class. Grades came easily to her in high school. Although her parents approved of her high achievement, Allie felt no pressure from them or from her less academically focused younger brother. In addition to her academics, Allie worked at an afterschool job, served as treasurer of the student council, played softball, and was active socially: "I never gave up anything that I can think of." She took physics and chemistry from a teacher she described as "brilliant," who guided her to a research university and a major in engineering. Being valedictorian was not really a goal for Allie, just doing well. Allie said she did not push herself hard enough and, indeed, found herself on academic probation after a poor record in her first college semester. Her grades improved as she became steadily more engrossed in her studies. After a series of undergraduate experiences doing research with professors and working in a national laboratory during one summer, Allie earned a doctorate in cancer radiobiology, completed postdoctoral work, and embarked on a faculty career of research and teaching. During her doctoral work, her mother told Allie, "you've gotten so far working so little, it would be amazing to see where you'd be if you had applied yourself." Allie worries about the funding climate in science and the difficulties of balancing a science career and hoped-for marriage and family. Still, she is dedicated to combining research and college teaching. "I feel I've been pursuing something most of my life, and I'm not sure whether I'll ever get it or even what it is."

Kate

Kate became valedictorian in a very different way. The first project interview with her took place ten months after her high school graduation. It was 1982 and Kate had enrolled in a prestigious public research university.

> Our family was rewarded [for good grades] only in encouraging words from our parents—a pat on the back and saying that they were proud of us.

My mom showed all of her friends my brother's report card saying he was second in his class. It just seemed it made her so happy to see that, and she just loved showing it to her friends. I would say, "Well, if she is that happy with that, I am going to beat that and I am going to be number one. And then we will see how happy she is." Mom made more of a deal about it. My dad is busy. Very, very busy. He works anywhere from fourteen to sixteen hours a day. . . . So my dad wasn't around that much, and if there was any way I could possibly make him happy, I was going to. And that seemed like the big one. A big, big majority of trying so hard in school was for my parents. Another one was pressures I got from my friends. Whenever I took a test or something like that, I would really be worried about how I did on it—even though I made a 98, if I had one wrong, it would worry me because I got pressured. I felt like I had to get a perfect paper on everything. I had to. Otherwise I would be letting people down and they would think, "Well, she is not really as smart as we thought she was." And that had a lot to do with it. Not as much as my parents though.

It was a goal I set for myself after freshman year [when] my class rank turned out to be number one. . . . I told myself that I was going to keep it that way [until] my senior year, all the way through high school. It was something I just went after.

I like the idea of teachers' thinking you are very bright. That appeals to me very much.

Honors classes were quite a bit more difficult, very much more in depth than the regular classes. I took every one that I could possibly take—all four years. My junior year, out of seven classes, I had six honors classes.

My freshman year I was on the varsity team. I swam, I played basketball, played field hockey, was going to be in track. I did a lot of running on my own. Halfway into my junior year I [stopped sports]. I was working at the time and I wanted to keep my grades up. Sports and work and keeping my grades up meant staying up until two in the morning and then getting up at six or seven A.M., and it was just too much. I couldn't handle it. . . . I went on a big, big diet right after I got out of school freshman year, and I dropped down to under eighty-five pounds. I would go to school during the day, get right out of school, go to basketball, go from basketball straight to work, and then come home from work and study until twelve at night. I would usually get off work at ten and study from then, and then I would get up and do exercises. Everybody else would be sleeping in this house. I would do exercises from twelve until two in the morning. . . . I missed out on a lot of school activities, probably a lot of friendships I missed out on. . . . For the first couple of years all I did was study—completely study. That's all I did. And work. That's all. I think in high school not only school is important but making those friendships and growing. That age is very—how can I say it—tender.

Being valedictorian? To me, it is no big deal. To other people, it may have been, but it is what I should have done. I should have had straight A's. . . . I can't say I'm smarter than anybody else because I know that I am not. It's just that I am capable of it, and I should use the brain I do have.

Kate left the university after one semester and enrolled in the community college in her home town. In addition to her nursing studies, she worked at a hospital and a retail job and prepared for her wedding to her high school boyfriend. She earned all A's in her community college courses. In 1984, she told us:

I kind of felt if I stayed [at the university, my boyfriend and I would] grow apart. He was north and I was south, and it was so far in between. I couldn't concentrate. I found myself calling him every night. And I'm a person [who] if I'm not going to do what I can do, I'm going to put my efforts someplace else. If [you] can't do it to the best of [your] ability, put that effort into something else that you can. And I felt—I don't know—I'm close to my parents. It was quite a bit of a change for me to leave them. I guess I'm so attached to the area and the people around here—that's me. And it scared me to death—it really did scare me when I went away.

Other people still expect very much from me. . . . I'm getting straight A's. . . . And I feel like everybody is watching you, every little move you make. And the second you get one wrong on that test, they all know about it. . . . I still feel like that. I really do. I don't like it. But I keep in there, hang in there.

After their marriage, Kate and her husband decided to begin a family immediately. She left the community college nursing program one semester before receiving her RN degree. In 1985 she said:

It was really hard for me to leave the university. It really was. Before then, I would have never done it. I would have never done anything my parents didn't want me to do. It was hard. . . . What will I miss? Probably learning more. Learning new things, I'll miss not doing that, but then again I pick up books and I sit down and read them. . . . [If I were a man], I would definitely be going for a bachelor's degree right now. I would have not changed my mind in the beginning. I would have stayed in school. To me, the man is the main one to support the family. And I know how important a college degree is these days [for] getting and finding a job.

People tend to put you on a pedestal. You are a valedictorian, you are so smart, you could be the president of the United States, you could win the next Nobel prize, blah, blah, blah. . . . I think people have the wrong idea of me. I can apply myself to anything, just about anything I read and learn and hear. I've got a very good memory. [Some intellectually gifted students] are ones that like to goof around and always had to goof around in high school and have a good time. They had the intelligence, had it coming out their ears, but just didn't apply it. I guess maybe they were going through that time in their life where it's that goofing around period. Some people have it in high school. Some people have it in college. I don't know if I have ever had it. . . . Am I sorry that I missed it? No, I'm not sorry whatsoever. That's something I could do without. I was really never that big in having to be out, having a good time, being a person that's always playing around. No, I've never done that. I guess I've always worked too much. I've always known the value of other things that are more important to me. Sometimes I feel like I'm forty in a twenty-one-year-old body. . . . . I'm getting to be more like my mother. I used to be a lot like my father, do nothing but work, work, work, work, and that's how my father is. He works from the time he gets up to the time he goes to bed.

Along with her husband and two children, Kate lived in the Rocky Mountain region, where she worked in the business office of two physicians and rode and showed quarter horses. She planned to return to college at some time in the future to study business management. The following interview took place the day after her ten-year high school reunion in 1991.

Even to this day, my brothers and sisters are very judgmental towards me. They're all accountants and in a big fast-paced life. Their careers are an extremely important part of their life. I find a lot of pressure from them, expectations, maybe, from them also. . . . We're so close in age. There's always been competition since we were small, and that's where this all started. Since I can remember, the three girls were competing in swimming. And then years of basketball . . . then through school years. We all did well in school, and it was competition there seeing who would be on top and who would have the most awards for this and everything else. . . . I was in the middle, agewise, coming through schools, and nothing really stood out about me. I felt very average, very plain, and very nothing. Maybe it was that being the fourth youngest out of five kids that [made me feel] I had to stick out. I felt I had to do something to let people know that I was there. But it did; it started way back then. It went through the high school years, and the high school years were really, really rough.

I can't say I really enjoyed high school. As a matter of fact, I can honestly say, looking back now, those were not by far any of the best years of my life—[they were] very confusing. I did what I thought people expected of me, and that was fuel for the fire. The more I thought was expected of me, the more I did, and the worse I got caught up in it and kept on going and pushed and pushed and pushed myself. And maybe that's why I never finished college when I got out of high school and when I got married. Because I was starting to do things for myself and had a baby even though people said, "Wait. Wait to get married. Finish school first. Wait to do this. Wait to do that. And wait, don't stop nursing school—you go finish it." "No," I said, "I want to do what I want to do now." And as hard as it was to tell them—especially my parents, which it always is—I did it for me. I don't want to be chained to my job. I've seen too many people like that. I like being a peon. It's nice. You put in your eight hours, you go home, it's not your problem when you leave. You leave everything there, and you go home, and you live your life, and to me that's what it's all about, the time after you're out of work.

I've always had the fear that people would look down upon me being that I was valedictorian and never did finish college. And I've always worried that I just haven't met up to people's expectations. I needed to come back for this [ten-year] reunion. . . . I needed to see everybody again. I should say that only one person last night asked me what I do. With other ones, it wasn't even in the conversation—all those people. They never asked. I'm finally at ease with that, not feeling like I haven't lived up to what people expect of me. I'm definitely a much better person, and I'm much happier with my life now than I was ten years ago.

I have been through a lot of soul-searching lately, and as I came through it, I realized that there is nothing wrong. I haven't failed. I am where I want to be. I am happy with life. It's taken me ten long years to get there, but it's great. . . . Last night was a relief. If anything else, it was a relief to know that they're not out judging me like I thought they were. I was judging myself all these years, and it wasn't anybody else. I was living up to what I thought everybody expected of me, whereas nobody expected anything of me. Nobody expected anything at all. They're all busy with their lives and making themselves happy and doing what's right for them. Now I more or less know that I can choose what I want to do. It's my decision from this point on, not anybody else's, and it's what I want to do, not what somebody else wants me to do.

There are people who are like myself that get caught up in the motivation, the expectations, and I wish them all the luck in the world. I hope someday that they can go through the things I've recently gone through and be able to like themselves for who they are and what they are, not what people expect of them, because that is the hardest thing in the world to live up to. . . . I think there are a lot of people like myself that just, one time in their life, want to be average. That's how I want to be. I don't want to stick out. I don't want to be on top. I don't want to be the top dog anymore. I don't want that.

In 1994, Kate and her family moved to another state in their region. Kate returned to a local community college and finished her associate's degree in nursing, planning to continue in the future to a four-year nursing degree.

Family

Like Kate, most of the valedictorians grew up in two-parent families. Only three students lived with divorced single parents, a much lower percentage than their age peers nationally (Bachman, Johnston, and O'Malley, 1981). (This is one way that valedictorians differ from eminent creative individuals, who are more likely to have experienced the death of a parent [Albert, 1980], and to have faced early adversity [Ochse, 1990].) For all of the valedictorians, one or both parents were vital influences on achievement. Kate clearly internalized her parents' high expectations. Yet her self-imposed pressure to achieve was almost certainly more extreme than anything her parents desired. The drive to make her place in the family among competitive siblings was another source of motivation, as was the deeply rooted work ethic of her father.

Valedictorians' families communicated and modeled the importance of working hard and doing one's best. Praise and encouragement followed achievements, although very few valedictorians received tangible rewards for getting good grades. Kevin told us: "My dad offered me a nickel, in grammar school, for every time I asked a question in class. I never took the nickels. I was kind of intrigued by [his offer]. 'Why would you want me to ask questions?' I always asked." Becky initially worked for a reward but soon came to prize her identity as an A student. "I hit sixth grade, and one of my teachers called my mom, and she said, 'Becky's really smart, but she's only getting C's in classes.' I had begged for a horse for four years, and my mom said, 'Becky, if you get straight A's, we'll give you a horse.' And I made straight A's, and then I guess after that I've always liked getting straight A's. My mom and dad really make a big deal out of it, and now it's for myself, I guess. I've gotten used to it, and I like to stay in the top level."

Becky described her mother as "not really pushy, but she's always just there; [she acts as though] you can do what you want anytime you want to do it." Allie's and Kate's families prized hard work and doing one's best. They gave verbal praise for high grades and showed they were proud of their daughters. Such stories were typical. As Becky said, "My parents really care how I do." Another college freshman, asked for whom she achieved, said, "My parents . . . because they supported me and encouraged me. I want them to be proud of me."

Overall then, the valedictorians enjoyed the approval of their parents, who communicated their high expectations without exerting strong direct pressure for good grades. Parents' high expectations and achievement values became part of the students' own view of the world. David, for example, never felt a conflict with his parents' high standards, which had become both part of his own identity and a cornerstone of his valued relationship with his father. "I never really felt as if I had a choice of getting lower grades than I could get. I always felt as if it were some kind of a duty to get the highest grades I could earn. First of all, it's a duty to myself and it's a duty to my parents. They've always wanted me to do well. They don't really put the pressure on to get straight A's, but they expect me to do well. And I've never not wanted to do well, so it's never been an issue of contention."

Valedictorians' parents paid close attention to school achievement, communicated a sense of responsibility, and set high standards for their children. Diane's parents exemplified this pattern. "There [are] just no excuses in my family. Whoever got in trouble at school, my mother would always take the teacher's or the principal's point of view or side of things, so there [are] no excuses. [They had] a high level of expectation, I guess." Xhou, the son of Asian immigrants, knew his parents came to the United States to provide opportunities for their four children. "Why achieve? It is just for my family. It's expected of me since I was a little kid. . . . My dad does kind of expect me to be wealthy and to succeed in whatever career I choose. It's kind of tough to live up to his expectations, because he was very successful back in [his home country]."

Some parents pressed their children not to settle for less than their best. "I don't think I pushed myself in high school," Lynn told us. "Sometimes I would slack off and say, 'I'm not going to study for this test because I know I'm going to pass it. So I don't get an A, I get a B.' Then my dad would really push and say, 'you know that you can do it. You're just not doing it because you don't want to; it's not because you can't do it.' So he would really push on that."

Parents expected hard work and good grades, but not every household was intellectually rich. For instance, Allie's parents, an electrician and a secretary, were delighted with her accomplishments but did not discuss science, current events, or intellectual ideas. It was the highly educated professional parents who tended to stress intellectual matters. David was a third-generation Ivy League graduate, a cellist, and a fluent speaker of French. His scientist father was "always reading a book. Usually something rather obscure." When asked how he resembled his parents, David replied that he and his father had many of the same interests: "I'm interested in architecture and interested in ancient Rome. Directly inherited." David and some other upper-middle-class valedictorians grew up in homes surrounded by books and ideas that were absent from the lives of students with less advantaged backgrounds or less educated parents.

Teachers

More than half of the valedictorians knew they were top students by the middle of elementary school and nearly all by middle school. Their identity as high achievers was bolstered by the attention and praise of teachers. Eric came from a family unusual in the study for not directly encouraging academic achievement. For him, it was his elementary school teachers who singled him out, praised his performance, and urged him to "keep working, keep working." Jeff was unsure whether he was a top honor student until his sophomore year of high school. "I wanted to wait for a challenging class and to compare myself against other students. This biology teacher we had was real strict—tough tests and all that—but a real good teacher. I respected him for that. The first semester, he complimented me. I remember he only gave one A—one A to the students, and it was me. I worked hard in there. When I got that A and they just put me above everyone else, that was a great feeling."

Virtually every valedictorian identified high school teachers who were important influences. Talented students valued the respect of teachers and tried "to please significant teachers." Students at small private and rural high schools were particularly close to their teachers. Kelly, the rural valedictorian who died in 1982, described her high school as "just a little school where everybody knew each other. Not a lot of classes offered because of the number of students. They couldn't afford to hire a bunch of teachers to teach different things like languages. Overall it was a pretty good school because you knew every teacher and every teacher knew you and you got more personal help." A Latina student, Monica, described her urban Catholic school as "a family." At larger schools, students were close to selected teachers, particularly in honors classes.

Like Kate, students valued their academic reputation with important teachers. As David said, "Most people, I think, don't feel that they owe teachers anything. For some reason, I do. I don't know why. Not all teachers, but some teachers. I really feel guilty if I don't participate in class and try to help them and talk to them."

As in Allie's case, many valedictorians found in their high school teachers guides and sponsors in choosing colleges, majors, and career paths. David said, "My favorite teachers in high school were sort of like my guys. They were kind of proud of me; they wanted to suggest that I read certain books and that I be sure to take a course with such and such a professor at Yale because they'd heard of him, and they really had the best of all hopes and intentions for me. They wanted me to learn about certain ideas and things."

Besides motivating students and strengthening their identity as academic achievers, influential teachers helped valedictorians become fascinated with particular subject matter and learn to enjoy grappling with challenging intellectual material. Allie became interested in medical applications of physics through her high school science teacher. Nick, who began his career as an accountant but then became a high school history teacher, recalled his early professional role model. "I've had teachers at school that have opened up my mind to different ways of thinking. [My history teacher] in high school . . . was nominated for a master teacher award, and she had to have a letter of recommendation from a student, and she asked me. And so I just really sat down and thought about it. I didn't write anything like, 'I think she knows her material.' I wrote that I think I learned how to think, to use my mind. She knows her facts, but that's not the important thing."

Several highly intellectual valedictorians particularly valued classes with greater student freedom, interactive discussions, essay tests, and creative projects. Rachel, who admits that "school was always pretty easy," took part in a special gifted program during elementary school that gave her "a lot of freedom. I enjoyed it. You're developed in a more abstract way." Unlike this experience, much schoolwork was a "duty" for the valedictorians. Nevertheless, even when classes were not intrinsically absorbing, high grade earners met the expectations of instructors and enjoyed the reward of a top mark.

School Smart

The top students readily identified themselves as "school smart" (Renzulli, 1986; Bloom and Sosniak, 1981). Academic talent, to them, meant the ability to excel at academic learning and school tasks like note taking, memorization, and testing. "I'm sure I have natural talent," said one, "but I always pride myself on getting the job done and just [having] the practical knowledge of what the teacher expects: how to study, what to learn, what to listen to; to sort out in your mind what's important, what's not; to really listen in class and to learn the concepts in class. Then . . . they won't be hard. Just listening and digesting material and then just sorting it out. It's more like a process—a study process."

Being school smart for the valedictorians was not the same as being highly intelligent or even clever in life. Many of them clearly attributed their success primarily to effort rather than ability. Barry said, "I can study for a test and get an A. But someone who gets C's in high school can be just as smart or just as wise, or even more of both than I am. I've never [equated] an A with 'smart.'" Many discount their ability to get good grades, as Jerry did: "I don't really consider myself smart. I just work really hard. There are so many more people smarter than I am, with natural intelligence, but [they] just don't use it." Barry and Jerry implied that any intelligent person could succeed at school by consistent effort and attention to teacher demands. Like Kate, they believed less successful classmates had chosen to emphasize nonacademic activities. (For a review of models of achievement motivation and attribution, see Weiner, 1990. The cross-cultural studies of Stevenson and Stigler, 1992, outline the positive educational effects when students, parents, and teachers regard achievement in terms of effort as opposed to innate ability.)

Conquering school was not only rewarded by parents and teachers, it provided top students with personal identities as achievers. Half the valedictorians said they knew they were top students by the fifth grade, three-quarters by the eighth grade. Rachel, who went on to earn straight A's in college and a Ph.D. in chemistry, clearly saw herself as academically talented. "I think everyone is special at something, and I think that if I can, why don't I be as good as I can be in this? [I think] 'I'm not an athlete, I'm not a singer, I'll be a student.' And it's nice to have something you can do better than some people. So that's what I do. I don't feel that I have to be popular or something because I have my own thing. So it's something to fall back on." For Laura, who has struggled with a mental illness, having been a top student reassures her that she is talented, "Because it makes me different from other people. Because I totally value my knowledge. No one will ever take that away from me. The most successful thing that I have done in my life is be a student." Luz, a Latina engineer, was inspired to persist in college by having been valedictorian: "I was successful before so I know I can be again."

Not only did valedictorians define themselves as academically successful, they carried a public label as achievers. Her high school and college classmates expected Kate to get top grades. Yet more students spoke of the pleasures than the pressures of being seen as an academic star. They enjoyed being known publicly as smart and promising.

What does being school smart imply for the talents and potential of academically able students? The students were wrong about one thing. Most are highly intelligent by any measure. Their college entrance examination scores ranged from the mean for college attenders to the top of the scale. Nearly 40 percent of those who took the National Merit Scholarship test qualified as finalists or winners. Students chose and excelled in optional honors and advanced classes.

However, the top students were correct that intellectual ability is only one of the talents needed for straight A's. Valedictorians had to perform well in every class, including courses that were poorly taught or uninteresting (Bloom and Sosniak, 1981). Not even demanding teachers of advanced classes always sparked the intrinsic interest of their best students. Students like Meredith described learning experiences of rote memorization and mechanical application of formulae and rules.

> [One teacher] taught us math well, but not love of mathematics. . . . I learned to do calculus well, but I never got excited about it. Nobody in my class [did] really. [If you admitted] that you like calculus, you'd be harassed, because we'd all say, "Oh God, we have another test, oh no," and we were all learning it well, but we didn't

really learn to like it. . . . Same thing with physics. I remember
when I was taking physics, I thought, "Physics is for boys," and "I
hate physics." The thing with physics is it has really neat applications to daily life if you think about it outside of class. It's something that I never thought about doing in high school. . . . The
work always seemed like a duty rather than something that
you would actually enjoy doing.

Even though Meredith's classes enrolled an elite group of students at a superb public suburban high school, the instructional
process reduced learning to decontextualized drill. Furthermore,
the school culture reinforced gender stereotypes about science and
discouraged open enthusiasm about learning. But Meredith met
her obligation, earning straight A's in advanced high school math
and science classes. To accomplish this kind of feat over four years
of coursework, straight A students needed to be able to study effectively, put effort into even unengaging tasks, and focus on school
instead of social or other activities. "Goofing off," "playing," or
"concentrating on something else" took many other bright students out of contention for academic laurels.

Valedictorians also had to play by the rules of the school system.

It's easy to study for the grades, I think. You don't really have to be
born smart. I'm kind of book smart. I'm not really born smart. . . . I
have an attitude for school—it's a system. If you know how to study,
you'll do well at school. I just pay attention in class. A lot of people
are in class and [only] going through the motions. But I think if
you're paying attention in class, that's half the battle right there.
And you take notes and you're there in class. To me, most people
aren't. I've never missed a class, cut a class. And I've never been
late to one. And I always have my homework done. It's just the
basics. Teachers give you the homework; you do it; you're going to
know it.

In short, valedictorians accepted the challenge of achieving
within the particular, peculiar structure of schooling.

High School Life

Commencement ceremony applause registered enthusiastic peer
recognition for athletes and class clowns but almost never for top

honors students. But even though wild applause for scholarship was missing, so was the image of the top student as a socially isolated grind who does nothing but study. Nor did highly ranked students attempt to conceal academic laurels. Their pleasure in public recognition was one of several indications that valedictorians were socially comfortable in high school.

Like Allie and unlike Kate, nearly all of the valedictorians enjoyed school. Jane reported: "I always had positive school experiences—always, from day one. I loved school. I was always such a model student. I loved to be in class. I always sat and took notes and asked questions." School was the center of valedictorians' lives. They played in school bands, wrote for school newspapers, and played on school sports teams. They were members and officers of academic clubs, student honoraries, and school governments. Kelly, for instance, was outstanding in academics, leadership, and athletics. In addition to being salutatorian, she was treasurer of her student body for three years, vice president her senior year, student council treasurer and secretary, and president and treasurer of the American Foreign Study Club. "Everybody trusted me with their money, I guess—always elected me treasurer." She played basketball for four years, ran track for two years, and was on the volleyball team for three years.

Although nearly all of the valedictorians participated in school activities, rural students like Kelly often reported particularly wide-ranging extracurricular involvement. Darren, a farmer's son, gave us the following list of his high school activities: "Chorus 4 years, president senior year; gospel quartet member; lead in senior play; church organist; band member (trombone) 4 years; student council officer; Academic Bowl team member 4 years, captain senior year; yearbook staff 4 years, school newspaper staff 4 years, editor senior year; letters in track (sprinter) 3 years; baseball manager 2 years; basketball manager 2 years; 4-H member; honor club member 3 years; Luther League president 2 years; community orchestra trombonist 3 years."

Sports, parties, dating, cars—the social world of U.S. high schools rarely featured intellectual life. Even so, valedictorians found social niches in high school. Their subculture often consisted of students who traveled as a group between honors classes, advanced placement courses, and optional electives in foreign language, music, science, and mathematics.

At many schools, top students like Kelly led their classes. The expectation that academic achievers would run the school was the subject of Rachel's valedictory address. She later explained the background situation that prompted her speech: "The class officers our senior year were not academic-oriented at all. It used to be that all the more popular people were the ones in the honors classes, but then there was like a big rebellion. Junior year, people started thinking, 'Oh, the honors kids have too much say,' and they started trying to come on. So then it was a big thing [that] they didn't want to elect honor students. It was a big controversy."

Rachel went to high school in an economically depressed industrial town. The honors students were both part of the mainstream of the school and separate from it. "You really are exposed to a lot at Town High. You know, you get pretty streetwise going to school there. The people are rough. You'll hear things, you'll see things that Mommy and Daddy don't want you to see or hear, but it doesn't have to affect you. People aren't out there pushing drugs on you. People are really cool. Everyone does what they want to do and they don't try to make other people do it. So there's a lot of acceptance."

Another valedictorian, Robin, found that her younger brother had experienced a different community than she had in the urban high school they both attended. "I think back on the fact that I was in advanced placement classes and honors classes. I think that made it for me. If I had been in that school in regular classes. . . . My brother had a very difficult time. . . . Drugs I really did not see in high school. I know they exist. My brother says, 'Oh man, yeah, they sold drugs in high school.' Well, where was I? He says, 'Well, you were hanging out in the honors classes.'"

A subculture of serious students provided valedictorians with an acceptable social alternative to anti-intellectual peer groups. Rachel found such a group at her diverse public high school. "I had competitive friends. No one looked down on getting good grades; none of my friends did. They all supported me, and they all were getting good grades themselves. They all helped me. It was a good situation with them." Barry found a similar group in his small town school in central Illinois. "I've always been with a group that was pretty smart. And to keep my standard, I had to stay a valedictorian."

Many valedictorians also had friends outside their primary social group of high-achieving classmates. Neighborhoods, sports, and employment were arenas for developing friendships outside the top academic ranks. Still, Robin was unusual in developing a primary social circle in which three of her closest friends did not go to college. (Atypically for the valedictorian group, she also married a man who did not continue his education beyond high school.) Most top students maintained their closest relationships within the small group of top high school students.

In addition to focusing on school activities and academically minded peer groups, valedictorians also avoided activities and groups that might have competed with academics. Top students were much less likely than high school students in general to drink alcohol and almost no valedictorian experimented with marijuana or other drugs in high school. (Comparisons of Illinois Valedictorian Project participants and all high school students are based on replication of a national survey study of 1981 high school seniors conducted by the University of Michigan Institute for Social Research; see Bachman, Johnston, and O'Malley, 1981).

Deep religious involvement also drew many high school students away from nonscholastic distractions. A third of the valedictorians were raised in the Catholic faith. One is Jewish, one Mormon, and one Nazarene. Three did not classify themselves. The remainder are Lutheran, Methodist, Baptist, and other Protestant denominations. As high school seniors, ten of the then eighty-two study members reported that religion was not a factor in their lives, but a third agreed with the statement "religion is absolutely central in my life." Several characterized themselves as born-again fundamentalist Christians. Although the degree of religiosity has decreased for most in the past fourteen years, the emphasis on religious beliefs and church activities during high school certainly affected many valedictorians' choices to accept family expectations, focus on school achievement, and avoid party life.

Valedictorians could be themselves with their friends. Only a few spoke of trying to conceal their class rank from peers, feeling set apart as a "brain," or hiding out in honors classes. Nearly all enjoyed their achievement and happily focused their lives on high school friends and activities. Although theirs was not the path of greatest popularity, valedictorians fit recognized, socially viable niches in the culture of high school.

Competition

From friendly contests to fierce rivalries, valedictorians achieved their honors in a hierarchical system of peer competition. Kate believed her academic performance was always under observation by classmates. For her, competition took the form of struggling to remain on the pedestal where she thought others expected her to be. She also competed directly with her older sisters and brother.

Several of the valedictorians and salutatorians competed head-to-head over the four years of high school or even longer. Diane, the salutatorian daughter of Mediterranean immigrant parents, was "just not going to let somebody else beat me out. . . . I like impressing other people, whether it's with my brains or my Cadillac or whatever it is. I think it is natural in everybody, but I carry it to an extreme." Diane lost to the valedictorian by one-tenth of a point, ending an intense rivalry that began before high school.

> I know for me, the reason behind me, driving me, is the competition. I don't like to say that because I like to say that I'm learning for the sake of learning, but I don't think I am. I beat [the valedictorian] out of eighth-grade awards. . . . And the first day of high school, I walked into study room and he said to me, 'I'm going to beat you this year.' Those were his exact words. . . . By the time we graduated. we had leveled out pretty much. In fact, we almost became friends, but he couldn't stand my guts for the majority of the four years.

Diane was unusual—although not alone—in avowing that winning and impressing others were her driving forces in high school. Other valedictorians acknowledged that they wanted to beat their high-ranked peers, but characterized competition as one among many motivations. Xhou remarked, "I've always had someone to compete with since I was a little kid." Several top-ranked students set the goal of becoming high school valedictorian during freshman year or even earlier. Kate decided to beat her brother's record of graduating second in his class. At age eleven, Alice attended her brother's high school graduation and remembers asking her mother about the meaning of the word "valedictorian." After learning that the honor marked the number one student in the graduating class, she wrote a note to herself to become high school valedictorian. "I have always made lists of my goals. So that day I put on my list the goal to be high school valedictorian."

For most of the students, gentle competition was a constant spur to achievement and a generally pleasurable aspect of high school life. At least a dozen of them were also serious athletic competitors. Although nearly all competed academically, a few said they were surprised to find themselves at the top of the class. But academic rivalry was an accepted part of valedictorians' social groups. Most valedictorians and salutatorians enjoyed the contest because they were such successful school competitors.

Pragmatism

Stereotypically, extraordinarily intellectual people have a hard time in high school. Such students find formal schooling at best irrelevant and at worst in conflict with their intense individual interests (Bloom and Sosniak 1981; Bloom, 1985). Finding their classes intellectually unengaging and the school culture anti-intellectual, extremely gifted high school students often fail to fit in socially and underachieve academically. Clearly, valedictorians did not fit this profile of school outsiders with driving intellectual interests. Valedictorians certainly viewed themselves as top students, an identity fostered by parents, teachers, and peers. However, although some saw themselves as intellectuals, most did not. Instead of being motivated by intellectual considerations, the best grade earners in the high schools were surprisingly pragmatic in their approach to school and career planning.

Valedictorians' values and interests were similar to the general profile of high school students in the early 1980s (Astin, Green, and Korn, 1987). High grade earners were practical and materialistic. Paul observed that "all the teachers say, 'the world is yours; the future's yours.' Except that the circumstances don't always work out. . . . You make your own luck and that's why I want to cover the ground. I want to get a good education and try to make my own luck." Richard stated, "I don't want to teach. There's no money in it." Diane said, "I see college as a job. . . . I'm here for one purpose and that is to learn, study, and do the best I can. And my parents' job is to pay for it."

Almost all of the valedictorians were either content with the educational system of grading and ranking or unable to consider an alternative. "I can't think of a better way" was a common response to project queries about the practice of recognizing the top high school student on the basis of grades. They approved of numerical weighting of grades for honors classes; otherwise, "people could have gotten valedictorian over me by taking easier classes!"

Overall, this was not the group to question the practices of schooling or the structure of achievement in society, but there were a few notable exceptions to this uncritical stance. When asked at age eighteen to reflect on the practice of grading and ranking in high school, Deborah said: "I feel like you plug into the system and it spits you out at the end. You know, you just kind of play along. You have your role to play, and you play out that role. I regret it. I resent having been through that. I felt that way at graduation, like it was just essentially a giant machine. You put in the person, and they're turning out products." As the years went by, several more students came to question their allegiance to the system they had accepted so wholeheartedly. In high school, though, nearly all valedictorians were committed to continuing their uncritical, pragmatic approach to mainstream American success.

Work

Whether they achieved for parents, teachers, or peers, valedictorians were workers. Even those who easily earned top high school grades put in enough effort to ensure superior school work. Considering themselves school smart meant most of the valedictorians attributed much of their success to hard work. Kate, of course, studied for hours every night in high school. Diane also studied extremely long hours: "There was a time in high school when it was just an effort to get me out of the house. [I'd say], 'No, I [have] to study.' I couldn't go out and go to a movie or something like that. But I'm not sorry for it. I'm really not." Lisa was covaledictorian with seven other straight A seniors at a central Illinois public high school. She worked hard for her rank but perceived that two other valedictorians were "on a higher plane," where grades came effortlessly. One of those two, Sophie, reacted strongly to this comment.

> I consider myself someone that worked hard and reaped the benefits of working hard. I studied hard in high school and did well because of it, but I don't think I'm academically talented. Rachel [the valedictorian mentioned earlier] never studied in high school and if she told you she did, she was lying. She's someone who is academically talented; she never studied in high school and did very well. If I didn't study in high school I would not have done well. . . . I studied four hours a night. . . . I took a flashlight with me when I was on the volleyball team to study on the bus coming home. I think it was the first time they had seen anybody do that.

Sophie's comments show her capacity for hard work and her initial willingness to make sacrifices for academic attainment. Working less than her hardest or aiming for a B was difficult for Sophie to imagine.

The pressure expressed by Sophie and Kate was not felt by the entire group. Many of the valedictorians felt high school was not particularly difficult, but most deeply enjoyed working hard and being productive. Matthew was indisputably an intellectual. As a first-year student and varsity football player at one of the country's top universities, he perceived work as a natural, enjoyable part of his achievements: "I'm a hard worker and I really enjoy putting forth a big effort towards whatever I take. I worked hard in high school and as far as athletics went, I worked hard in that, so I enjoyed that. I enjoy hard work actually. And in college, I'm doing the same thing pretty much. It's nothing out of the ordinary." Many valedictorians agreed with Xhou: "My main belief in life is that if you work hard, you will succeed." Students told us of spending hours on a homework problem in mathematics, confident and eager to solve it without asking for help. Even outside of school, valedictorians worked hard and accomplished their goals. Lynn reported: "I've always wanted to get things accomplished. I'm always [the one in the group who says], 'come on, let's get busy and let's do this. . . . Let's get it done right now.' Sometimes they get mad at me, but you have to get things done." Robin was equally motivated, in and outside school: "I'll decide something and just do it. . . . I think that I don't have to do as much as I do. There's really no need. But I enjoy it. I enjoy being busy."

On occasion, these top students procrastinated or resisted work, but in general, their strong work ethic underlies their identity and achievement. In a comparison of achievement motivation between the study group and national representative samples of college students, athletes, and professionals, the valedictorians far outscored every other group on motivation to work hard and keep busy. (Comparisons are based on results from the Work and Family Orientation questionnaire, which measures work, mastery, and competition motivation [Spence and Helmreich, 1978]. While their work scores were very high, valedictorians' competition scores fell slightly below and mastery motivation scores slightly above those of norm groups of college students [Arnold, 1987].)

The Legacy of Schoolhouse Intelligence

Achieving at first for others—parents, respected teachers, and competitors—valedictorians left high school with the task of learning how to achieve for themselves. Hard work, purpose, and desire for accomplishment continue to anchor valedictorians fourteen years after college. In contrast to their stability in these qualities over time, many top students have become increasingly torn about the place of rewards and responsibility in their lives. With the disappearance of grades as the sole marker of success, many students found they became engrossed in the intrinsic challenges of academic disciplines and career paths. Others sought new external rewards: money, prestige, security. Still others questioned their desire to continue striving.

Meg, a high school biology teacher for eight years, entered therapy in her late twenties to explore the conflict between her desire for a radical career shift and her need to be secure and to avoid risks. As a student, Meg said, she relied on grades as assurances of success. "I think everybody wants to be appreciated. They're valued, they're honored, they're important. Everyone wants to feel that. I think I worked for [recognition] because . . . I may need that more than other people do. That's something that after getting out of school you don't get any more. I really miss that. I liked 'here's the A, here's the A+, here's the A–, here's the A.' It is a constant reassurance that you're doing whatever it is that is necessary for success." In the absence of outside recognition for her teaching, Meg relied on her own high work standards. "I expect myself to be an achiever in whatever it is that I do. I think in some senses that can be negative. You push yourself in an unhealthy way. It's also positive in that you care about what you're doing. You're not just slipping along, doing what's necessary, putting in your eight hours." Outside recognition was obviously not essential to Meg's professionalism as a teacher, but she missed the clear rewards of good grades. She saw herself as an achiever yet struggled to maintain reasonable expectations in a professional situation with little feedback and potentially endless demands.

The legacy of what Meg calls "hyper-responsibility" often poses problems for the valedictorians as adults. Having worked originally to meet school and family expectations, talented students are sometimes unpracticed at examining their own motivations and desires. At thirty, Meg questioned her life of "hoop jumping."

> I've been thinking a lot about the whole motivation process in terms of why you do what you do. Are you doing it to seek approval? Someone else's approval? Are you doing it because it's what you want to make you happy? I think I've done a lot of doing something else because I think it's what I'm supposed to do. I'm almost thirty years old, and for the first time, I feel like, wow, maybe I really don't have to do that. . . . I am still too much ruled by "shoulds." I think I'm learning to block it, but not . . . as well as I will.

Most of the academically talented students followed a normal development path by moving from performing for others to achieving for themselves. Like the other valedictorians, Meg eventually progressed beyond achieving for her parents: "At this point in my life, it's become a part of me, and I don't think I'm working anymore for anyone but myself." In 1994, Meg left teaching to retrain as a physical therapist.

Sophie earned all A's in college, continuing her high school pattern of working harder than nearly all of her classmates. At age thirty, she regretted working so hard on academics in high school and college.

You got so used to it in high school and in college, always having
to get A's, that you do that for every class. I think, looking back,
I probably would have gotten a lot more out of different classes if I
would have let other ones slide. . . . When I look back at the time
I studied in college, I could probably have done just as well in
college with half the effort. If I would do college again, would
I find it necessary to come out with a 4.0? I don't think so. I would
probably try to do different things and broaden my horizons a
little, but I didn't know that going in.

More than a decade after high school, Dale also wrestled with
his past of duty and responsibility.

I was the oldest and I was the one that was always the
conformist. . . . I'd be fooling myself if I didn't say that I'm very
affected by adoration and grades, and I like that stuff, but if there
wasn't grades and there wasn't all that stuff, I'd be exactly the same.
I'm just curious. I've just always been a curious person. I always will
be. . . . I have a very high sense of quality, and I can't hand in anything mediocre. I just can't do it. In that way I'm a perfectionist
and I work hard. I think that's why I was valedictorian. I mean, I
took classes seriously that were such a waste of my time. Like home
ec—I probably got an A in that because everything I did was beautiful. But I could have been out carousing. A lot of the energy that I
put into being a good student should have been put in other
things, I think. All of that creativity should have been going into an
art class, not in doing this very mundane class that was very mean-
ingless for me, but I would still put so much effort into it. . . . I'm
paying for what I did for twenty-four or twenty-five years in not
being who I was—being a good student, being a good everything, a
good son. And I tell you, when you don't have your youth in the
teenage years, you want it; you want to capture it somehow. I mean,
I have no pride in saying that I didn't do drugs and all that stuff. I
hate it. I'm embarrassed by it. I mean, I don't find any of it virtuous
at all. I need to get the nerve up to go out and experiment. I need
to go out and get it out of my system so I don't feel like I've missed
life. I need to go out and do drugs. I need to go out and meet a
man. I need to go out and meet women.

Dale, like Meg, began wrestling in his late twenties with the
legacy of hyper-responsibility. Also like Meg, he found therapy an

important vehicle for questioning his conformity to others' expectations. Exposure to unconventional life-styles and radical intellectual ideas in graduate school also influenced Dale's eventual choice of creative work and an openly gay life. Most of his fellow valedictorians lead more conventional lives, but many have struggled since high school to find personal meaning in achievement.

How to Become High School Valedictorian

Valedictorians were not falsely humble about their ability—they knew they were bright. They also knew that intellectual gifts were only one part of getting perfect grades. According to the Illinois Valedictorian Project, the cliché is true: schools reward students who work hard and do their best. Valedictorians' families stressed precisely these qualities. Top students were willing to play by the rules of the academic system, and they were expert at those rules. Valedictorians both focused on scholastic pursuits and avoided the distractions that compete with serious study. School was the center of valedictorians' activities and identities. Finally, valedictorians enjoyed learning, although intellectual engagement was not the primary motivator for most star students or for their high-achieving peer groups. Working hard, trying your best, conforming to the system, excelling at academic tasks, focusing your efforts, avoiding distractions, enjoying learning: these items form the short list of how one becomes high school valedictorian.

Valedictorians were "good kids" whose laurels resulted from conforming to the system of schooling. Pragmatic, all-around high schoolers, they enjoyed personal and public identities as high achievers and fit comfortably into the social culture of their high schools. The best grade earners in a school traveled the road to the head of the class in company with peer groups in which it was acceptable to be a good student and in which competition spurred them on. Most of the valedictorians followed this path with pleasure. A few, like Kate, felt trapped by good grades and the pressure to achieve, but most perceived their efforts as voluntary and worthwhile. Yet it was pleasing others through good grades that started top students toward school success, and very few academic standouts had completed internalizing the motivation to achieve as early as high school.

Fourteen years beyond high school, some valedictorians like Barry still struggle to find and follow their own achievement path: "Since high school, I had a general direction that I lived by, certain rules that all I had to do was do them: go to school, classes, do what they tell you to do. I did that well. I functioned well within that environment. But it didn't create much of an individuality or creativity within myself. I never really explored what I really wanted— what did I really want in life?"

The many valedictorians who have found new, personal meanings for achievement happily abandoned the old conformity to school demands and academic definitions of success. As Beth wrote ten years after high school: "I see so many more different ways to think and to learn and to experience and to 'be smart' than I did at age 18."

Chapter Three

What Is Success?
Envisioning the Ultimate

Success is the one unpardonable sin to one's fellows.
AMBROSE BIERCE, *THE DEVIL'S DICTIONARY* (1911, P. 333)

Are valedictorians successful a decade and a half after high school? Yes is the simple answer to this straightforward question. As a group, valedictorians continue exceptional accomplishments into their early adult lives. (See the valedictorians' educational attainments in Table 3 and their occupations in Table 4.) Yet the answer becomes infinitely less simple when we examine what society and the valedictorians themselves mean by "success." The outer layers of success—how well outstanding high school students fare educationally and professionally—are the most easily observed. Many definitions of life achievement stop here. Most Americans, though, would consider at least one more level in measuring adult success: a person's happiness and satisfaction with life. And further layers remain: How well have valedictorians met their own personal ambitions for adult attainment? As individuals and as a group, what did high academic achievers envision as ideal future lives? In what ways and under what circumstances did their early visions of success change over time? At the core of these questions are social and individual values about what it means to lead a good life. Consider Marilyn, the successful scientist described in Chapter One, alongside another rural valedictorian, Emma.

Marilyn is a single postdoctoral fellow in science. Having completed her Ph.D. and an initial postdoctoral appointment in animal nutrition, she was unable to find a research position in an extremely competitive job market. Taking a second postdoctoral position meant her fourth interstate move in ten years and a switch to human nutrition research. Marilyn is dedicated to remaining a research scientist in nutrition but will tailor her research to the job she finds. Meanwhile, she longs to be geographically stable and to stop leaving friends behind. Marilyn would be happy remaining single. Ideally, she would like to marry but not to have children.

Emma is a married homemaker with two small children. When she became pregnant around the time of completing her Ph.D. in engineering, she declined the postdoctoral fellowship she had been offered in the city where her husband had received an excellent research position. She never considered working full time with preschool children. Instead, she teaches science to children two days a week and volunteers at the city science museum. She deeply enjoys raising her sons as well as introducing children to active discovery in science. She plans to broaden her involvement in science education as her children enter school but has no expectation of practicing her engineering specialty.

Is Marilyn successful? Is Emma? The outer layer of success shows both women have attained exceptionally high educational levels. Both received doctoral degrees in prestigious, male-dominated fields. Emma, in fact, was one of the first women to receive a Ph.D. in her department at a major research university. Both conducted research before age thirty that holds significant potential to contribute to food production and biomedical advances. Clearly, both are successful, yet measuring their adult accomplishment by their current professional status, the picture becomes more complex. Marilyn is a practicing scientist; Emma works in the home and teaches science part time. Through this lens, Marilyn appears more successful. Disentangling the career measure of success from the social measure of prestige is impossible, however. Is scientific research more important than raising children or teaching science? More worthwhile? To distract us from such questions, we can ask whether Marilyn or Emma is happier. In 1994, Marilyn answered a questionnaire item on this topic by saying she was "quite satisfied" with her current life. Emma said she was "completely satisfied" with hers. Does this prove Emma is more successful by the measuring stick of self-reported life satisfaction? The delights of intellectual discovery differ from the joys of motherhood but comparing and ranking them seems fraught with difficulties.

Continuing to peel away the layers of what it means to be successful in life leads to the question of how well valedictorians match their own visions of success. At each interview and in each questionnaire, we asked valedictorians "What is the ultimate for you?" In interviews, Terry Denny and I carefully avoided giving cues or even answering direct questions about whether the question concerned personal or professional goals. At nineteen, Emma said that the ultimate life for her was to be happy by helping others. In her early twenties, she saw herself working ten years later in research development in a "large and exciting firm" or as a middle manager in a chemical company. Emma certainly has not met her specific ambition of working as an engineering researcher or manager. She has, however, repeatedly defined herself in terms of close relationships and service to others. Her specific ambitions remained unmet, but Emma currently lives according to the values she has consistently named as constituting a good life. Viewed from this perspective, Emma's changing career ambitions over fourteen years reflect her increasing maturity and self-knowledge, not a lowering of aspirations. It was with every opportunity for an unusually prestigious career that Emma chose family over paid work.

Marilyn's story shows an equally imperfect connection between early ambitions and adult attainment. Marilyn first wanted to become a veterinarian who also raised prize livestock. As she became more interested in animal research, she abandoned the idea of veterinary medicine and considered a master's degree. At the end of that degree, she was unsure whether she wanted to continue to the Ph.D. but did so after urging by professors and classmates. Currently, her work focuses on human rather than animal biology. Threaded through the story of Marilyn's ambitions over time are consistent interests in intellectual work and friendships. She has never placed a high priority on marriage or children. And she still wants her own farm and sheep.

When viewed through the frame of their own ambitions and their own visions of success, Emma and Marilyn have not matched their aspirations in the narrow sense. Emma is not an engineer and

Marilyn is not a veterinarian. As they matured and continued their education, however, the two women's aspirations changed. The circumstances of their lives affected their ambitions: Marilyn became more and more successful in research, and Emma met and married a man who philosophically and financially supported her full-time childrearing. More important than early ambitions and even more vital than circumstance was each woman's system of personal values. Measured in terms of their own values for a good life, Marilyn and Emma are enormously successful.

Each valedictorian's own view of success determines his or her choices and the arenas of his or her accomplishments. In addition to individual beliefs, social values determine individuals' assessment of these choices and arenas. If we consider an accomplished life in terms of high (that is, socially admired and highly materially rewarded) career levels, Marilyn is more successful. If we consider a fulfilling marriage and motherhood as marking a life of achievement, Emma is more successful. The success of valedictorians fourteen years after high school, in short, is a complicated, multilayered picture. Considering each layer in turn permits the valedictorian success story to be viewed through "overlapping readings" (a term from Susan Chase's work on high-achieving women school superintendents, 1995), readings that must be considered through the filter of social and individual values.

Reading One: Educational Success

The valedictorians themselves questioned whether perfect grades reflected the highest level of ability or the deepest understanding of academic material. Still, straight A high school students are certainly educationally successful. All eighty-one valedictorians were highly accomplished secondary school students, and by any measure, they continued to achieve outstanding levels of educational attainment beyond the time of the valedictory address.

The comparative fate of the U.S. national high school graduating class of 1980 illustrates just how extraordinary the educational success of the valedictorians has been in the fourteen years since high school. According to the pattern of same-age high school graduates nationally, forty-four of the eighty-one valedictorians would have been expected to go to college after leaving high school. Twenty-two, or half of them, would have earned a four-year college degree seven years after high school. One would have gone on to graduate school and two to professional schools like medicine, business, or law (Educational Testing Service, 1991). Or for a more meaningful comparison, consider the patterns of attainment among age peers in the top ability quartile. If the eighty-one valedictorians had been typical of all high-ability secondary school graduates, fifty-eight of them would have entered college. Seven years after high school, forty would have completed four or more years of college and ten would be enrolled in graduate school (Educational Testing Service, 1991).

In reality, high school valedictorians far exceeded the educational attainment of even their high-ability classmates. *Every* valedictorian entered college in the fall following the May 1981 high school commencements. Ninety-five percent of the study group, seventy-seven of the valedictorians, completed a college degree. (This high level bears out the finding, reported in Tinto, 1993, that high ability is a more powerful predictor than socioeconomic status of four-year degree attainment.) Kate's associate's degree in nursing and Carol's three-year RN credential were the only nonbaccalaureate undergraduate degrees; all the other completers earned four-year bachelor's degrees. That is, the valedictorians were twice as likely to finish college as high-ability peers of all class ranks. The best high school students succeeded magnificently in college academics. Three out of four won academic awards or honors in college. On the whole, the group earned a mean college grade point average of 3.6 on a 4.0 scale. Many did undergraduate research. Several were college teaching assistants. At least two valedictorians were cited as the outstanding graduates of their colleges. Six valedictorians graduated from college with straight A's.

Now that the valedictorians are in their early thirties, forty-six of them (57 percent) have earned degrees beyond the bachelor's or were active graduate students in 1994. One in three holds a doctorate, medical, or law degree. The record is clear; nothing succeeds like success and there is no predictor of academic success better than a history of academic success.

Reading Two: Career Success

Is outstanding academic success the gateway to eminence? The valedictorians have also succeeded in their professional work, although not as universally as in academics. The general catalogue of their career accomplishments can be listed: six attorneys, three physicians, twelve engineers, four CPAs, ten businesspeople (with M.B.A. degrees), five professors, five scientists, four researchers, three teachers, and eight individuals in other helping professions. (Also see Table 4.) Lists cannot communicate the essence of valedictorians' work accomplishments, however, nor the complexity of their professional choices. A sampling of their career successes gives a clearer idea of their outstanding attainments:

Hope followed her Phi Beta Kappa studies in chemistry with a master's and Ph.D. in theology, desiring a university teaching career related directly to students' lives and social challenges. Hope now works as a medical ethicist. In addition to her grant-funded work on the ethical dimensions of biogenetics research, Hope writes, travels, and consults on a number of medical ethics cases. She has also been a guest expert on television programs considering dilemmas in medical ethics.

David graduated Phi Beta Kappa in three years from Yale and spent a year in Europe as a Fulbright scholar. Upon his return, he attended a prestigious law school, where he was elected to the *Law Review*. After clerking for a federal judge, David took a position in one of the top law firms in a major city and anticipates becoming a partner in the near future.

Yvonne went to medical school after completing a double major in biology and religion. After medical school, she chose a residency in her home city, turning down more prestigious university hospitals to remain near her family and continue in general medicine. As a medical student and physician, Yvonne has worked extensively in developing countries. Her current practice centers on the inner-city clinic she recently opened in a severely economically depressed urban area.

Bruce is a Ph.D. theoretical mathematician and visiting assistant professor at a prestigious liberal arts college. He studied classics as well as mathematics in his undergraduate years, adding Greek and Latin to his knowledge of French and German. After graduate school, he chose to take a postdoctoral fellowship in Japan, where he became extremely proficient in Japanese. For over a decade, Bruce has also spent considerable time on his passion of folk dancing, which he has taught in several cities.

Equally outstanding valedictorians can be found in architecture, science, engineering, and business. Although such professions clearly fall at the top of the occupational hierarchy, valedictorians are also extremely successful teachers, physical therapists, nurses, and managers. One is an industrial filmmaker for a large company; another is a poet who works part time as a substitute teacher.

Are any of the valedictorians unsuccessful in their careers? Again the answer to this question depends on social and individual views of success. One valedictorian, Laura, is chronically unemployed. A second, Charlotte, reported a period of several years in which she could not hold a steady job. For both women, health problems hindered their ability to work. Ten of the eighty-one valedictorians currently fill nonprofessional positions not requiring a college degree. Three of these are college dropouts. Jonas is a good example, however, of the problem in defining these nonprofessionals as vocationally unsuccessful. Jonas is a supervisor in a large delivery company, where he has been steadily promoted to increasingly responsible positions. He earns a larger salary than some of the valedictorians with doctorates. And what of Alan, the sole farmer in the study? After receiving nearly all A's as an undergraduate in business administration at a highly selective research university, Alan decided a life of farming fit his central commitments to God and family. The nonprofessional valedictorians are service representatives, bookkeepers, and retail and banking workers. Some of them have deliberately avoided professional work, concentrating instead on community service, art, or family. Sally, for instance, left agronomy to follow her military husband from post to post. She operates her own exercise school, part of a franchise, in each town she reaches.

Mothers who currently work in the home full time similarly resist classification as successful or unsuccessful professionals. Five of the six women currently outside the labor force hold graduate degrees. Besides Emma, one other woman in this group holds a Ph.D. in science. Clearly, the full-time homemakers chose their current life-style within multiple work options. Just as certainly, most will reenter the labor force in the future, bringing with them high potential for professional success. In the future, other women (and perhaps some men) will interrupt or reduce their paid work for childrearing.

The second layer of success, career attainment, is slightly more complicated than simple educational outcomes. For the most part, however, the valedictorians are highly successful in their work lives.

Reading Three: Life Satisfaction

Since 1982, the valedictorians have responded every four years to the question: "How satisfied are you with your life as a whole these days?" The profile of their answers over time depicts academically talented men and women as generally quite happy with their lives. Nearly 90 percent have consistently said they are satisfied with their lives. Like other dimensions of their success, levels of happiness among former valedictorians vary over time. Only eight have ever reported being completely satisfied with life. Of these, only Alice and Marlene have checked the highest level of life satisfaction on more than one questionnaire. These two consistent top scorers are remarkably similar. Both are women who chose to major in physical therapy because of their interest in science and their desire for a career that could be combined with childrearing. Both married soon after college graduation, both are parents, and both work as part-time physical therapists. The unusually satisfied pair have met their ambitions for a life that emphasizes family but includes fulfilling and respected professional work of helping others and working with people. Marlene believes she has already achieved her ultimate: "A balanced lifestyle of family, profession, and time alone to continue building a relationship with my husband."

Slightly more than half of the valedictorians have classified themselves consistently as "quite satisfied" with their lives. For those whose ratings have changed slightly, most have become happier with their lives over the fourteen years since high school. Seven other students reported being unhappy during college but quite satisfied since. Like the two physical therapists, many of the most satisfied valedictorians describe their lives in terms of both career and personal achievements. Kevin reported, "I'm working hard and devoting a lot of energy to my career, and I'm spending a lot of time with my family. It's a pretty good mix." Bruce said, "One of my biggest highs is teaching people something so that they really learn it. In the long run, I would like to be in a position where I could teach, say, math and folk dancing but still be involved in challenging learning experiences and travel." Beth said, "I am completely satisfied with myself as a whole these days." A small group of four students has consistently reported being only "somewhat satisfied" with life. Notably, all four are exceptionally high educational and career achievers, including a high-powered lawyer, a physician, and two doctoral students.

Among the rest of the valedictorians, twenty-eight have fluctuated over the years in their reported happiness and ten have consistently reported having mixed feelings or being somewhat or quite dissatisfied with their lives as a whole. Significant changes in life satisfaction over the years can nearly always be traced to problems at the time the valedictorians responded to surveys. Gordon, for instance, listed himself as "quite satisfied" with his life in 1982, 1986, and 1994. However, he answered the 1990 survey after dropping out of his science doctoral program and losing both of his parents to cancer within the same year. Miserable in his work at an insurance agency, spending most of his time alone, Gordon reported he was "somewhat dissatisfied" with his life at this time. He wrote that the ultimate for him was "death, of course. The penultimate would be to have enough guts (and talent) to write fiction for a living. Sadly, I lack one of the two, if not both." By 1994, Gordon was once more quite satisfied with his life. A year after the 1990 survey and two years after his parents' deaths, he had married and started law school part time. He enjoyed law school, excelled academically, and became a father. The best part of the past five years, he said was "marrying my wife, Mary. This relationship has been very healing and fulfilling for me. For the first time in years, I can say I am happy, and Mary is the main reason. My son is also on the Best list, but honestly, I can't say he is *THE* best." The ultimate for Gordon "is still to be happy and content. I think I am beginning to find it."

Other valedictorians have fluctuated in their reported happiness as a result of relationship or family problems. Some, along with Gordon, have lost parents over the past fourteen years. Others have seen serious relationships end. Some have suffered professional setbacks that have caused them temporary dissatisfaction. Jane and Meg, for instance, both reported being less happy when their husbands' career moves left them temporarily unemployed. During her postdoctoral work, Allie was deeply distressed by her career prospects in a poorly funded area of science research. Like some other valedictorians, she has also been sharply dissatisfied when employed in a position she disliked. Gordon, Jane, Meg, and Allie are typical of the one in three valedictorians who have generally been content but who have fluctuated in their satisfaction with life. It is perhaps notable that many of the highest career achievers in the study fall into this group. Possibly the demands of high-level study and work, the challenges of career establishment, and the difficulties in finding a balance between personal and work spheres make these men and women less stable in their reported happiness. Or perhaps these valedictorians report their feelings more honestly. In any case, even the fluctuaters generally report being somewhat or quite satisfied with their lives.

Only eight men and women have consistently reported being dissatisfied with life. This group completed less postsecondary education and reports lower work satisfaction than the valedictorians as a whole. Only one holds a graduate degree. Beyond these characteristics, few generalizations fit the dissatisfied group. They are male and female, married and unmarried, parents and nonparents. Their individual situations range from a student who suffers from bipolar (manic-depressive) disorder to a financially struggling poet, to a male engineer who has unsuccessfully sought someone to marry. If anything ties the members of this small group together, it is their perception of being unable to control their progress toward life goals. Such feelings of helplessness have been relatively rare among former valedictorians over the years leading to their middle thirties.

As measured by happiness, therefore, the valedictorians again emerge as highly successful adults. Almost all are consistently or usually happy with their lives. The question of life satisfaction is even more complicated than work success, however. Not only do a third of the valedictorians fluctuate in their reported happiness, many of the highest career achievers and most intellectually focused men and women are not consistently highly satisfied with their lives. Whether their expectations are higher, their challenges steeper, or their role balance less manageable, these valedictorians do appear to lead particularly demanding lives. Probably not best measured during the peak years of career establishment, their levels of happiness might equal or surpass those of their peers once they, too, establish a satisfying personal and professional balance.

The Core: Valedictorians' Visions of Success

Judged by educational attainment, career status, and personal happiness, valedictorians are indeed successful fourteen years after high school. Like Marilyn and Emma, most individuals in the study group have held to consistent values but shifted particulars in planning their futures. Their own visions of the ultimate life show the evolution over time of valedictorians' ambitions. Staying faithful to high school dreams produces success only when students manage to deepen and personalize their initial aspirations. Remaining open to possibilities has characterized some of the most outstanding achievers in the study; a few of the least content have fulfilled their early ambitions exactly.

Following the career aspirations of valedictorians over the decade and a half since high school demonstrates whether they have achieved their own ambitions. At age twenty-one, the valedictorians reported what they expected to be doing in their thirties. As they approach their mid thirties, fully three-quarters of the academic achievers are pursuing the general professional or family lives they anticipated at twenty-one. Women are less likely than men to be carrying out their plans of a decade before. Forty-four percent of the valedictorians currently do precisely what they envisioned in college.

Richard is an example of a valedictorian who matched his general early career vision but not his specific occupational plan. At eighteen he talked about architecture and wanting to raise a family. The next year, his plans centered on an enjoyable, financially comfortable life-style. As a college junior, the ultimate for Richard was building his own house and working at a decision-making job. At age twenty-one, Richard wrote that in his thirties he expected to be in "management or possibly owning and operating my own business." At twenty-five, married and selling computer software, he again spoke of owning his own business "and still having time to travel and enjoy life." His 1990 ultimate was "to run my own company or division. I'd like to be a vice president of sales or marketing. I'd be very happy if I were a regional manager, managing a group of salespeople." By 1994, Richard was indeed a manager, writing that the ultimate for him was "being able to live comfortably, enjoy all activities, travel, and enjoy them all with my wife and friends." Although Richard does not head his own company, he has consistently sought work with financial rewards, decision-making responsibilities, and time for personal activities. His general career plan became more specific over time, but his ultimate has come to focus increasingly on nonprofessional goals. His architecture interest has also remained alive with his participation in designing the house he and his wife built.

Examining the level of the valedictorians' aspirations over time also demonstrates which men and women have achieved their own ambitions. Like Richard, half of the academically talented group has maintained the same level of professional aspirations over time. In general, men are more consistent in their career aspiration levels than women. The group of consistent aspirers includes women who have always expected to subordinate paid work to family and who are carrying out that plan. A second consistent group includes valedictorians who deeply enjoy the career paths they first envisioned in their early twenties. Industrial video producer Darren wrote in 1986: "I will hopefully be a television producer/director of non-broadcast programs. . . . Instructional programming interests me at the present. It's nice to slip into a job which fits perfectly the expectations I had." Jane, a community college professor, said as a college sophomore that college teaching in biology would "combine my fascination with the biological sciences with my interest in working with people."

A third set of valedictorians who have achieved their aspirations are unhappy in their work. Al has successfully achieved his longstanding ambition to become a computer systems analyst. His ultimate now would be "to be a head football coach for a high school boys team and be able to work with people in a capacity (I don't know what) where I didn't have to worry about economics." David, the fast-track lawyer, wrote in 1994 that one of the hardest things in his life has been "coming to grips with the less attractive aspects of my work. My work is often more a job than a calling and much of it seems pointless and devoid of meaning."

A third of the valedictorians have lowered the level of their career aspirations over time. Some of this group are women like Emma who have left their professional fields to raise children full time. Jake has decided not to pursue promotion into engineering management so he can work regular hours and continue to devote himself to his family and church activities. A few other valedictorians who have lowered their aspirations over time have chosen alternative life-styles or a greater family emphasis than they anticipated in college. A very different subgroup comprises men and women who have not achieved their desired ambitions. Jonas, who wanted to become a television technician, is one of this group. Others are students who desired glamorous careers in entertainment law, sports broadcasting, and journalism but found themselves unable to implement their plans.

The remaining valedictorians either raised their aspirations over time (seven women and one man) or changed the level of their aspirations at several points since high school. Those with increased aspirations, like Marilyn, were mostly women who experienced recognition, mentoring, and increasing career commitment over the college years. Those who wavered in their aspirations included four female engineers who disliked their profession and considered various other fields and a woman who is a high career achiever but would prefer to be married and out of the labor force. Kate also fits into this group, having vacillated in her desire to work, to finish college, and to become a nurse.

The valedictorians, then, meet the test for success of matching their ambitions. Most are leading lives that match their general aspirations. Carrying out plans made in college does not always indicate occupational distinction, however, nor does reaching specific goals guarantee life satisfaction. Even the valedictorians who happily follow the lives they envisioned have deepened and changed their views of the good life. Jeff met his consistent desire for a career of college teaching and a fulfilling marriage and family life. By 1991, his view of the ultimate had deepened beyond a prestigious, intellectually challenging job. "I guess what I really dream about is a world where people respect the world more. . . . I guess that's part of the reason that I really want to be a teacher . . .

because I can influence enough people. I can say to them, 'Look, this is what you can do; this is what you think; you can do something about that. Do it. Don't just think about it. You can actually go out and make a difference.' I think that's what I really dream about."

Examining the evolving aspirations of the entire valedictorian group masks the ways in which each individual followed a unique path. An extended single case more clearly depicts the interweaving of experiences, choices, and values in the life of an academic achiever.

Matthew

It is an early evening in June of 1990 in an upper-middle-class suburban neighborhood. Matthew and I are seated on overstuffed couches in the den of his parents' house. The room seems full of furniture, books, contemporary two-dimensional art and sculpture. Matthew's father is with us, talking animatedly. He has greeted me, pressed refreshments, told me his thoughts on the valedictorian study and on his own academic background. I am finding him the sort of terribly outgoing, gregarious, overpowering person you have to fight with to get a word in edgewise. Matthew has not been very helpful in ending this conversation so we can start the interview, staying mostly silent as his father chatters on. You would pick Matthew out on the street for the football player he was in high school and college. His silence fits the blocky physique, the broad neck, the lantern jaw.

Finally Dad leaves, extracting my promise to have dinner with the family after the interview. The football stereotypes fade with Matthew's first words, leaving the fascinating presence of an Ivy League philosophy graduate. Unlike his father, Matthew speaks slowly and quietly, with hesitations, restarts, and careful elaboration. One of the most introverted, intellectual people in the study, Matthew is a very private person but not asocial. He socialized with friends in high school and college and once invited a fellow Harvard athlete who was having problems at home to spend the summer with him. Matthew can be a difficult person to interview, a young man who does not put on public display his innermost thoughts and feelings. Maybe more importantly, he sees so many dimensions to every general question I ask that he needs to contemplate, sift, and develop his responses.

After graduating in philosophy at Harvard, Matthew took a year off to travel around the United States. In 1986, when asked on a survey what work he expected to be doing in his thirties, he wrote: "If only the oracle would reveal the latent and benighted truth! (Or is a truth something already revealed? I think Plato might have problems with that one.)"

Matthew had always shared his family's interest in the stock and commodities markets. A friend showed him around the Board of Trade one day, and to Matthew, "it seemed like not only an intellectual challenge but also being on the floor would have been a sort of physical thing too. It was something I wanted to do, and so I did it. I guess that's the simplest way to put it. . . . I was totally uncertain about what I wanted to do or how I wanted to do it or whatever. This was something that just came along." Four years later, after a time as a novice floor trader, Matthew was trading commodities "off the floor," via computer, on the Chicago commodities exchange. Again stereotypes leaped to my mind, of competitive aggression and shouting and wild pursuit of money. Again the stereotype was completely off base. Matthew was living an ascetic existence in his parents' comfortable house. His interest in the market was deep, but its source, he said, was intellectual fascination with the art of financial prediction, the psychology of human performance.

> There was a guy who wrote a book called *The Master Game* and defined games as being either meta-games, which were games for basically self-knowledge or beauty and truth, those sorts of things, and object games, which were games that concerned money and power and worldly things. To me, to excel at the meta-game is much more difficult because it takes a tremendous amount of discipline and you're trying to control your thoughts and you're trying to control your life and actions and these metaphors that society is throwing at you and that you're trying to use to define yourself. I think every day I try to deal with those problems.
>
> The interesting thing about what I do is that it's a meta-game and an object game. The pure object of trading is to make money. It's dollars and cents, but . . . Every day when I wake up I have to

ask the question: am I willing to lose everything I have today? How many people are going to ask that question? . . . I have to be willing to say yes. Now to go in and approach the market as if your money and your reputation and your skills and all the things that you've been working up to don't matter takes a lot of discipline; it takes a lot of self-control. You have to be able to put aside fear; you have to be able to put aside your past. If you're going to be controlled by the metaphors that you use to define yourself, you're going to be limited to the extent that you can excel at the game you're playing.

The money made a difference, Matthew said, because it made the game real and the consequences significant. Still, the magnitude of his trades was unimportant in comparison with the intellectual challenge of the process.

I have a personality such that if I were making, say, $20,000 a year and being totally independent and had the ability to survive, I would choose that without question over working for IBM or Merrill Lynch or whatever, making $200,000. As far as the money goes, it was enough for me. I'd take my independence any day. The offshoot was that I started getting into all of these areas that people had, over the course of hundreds and hundreds of years tried, [in order] to read the markets, and I started getting into the language of the marketplace and the metaphors that people would use, the techniques, all that sort of thing. It was and still is a fascinating area. To me trading is artistic; it's aesthetic. So often, the stuff I'm doing involves a lot of visual work, charting and that sort of thing. I think of artists, and to me, that's the way trading is.

Matthew considered the psychology of trading deeply intertwined with the aesthetic dimension. Among the books he was reading at the time of the interview were two scholarly texts on popular culture, a biography of a Zen monk, the Carlos Castaneda "Don Juan" series, and the work of University of Chicago cognitive psychologist Csikszentmihalyi on optimal human performance. There was a strong intellectual tie between how Matthew defined himself and how he played the market. "If you're going to make money as a trader, and again I'll use the term *metaphor,* your fundamental view [your system for playing the market], is going to be skewed because you're going to carry it around with you; you're going to be married to it. It's going to be a metaphor that's going to dictate your view of the markets." The human effects of adopting particular, limiting metaphors tied together Matthew's reading. "It's only when you get to the point that you can quiet the internal voice that keeps saying, 'you can't do this, you're not going to make it,' it's only at that point that you're going to make it. I think that's one of the common threads that I see in these works, and it's true of structuralism and poststructuralism and all those others—they're all going after these metaphors. It's true of Zen; it's true of all the great religions: they're all basically attacking language and some of the constraints that language puts upon you." Matthew was looking for ways to remain tightly focused on the micro-level variables in trading while taking in the larger complicated patterns in the market. The complexity of this task meant Matthew needed to concentrate completely on what he was doing while remaining open to alternative possibilities and unconsciously perceived designs. His approach had brought Matthew some financial success and the attention of a major West Coast trader with whom he conferred frequently about specific trades and market philosophy.

In college, Matthew had also tried to resist narrow visions of who he was.

> At [college], and even now, I constantly find myself searching for new metaphors to define myself, or new parameters, new identities that might expand my understanding of the world or of myself or whatever. . . . It seemed like, for me, I was always trying to balance the various sides that define me, and it was a very difficult thing to do. I wanted to be like the investment bankers, and I wanted to be like the people protesting apartheid, and I wanted to be the brilliant academic, and I wanted to be something. So in terms of the roles that you constantly are exposed to or what you're supposed to be, it was difficult.

Two of his sides, Matthew said, were the intellectual who was always reading ten books at a time, and the pragmatist "who always felt the need to make money or do something very practical." Matthew was highly successful academically, winning the university philosophy prize for his senior honors thesis. A professor had earlier awarded Matthew an A++ for a paper that presented Dewey, Nietzsche, and Freud discussing life over a game of pocket billiards. Socially, Matthew enjoyed friendships with classmates and teammates. Asked whether he had spent enough time during college having fun, he answered that it depended on what I meant by fun. "To me, it's fun to read. To me, it's fun to learn."

As early as his first interview, Matthew had spoken of enjoying hard work and discipline. His varsity athletic career had been arrested by a series of injuries, but he continued to value physical self-discipline and effort as well as intellectual endeavors. Observing his life as an off-the-floor commodities trader, he said, would be like watching someone play "a glorified version of some kind of a video game or something." Most of his twelve- to fifteen-hour day was spent in his room, surrounded by charts and printouts, watching the computer screen intently as he followed and made trades, or charting and analyzing the day's data. He slept on a small fold-out couch in the same room. Matthew described a typical day:

> I'm up at 5:30, go through the morning ritual, jogging, getting ready, seeing if I'm ready psychologically, going over the scenario that I might anticipate for the day. The markets open at 7:20, they close at 3:15, 3:30. I follow basically twelve commodities, so I have to print out all the data; I have to go over it and analyze it; I have to update some of my longer-term charts—all that takes two or three hours. In fact, just to print it out generally takes me about an hour. To get in and further review it takes more time, then frequently I'll go back and pull some of the patterns and try to identify certain themes that keep recurring and how they fit into the context of the research that I'm doing, that sort of thing. . . . I always get in a couple of hours, two or three hours, for extracurricular reading, fiction, philosophy, or whatever else I'm trying to do.

Matthew acknowledged that his life was a lonely one but saw this period as a professional novitiate demanding all of his time. He would like to marry and have children sometime in the future, he said, but not until his financial security was established. Meanwhile, he was looking forward to moving to the Southwest. The beauty and austerity of the desert had deeply impressed him during his cross-country travels after college, and he could continue trading from there through computer lines. Along with his commodities trading, Matthew intended to begin a graduate degree although he was not sure what area he wanted to pursue in depth: "One of the problems with having time to read all that you want is that your interests become so eclectic it's hard to focus."

Tracing Matthew's vision of success during the fourteen years since high school is not particularly illuminating. In his first year of college, he aspired to professional football and politics. In his sophomore year, he spoke of becoming a Rhodes scholar. After that, Matthew avoided answering the question of what the ultimate was for him. At the 1990 interview, Matthew described short-term goals like deciding on graduate school and moving to the Southwest. When pressed about the ultimate, Matthew resisted the question: "That's like asking me to say that this is the guiding metaphor of my life. It's difficult for me to answer that because it asks me to put constraints on who I might be or what I might be." I said, "So you don't believe in the question?" Matthew replied, "Yeah, I guess that's fair. I guess now I'll contradict myself and tell you some things. Ultimately, if I made enough money, there [are] certainly things I'd like to do, contributions I'd like to make. Aside from security, money also can have some positive aspects, and if I was good enough at this game, I certainly wouldn't be adverse to giving some of it back to society in some ways. That's a long way down the road. Possibly, I'd like to teach. I'm not sure what or where or when or how, but it's something I might consider doing."

Asked directly about valedictorians and success, Matthew reiterated his difficulty in defining and using the term *success*.

> I think that probably what's at stake is the notion of what society expects of [valedictorians] and what they expect of themselves. Obviously, being valedictorian means . . . that you're supposed to be something in terms of intellect, in terms of achievement, or success, or whatever words you want to use, and yet it may mean something totally different to someone who's on a path to find the Dalai Lama in Pakistan or wherever. . . . It strikes me that there are all sorts of externals that are influencing people, like Phi Beta Kappa, honor roll, those sorts of things. Not that those are bad, but it turns out for me that my best grades came in circumstances when I didn't care [about the grade]. When I really loved the work and was doing it at very high levels, the grades just came naturally as a consequence.

Matthew continues to wind his central quest through reading, market trading, and personal life. He has gone mountain climbing because he feared heights. He has begun a Ph.D. in psychology as he continues commodities trading via computer. "How can I redefine myself and what I'm capable of doing? Or how am I limiting myself? I think those are issues that I'll be working on for the rest of my life. . . . To borrow from T. S. Eliot, it's the journey, it's not the arrival. And I believed it then and I believe it now, that the process is eminently more important than anything else."

Learning from Matthew

Matthew stubbornly resists the label of success for himself or for anyone else. He cannot take seriously the notion of describing his ultimate life because of the limits inherent in defining himself in terms of goals instead of processes. To Matthew, a successful life is one in which he continues redefining possibilities, continues reinventing himself.

How does Matthew fit an analysis of valedictorian life success? His large contributions to this theme are an intellectually reasoned reminder that success must be determined in the context of individual lives and a strong vote against the attempt to generalize beyond this. We can, however, assess Matthew's attainments according to public and individual readings of success. With a Ph.D. in progress and a distinguished undergraduate career, he is certainly academically successful. He has attracted the professional admiration of leaders in his field and has prospered in a highly competitive, uncertain occupational arena. Matthew has lived his life according to his values and intellectual commitments and is fascinated by what he does. He has consistently reported being "somewhat satisfied" with his life, a response that fits his resistance to categorizing himself.

Among all of the valedictorians, Matthew is one of the half-dozen or so indisputable intellectuals and one of the study members I believe to be most likely to become eminent. Terry Denny agreed when in 1984 he wrote the following about the twenty-one-year-old Matthew:

Because Matthew is so mysterious and because of his enormously powerful physical countenance and his intellectual prowess and his intellectual curiosity and knowledge as a result of that curiosity, he has all the makings of a leader. I doubt that he sees himself in a leadership role, but he could very well be the sort of person that people would turn to. The leadership qualities are there. . . . I have no concerns for Matthew's future. He will be a success in his own eyes and in the eyes of others. The best predictor of tomorrow is today.

Success: Themes and Variations

There is a remarkably consistent emphasis in the valedictorians' views of their ultimate. Over time, most of these academically talented students have shifted their primary view of the future from career to a balance between work and family. Nearly all see their ideal life as combining fulfilling work and significant personal relationships. These evolving priorities reflect the strength of undergraduate career socialization, the beginning of serious relationships, and the increasing maturity of young men and women in their early adulthood.

As the study began, many of the valedictorians spoke of the ultimate in terms of money and material well-being. "I'm striving to be a chemical engineer, so I'll make $40,000 a year right off, you know, so I can have my Cadillac, nice house, whatever." Even at age eighteen, nearly all of the group wanted a comfortable life rather than exceptional wealth. As valedictorians began college, their ideas about what it meant to be successful were often limited to stereotypical visions of the American dream. Soon after high school, one young man gave this definition of his ultimate: "I just want to get on the commuter train in the morning like everybody else."

Material security and interesting, prestigious jobs dominated the long-term aspirations of students under twenty. These ambitions fit the national ethos of the early 1980s and the developmental levels of most first-year undergraduates. Working to correct social and economic inequalities was an important goal for practically no one. As a college freshman, Dan was uninterested in exploring the liberal arts: "Life's been planned. I've had things planned since I was about fourteen. I knew what I was going to do and how I was going to go about it."

Nevertheless, there was variation in the valedictorians' visions of success. The forty-two men and women who saw God as a solid or central part of their lives also envisioned religious faith as an important part of their ultimate. Two first-year college students defined themselves in terms of creative accomplishments and another in terms of service to others. Another half dozen, like Matthew, defined themselves in terms of intellectual passions.

Although nearly all began with stereotypical ideas of the perfect life, most valedictorians examined and personalized their early ambitions during the early college years. As Barry said:

> From high school, all I wanted was to be like my father, to do what he did in his lifetime—to get married, have two children, to get a good job in a managerial position, . . . paid well enough to cover the family. . . . There were certain specifics that I liked. I liked things that dealt with international trade so that was the flavor I was going to get out of my life. But, as I said, I changed. I didn't want that anymore, or at least, I told myself I didn't want that anymore. To tell you the truth, I don't want to marry. I don't want any children. Maybe it's because I don't want to have certain responsibilities, and maybe it's because I want to live a certain set life that I've now created—one that will be my own.

Barry was typical in redefining his ultimate to fit his own desires rather than stereotypical social roles. He was unusual, however, in eliminating family from his ideal future life. The valedictorians as a group came to see the future as including both work and family. Sophomore year of college saw a turning point in their discussions of the ultimate. Women, in particular, began describing their ultimate as a life combining satisfying family and work roles. As the years continued, the emphasis on careers and material security evolved into a group preoccupation with balance between life roles. In short, with only a few exceptions, valedictorians were initially quite similar in their stereotypical portrayals of the ultimate. More internally motivated choices came with increasing maturity.

Although most of the group has come to value a balance between personal relationships and professional achievements, the weight each assigns to family and work varies considerably. Matthew, at this point, cherishes intellectual challenge as a central focus of a satisfying life. Emma sees her children's healthy development as her most important personal goal. Farmer Alan has consistently spoken and written of the ultimate in terms of religious faith, "that the great treasure I have found in Jesus Christ can be understood and received by others." Barry, who works as a nonprofessional, sees personal serenity as his goal: "I have accomplished what I have wanted, and I've come to a peace of mind that is an end within itself." Nick, the former accountant who became a high school teacher, sees his ultimate in terms of his community roles. "I'm much more driven by family values and small-town type of values than driven by having a big job in a big city and making a lot of money and driving a nice car." David values family, but he also desires a big-time career. "If you are going to go to a good college and go for a big career, why not go for the best?" Recognition of professional peers, scientific discoveries, political activism, artistic expression: the valedictorians differ considerably in the configuration of their life goals.

Some valedictorians see themselves as locked into choices they made before understanding their own deepest values. Sophie, a physician, embarked on the premed trail without really asking herself if medicine would fulfill her.

> I think there's something, especially in high school and college as well, if you [were] in the top of your class, you had to go to medical school. Or you had to go to law school. . . . 'The top of the class—oh, they're the ones that are going to go to medical school.' If I had it to do all over again, I [might] not go to medical school. I would probably go back and be a French major or something and teach French at a small liberal arts college or something. That's probably what I would do. I see lots of things that I think I would like to do. I read a really interesting article in the *Smithsonian* about this group of people that are in the rain forest and studying birds and plants and things like that, you know, that's interesting. That's biology or science. I could do that. Or [I] read about the digs in Egypt—it would be neat to be an archaeologist. . . . I don't know if I had it all to do again if I would go to medical school.

Extremely talented students face an odd danger: they do so well in the paths they choose that they might not question whether the direction really fits them. Because professions like medicine, engineering, science, and accountancy require such early academic commitments, some men and women find themselves remaining in areas that they would not have chosen with a more highly developed sense of who they are. Most, like Sophie, find ways to adapt and shape their lives around the early choice. A few remain in jobs they actively dislike. And some leave career paths after investing years of training or practice. Emma, for instance, left engineering after her doctorate; Rachel never plans to use her Ph.D. in chemistry to practice as a research scientist.

Like adults in general, valedictorians are more different from one another now than they were in their early twenties. They continue to have much in common, however. Part of their similarity arises from their valedictorian traits. These are hard working, achievement-oriented men and women who set and meet high goals for themselves in the arenas each values. And part of their similarity derives from the experience of being the same age at the same historical period of time. At the leading edge of the so-called Generation X, the valedictorians are part of a cohort that found their twenties to be a time of turbulence and continuing self-definition. Amid difficult economic times and increasingly complex options for women's roles, high-achieving students have faced a social context of multiple, often indistinct possibilities for personal goals and career routes. Most struggle to find a pathway that accommodates their strongly held values for meaningful relationships and personal achievement. Some, like Valerie, currently define the ultimate mostly in terms of family: "to raise happy, healthy, socially responsible children; to have a happy marriage; to enjoy myself and my personal, professional involvement in my community." And although valedictorians disagree on exactly what it means to lead a successful life, many would second Bill's ideal of both family and work: "The ultimate is to lead a happy, content life where I feel like I've been successful personally as well as professionally. The two are intertwined."

Chapter Four

Life After the First B
Going to College

*The 1980s image is a tidy, cheerful, and self-centered
student milking higher education for all it is worth to get
ahead in the world.*
KATCHADOURIAN AND BOLI, *CAREERISM AND
INTELLECTUALISM AMONG COLLEGE STUDENTS* (1985, P. 1)

The eighty-one valedictorians and salutatorians of the Illinois Valedictorian Project arrived at college in fall 1981. They brought with
them flawless high school academic records, strong work motivation, and effective study techniques. As undergraduates, valedictorians continued to take school seriously, continued to be top
academic performers. Their achievements included spectacularly
high levels of four-year degree attainment, postsecondary grades,
college honors, and graduate study. Not all these academically talented high school students achieved top college rankings, however,
and group members followed many college paths. They fanned out
across the country to community colleges, liberal arts schools,
regional and national public universities, and the most selective
private postsecondary institutions in America. Their choices of college and major, path to the degree, and approach to undergraduate education began to differentiate these top high school
achievers from one another.

Did the top of the class head for the best colleges? Unlimited
college options were not the reality for most valedictorians. Money
and distance from home ruled the choices of many. Lack of

sophistication about financial aid and college choice barred others from considering a full range of possibilities. For a few, fear of moving from a limited arena into national competition reduced the college pool.

A quarter of the valedictorians attended religiously affiliated colleges and universities, feeling most comfortable at such institutions; several considered only colleges run by their church denomination. Another quarter of the group attended private nonsectarian institutions. Half of the valedictorians chose public four-year postsecondary institutions, and a strong tradition of state-assisted universities in the Midwest probably affected the college choices of the group. Two-thirds remained in Illinois for college, and twenty-two of these attended the University of Illinois at Urbana-Champaign, by far the largest single group of valedictorians at any campus.

Family social class affected college choice. Ten years after graduating from high school and going on to a local university, Luz, a Latina valedictorian, reflected on her limited college search.

> I was talking to somebody the other day [who was taking her daughter] to visit colleges and universities so that they could make a good choice for her. Her daughter is being prepared for college by going to a prep school away from home. Now that's something that I didn't have and very few minority students have—certainly students who come from financially impoverished backgrounds never have. Also, I never had a parent who could give me advice on college choices or on professional matters. I never had role models that I could look at and talk with about such matters as college.

Parental education and family income affected college choice in complex ways. There was no difference in the socioeconomic status of male and female valedictorians and no overall gender difference in the selectivity of the postsecondary institutions they attended. Mothers of female study members, interestingly, were more highly educated than males' mothers. Men from more privileged backgrounds attended more selective colleges and universities than other male valedictorians. However, women from families with higher socioeconomic status were not more likely than other women to choose highly prestigious colleges. Male valedictorians attended Harvard, Yale, Princeton, MIT, and Stanford. Only one woman chose an Ivy League university—Cornell. Other researchers have also found that girls choose slightly less prestigious postsecondary institutions than boys with the same grade point averages (Rosser, 1989). But why women valedictorians favored schools immediately below the top rank is unclear. Beth, for instance, said she turned down Duke in favor of a public research university to stay closer to home and to avoid heavy loans. She had already decided against applying to an Ivy League school. Her mother had recommended Yale, but when the application form arrived, "it seemed presumptuous that they [said they] were the best school in the world. And I threw it in the garbage and said I'm not going to apply there." Beth came from a highly educated professional family. Her disdain of Yale's self-promotion was in direct contrast to the reaction of David, another upper-middle-class valedictorian: "Why not go for the best?" A middle-class valedictorian, Dan, would have preferred a much smaller school but attended the University of Illinois because of its excellent academic reputation and reasonable costs. Like many U.S. high school seniors facing the realities of rapidly increasing college tuition, Dan viewed the state university as optimizing educational quality and cost.

The top high school students met increased competition in college. First-year adjustments included facing the first B, making friends, and becoming a part of the institution's academic and social systems (Tinto, 1993). A few students never achieved a sense of belonging on campus. Kate and Melissa were home before Christmas, both feeling alienated from academics and pulled toward boyfriends at home. Melissa is one of the four students who never returned to college, her higher education by far the briefest of any study member.

Eleven students transferred from their initial campus to another institution; two students transferred twice. Among the transfers were three students who began their college education at community colleges before continuing to four-year institutions. A rural valedictorian, who wrote that he wanted his pseudonym for this book to be "Dittohead" or "Cobra Jet," turned down his initial acceptance at a Big Ten university. Worried about his ability to compete at the university, he earned a two-year community college degree with all A's. Transferring as a junior to the same university he had initially turned down, this young man nearly left school several times in the initial weeks of the first semester. Genuinely surprised to find that he could compete in a national institution, he graduated in engineering two years later with a 3.9 average.

Some valedictorians found college academics considerably more difficult than high school, but many were pleased—and some displeased—to find few genuinely tough challenges in the classroom. All found that their work ethic and academic skills were equal to undergraduate demands, although a very few experienced some academic struggles that caused them to modify their study habits or change their majors.

As valedictorians moved into the second year of college, their preoccupations turned to choosing or confirming choices of majors and settling into academic courses and study routines. They continued to lead full lives outside the classroom. Friendships were important to virtually all of the academically talented students; dating and romantic relationships preoccupied many. Over a third of the group played intermural athletics; a half dozen competed in varsity intercollegiate athletics. Two-thirds of the valedictorians pursued performing arts activities, and about half joined fraternities or sororities. Most members of the group attended church during their undergraduate years, a reflection of the high incidence of religiousness among them.

Nearly all the academically talented students worked for pay during college. Most worked part time during the academic year and full time each summer. Thirteen students were employed only during the summers, and three students worked full time during the entire year. Most performed unskilled or semiskilled work—what one valedictorian called "pizza jobs." Pizza jobs ranged from farm and factory labor to secretarial and food service jobs on and off campus. Many were employed by their colleges as residence hall student assistants or as library or office aides. Sixty percent of the men and 40 percent of the women gained professionally related work experience during college as undergraduate teaching and research assistants, interns, and off-campus skilled employees. Women were more likely than men to experience a professional internship but far less likely to hold an off-campus paid job related to their academic field.

Two-thirds of the group majored in just four academic areas:

business, engineering, science, and applied health (nursing, physical therapy). The remainder of the valedictorians chose majors in communications, social sciences, and mathematics. Three students majored in education, four in the humanities, and one each in art and architecture. Eight students completed two majors, including a man and a woman who earned double bachelor's degrees (see Table 2). Seventy percent of the valedictorians finished undergraduate degrees in four years, a few graduated in three years (5 percent), and the remainder took five years or more. On average, valedictorians earned college degrees in fewer years than college completers in general (Tinto, 1993). In 1994, only two men and two women lacked college degrees.

Although their academic achievement remained exemplary, the top high school students looked more and more different as the college years progressed. Grouping college pathways into patterns helps make sense of the valedictorians' undergraduate years and the relationship of college to careers. The patterns I use were developed in a four-year study of 320 members of the Stanford University class of 1981 (Katchadourian and Boli, 1985). Like the Illinois Valedictorian Project, the Stanford Cohort Study discovered distinct groups of students among academically talented secondary school students. Exploring the degree to which students identified with career or intellectual aims of higher education and the factors associated with these patterns, the study identified "careerists," "intellectuals," "strivers," and "unconnected students" (see Table 5 for a direct comparison of the valedictorians and the Stanford cohort).

Here are examples of each pattern among the valedictorians who have been featured so far.

Jonas lived at home and attended the urban public university recommended to him by his sister's boyfriend. An African American from a poor urban neighborhood, Jonas financed college with scholarships and loans. After deciding that his initial major in mechanical engineering was not leading to an attractive career goal, he transferred to another institution to pursue a major in television broadcasting. Career attainment was clearly Jonas's reason for going to college. His interest in the liberal arts remained relatively low, and Jonas left college when his occupational goals became impossible to meet. *Careerists attend college primarily for vocational reasons. Although at times genuinely interested in their academic work, careerists choose majors and occupational fields for the instrumental purpose of furthering vocational goals. Jonas's utilitarian view of college qualifies him as a careerist.*

After wide consideration of college options with his highly educated parents, Matthew chose one of the top private universities in the country. The East Coast Ivy League college was ideal for pursuing both intercollegiate athletics and challenging liberal arts study. Fascinated by ideas, Matthew read widely for course requirements and recreation. He did not declare an academic major during the first two years of college. Instead he took courses in a wide range of fields, settling on philosophy at the beginning of his junior year. Although Matthew was unsure of his future career field, he was content to let his intellectual interests guide his educational choices. He chose a field for graduate study several years after graduating from college. *Intellectuals are the opposite of careerists, choosing majors and careers according to personal interest with little emphasis on vocational ends. Although often interested in finding fulfilling vocations, intellectuals focus on liberal arts learning during the college years. Matthew clearly falls in the intellectual category of undergraduate students.*

Marilyn attended a public regional university recommended to her by a guidance counselor who thought the state research university would be too competitive. Private college was not an option for Marilyn according to her rural, working-class parents; her father was proud of his daughter's academic achievement but dubious about her seeking a career instead of marriage and children. Besides, Marilyn's focus on animals fit ideally into Midwestern public universities. In college, Marilyn broadened her original interest in veterinary medicine when she found herself fascinated by animal science and research. After transferring to the public research university, Marilyn pursued animal science as a future career. Her choice of major and subsequent graduate study derived equally from Marilyn's career goal and her intrinsic interest in science. *Strivers desire a college education that will both prepare them for careers and allow them to fulfill their liberal arts interests. Although sometimes overextended and lacking intellectual depth, strivers desire intrinsic interest and occupational utility in their college experience. Marilyn is an example of a striver who emphasizes both intellectual engagement and career orientation.*

Before the end of the first semester, Kate left the large public university where she began college. She had chosen the university because of its excellent reputation and location in her home state. An education major, she was unsure whether she wanted to be a teacher and unhappy with her general liberal arts courses. She also missed her family and her high school boyfriend. After spending several semesters in a local community college nursing program, she was relatively unengaged in her courses and ambivalent about becoming a nurse. Kate left school, married, and began a family. She spent the next ten years working in the home, rearing children, and working as a medical office manager before completing her associate's degree at age thirty-one. *Unconnected students are not focused on career ends or on liberal education. Failing to engage fully in their college educations, unconnected students can have difficulty making academic or career choices, be alienated from the college, or hold competing interests to college. In her first two educational institutions, Kate was clearly an unconnected student who was neither fully committed to teaching or nursing nor genuinely intellectually engaged by her classes.*

I have also considered the possibility that the four college types might be additionally understood in terms of identity development. In Marcia's (1966) elaboration of Erikson's late adolescent identity stage, careerists might be classified as "foreclosed," or committed to unexamined parental values and goals; unconnected students as exemplifying identity "diffusion"; strivers as actively examining identity issues and commitments, that is, in a "moratorium" period; and intellectuals as having reached "identity achievement" after a process of exploration and testing of opportunities. However, patterns of stability and change in the types and the important associations with socioeconomic status, specific college context, and historical era (some of which are demonstrated below) argue that achievement status and career type are overlapping but not synonymous concepts.

Jonas, Matthew, Marilyn, and Kate shared straight A high school records but approached college very differently. Their postsecondary institutions included private and public community colleges and universities. Three attended school in Illinois, the fourth on the East Coast. Even those who remained in public universities in their home state experienced institutions with widely differing geographic settings, academic selectivity, and student populations. The four valedictorians diverged in the sophistication of their college choice process and focused on different parts of the college experience. A closer look at the four college types shows the connection between each type and the backgrounds, values, and undergraduate experiences of academically talented students.

Careerists: College as Instrument

Jonas saw college as career preparation. Having dropped out to support his family, he found work at a company that offered him a job ladder of increasing responsibility and salary. A well-paid supervisor, Jonas now considers himself as successful and sees no need for a college degree. He stands out among the valedictorians in not finishing college, but he attained his objective of a secure, well-paying job without completing a degree. Jim, the only other male valedictorian who still lacked a degree in 1994, followed similar reasoning when he dropped out of a top research university in 1984 to pursue an entrepreneurial career in computer science.

Jonas shared his utilitarian approach to college with nearly half of the valedictorians—51 percent of the males and 41 percent of the females. In other words, careerists made up the largest group within the Illinois Valedictorian Project. These thirty-seven students focused on instrumental purposes in choosing colleges, majors, courses, and careers. They chose vocationally oriented majors that matched their careerist view of higher education, two-thirds studying business or engineering and the rest studying nursing, physical therapy, education, and communications. No careerist focused on arts or humanities.

The preponderance of careerist valedictorians fit the times. The 1980s saw dramatic increases in vocationally oriented college students (Levine, 1980). Freshmen were increasingly preoccupied with financial well-being and careers in business and engineering (Astin, Green, and Korn, 1987). Ronald Reagan was elected president as the valedictorians graduated from high school and became eligible to vote; the prevailing business ethos paralleled rapidly rising tuition costs, economic recession, and diminished social mobility for the small birth cohort following the baby boom generation. Not yet named Generation X, the valedictorians' age group faced genuine constraints on their financial futures and career opportunities. A female engineer, Patricia, captured the careerist sentiment in reflecting on her accomplishment: "I have a very mercenary attitude in life. You have to be good in grade school to be good in high school, to get to go to college, to get a job, to make money."

Valedictorians might have fit their times, but did the head of the high school class differ from other college students? Again, the Stanford Cohort Study of the class of 1981 provides a comparison group, although not a perfect match (Katchadourian and Boli, 1985). Members of the Illinois Valedictorian Project were twice as likely as 1980s Stanford students to fall into the category of careerists (46 percent as opposed to 23 percent). Stanford men were much more likely than Stanford women to be careerists; valedictorian men were only slightly more likely than valedictorian women to see college mostly as vocational preparation. The Stanford researchers' list of careerist traits echoes many characteristics of students who reach the top of their high schools: determination, hard work, high aspirations, single-mindedness. Careerists were independent, self-sufficient, and sure of their goals. They could also be narrow, materialistic, driven, and worried about the future.

Some Stanford careerists were genuinely interested in their academic fields and related courses. Most though, "let practical and tactical concerns overwhelm broader educational purposes" (Katchadourian and Boli, 1985, p. 101). Like the valedictorians in general, Stanford careerists demonstrated admirable talent, effort, and ambition. With an eye on the prize, they were willing to persevere and intent on controlling their future. Responsible, stable, and academically successful, careerists were an excellent bet for continued achievement in mainstream occupations. As the Stanford research team concluded: "Careerists convey a soothing image as a serious and solid group of young men and women who will do the work of the world and effectively look after themselves. If one needed a doctor, engineer, banker, or lawyer, one would be glad to have them around" (p. 92).

The Stanford investigators also predicted that careerists would not reach the top levels of professions, regardless of their single-minded focus on occupational advancement; however, this view was not supported in their ten-year follow-up (Katchadourian and

Boli, 1994). The Illinois Valedictorian Project provides another investigation of the effects of concentrating on vocational preparation at varied colleges and universities.

Martin: Future Accountant

A closer look at a typical careerist reveals the pressures, strengths, and liabilities of this undergraduate approach. This careerist's college story also illustrates some of the themes of the valedictorians' undergraduate years.

Martin grew up in an urban neighborhood as the oldest of three children in a lower-middle-class Catholic family. His father, who had attended a specialized arts college, worked as a computer programmer. His mother was employed as a retail service manager. Martin was keenly aware that his father's chronic depression and problem drinking related to job unhappiness, and he was appreciative of his parents' unrelenting efforts to support the family and contribute to their children's college education. Martin attended parochial schools, graduating as salutatorian from a Catholic boys' high school. A tall, attractive, friendly young man, Martin was active in sports, student government, and academic clubs.

Martin never considered leaving the Midwest for college. He sought a good business department, choosing eventually to attend a midsized Catholic university in his home city. Its scale was not as daunting as the University of Illinois, and Martin wanted to stay in the city with his family and friends. "I knew it was a good school for what I wanted to do, accounting. . . . And it's a smaller school, and I think it's a closer environment."

As a high school senior, Martin knew exactly what he wanted to study and held a precise picture of his future career goal: partner in an accounting firm. He even reported a specific figure for the salary he expected. Accountancy, he decided, offered a practical outlet for his talent in mathematics. "When I left high school I thought of what I wanted to do and I took my strong points, which were an understanding of mathematics, math theory, applications in math, and I thought, 'Well, what can I do with that?' At first I thought math major . . . [but] I said, 'Well, what am I going to do with a math major?' Not too much unless I wanted to teach math. So then I thought . . . accounting. [And I] said, 'Well, that's a pretty good field, it's an expanding field, it's a profitable field.' So I decided to get into that."

In his first year of college, Martin was pleased to begin the accounting curriculum immediately but worried about doing well in the two difficult core courses in his major. When asked what was motivating his continued hard work, he spoke in terms of the connection between his major and career. "My motivation now is to become a successful accounting student, pass the CPA [exam] well, get myself well entrenched with a good firm as quickly as possible, and then work from there." The first B in Martin's college life arrived in his first year, but not in the accountancy courses. Martin took the grade in stride. He tried to avoid competing with other students, he said, concentrating instead on keeping up with the course material and doing his best. "I'm just not really satisfied with anything less than an A; still, I'll take B's if they come once in a while." Martin earned mostly A's and occasional B's during college, graduating with a 3.5 grade point average.

Later, Martin referred to his first year as a tough period of adjustment. Besides anxiety about his ability to make it in accounting, Martin withdrew in the middle of pledging a fraternity and began dating for the first time. He held a job ten hours a week and was active at his home church. Martin was particularly positive about his sports reporting for the college newspaper, an activity that was to become more and more important in his undergraduate years.

His sophomore year, Martin announced that his career decision was firm. He had gotten an A in both difficult core accounting classes: "That's it. I'm working at a Big Eight firm when I graduate." That year, he made another important academic and career decision. He accepted an invitation to enter a five-year honors program in accountancy from which he would graduate with a master's of accountancy degree. The fifth-year graduate degree would make it unnecessary for him to return to school later for an M.B.A., "so when I'm done in 1986, I'll just have turned twenty-three, [otherwise] I could be in school until I spent $50,000." Even with financial aid, Martin said, he would owe $30,000 at the end of five years.

Over the remaining years of college and the extra graduate year, Martin worked hard at academics, part-time academic year employment, and full-time nonprofessional summer jobs. He continued to date sporadically, to play sports, and to deepen his involvement with the college newspaper. After writing for the sports page during his first year, he became sports editor, and as a senior, editor-in-chief. Martin sent us clippings from the newspaper and sparkled when describing his journalism work. We asked Martin whether he had ever considered an alternative to accountancy. Both mathematics teaching and journalism, Martin said, were out of the question because they were financially impractical. "I went into business because it was something that I thought I'd be good at and other people thought I'd be good at. I knew that it could be profitable, meaning that it was pretty easy to get a job and a good paying job, something that I could be relatively successful in right away. . . . The only other alternative would have been to give all of it up and take a whole bunch of communications classes and journalism classes and go with the newspaper stuff. But that was always a hobby."

Martin never mentioned strong intrinsic interest in his business courses, but worked hard to be able to do "exactly what I wanted to do with limited barriers. I needed that up-front schooling, and I needed to do well in it to open the doors. Because if I don't [open the doors], then I work for account temps. I work for some small little tool and die maker. I work for—I don't know—a bank." Although he made strong friendships at college and developed some relationships with administrators as a result of his newspaper work, Martin never made a strong personal connection with a faculty member. His fourth-year summation was telling: "School—I really enjoy it. I mean if it weren't for the classes, it would be perfect. [*Laughs.*] But you know, even classes are good. You see the people you know, and that's always good."

Not surprisingly, Martin achieved his ambition exactly. He earned the master's degree, passed the CPA examination in fine style, and worked for a major public accounting firm. By the summer of 1990, he was unhappy in his job, complaining about the long hours, extensive travel, and tedious work. He no longer wanted to become a partner, he said, and was thinking instead about joining a smaller company as a financial officer. Martin also wanted to buy a house and to begin a relationship that would lead to marriage. His view toward education, despite his disenchantment with public accountancy, remained unabashedly careerist. At that point, he had no plans to return to school but said that stand could very easily change if he were to move to a company that wanted M.B.A.'s in the management track and would pay for the degree. Later in 1990, he moved to a large Chicago company as an internal auditor, moving up steadily over the next four years. Happier in his work, he also began a significant romantic relationship with a woman he married in 1993.

Lessons from Careerists

Like most of the Stanford careerists, Martin did not come from the highest socioeconomic level. Like most, he had a father who worked in a technical specialty. Careerists tend to be the sons and daughters of careerist fathers, highly influenced by their families to stress the practical side of higher education. Alice, for example, chose physical therapy on her father's suggestion. An Illinois prize winner in mathematics, Alice changed majors several times but retained a vocational approach to college.

> I didn't like spending all that time in the lab over there with the computers. So I dropped that. Then I was going into math or science education and that's what I wanted to do. But then I thought, "Well, health education, with the state budgets as they are, that's going to be one of the first classes that they cut because it's not required." . . . My dad and I kept thinking about it, and I was all upset for a while trying to think what am I going to do with the rest of my life. And I felt kind of discouraged—I was continuing to go to school but not studying. . . . And Dad kept his eyes open, and every time he opened the papers, he read, "physical therapist." And so he just mentioned it to me one day, and I started thinking about it. And then I talked to a guy in my church and I started calling around and talking to people. And I just kind of decided that's what I'd like to do.

Once settled on her career field, Alice studied hard and earned the excellent grades required to transfer to a prestigious physical therapy program. She continued to be influenced primarily by family and church friends rather than college professors. The importance of her father's influence and her relative disconnection from faculty mirrors the experience of the Stanford careerists. The scant faculty interactions of careerists, according to Katchadourian and Boli, probably result from lack of deep intellectual engagement in courses and from students' pragmatic view of college as the accumulation of practical knowledge and credentials. As another careerist, John, stated, he knew people who sought out professors outside of class, but he felt no need to do so: "There is really nothing I could go and talk with them about. I mean, there probably is, and I probably could talk to them about the class itself, but I get to hear enough of that as it is. I haven't met up with anyone that I'd really like to talk with."

The valedictorians' examples illustrate the importance for careerists of social class and family beliefs about education in choosing colleges and structuring the undergraduate experience. In common with all first-year college students, careerists face a period of adjustment to college. (For valedictorians, facing the first B can be an additional worry.) Like their undergraduate peers, these vocationally oriented students take part in extracurricular activities, including employment. They spend considerable energy on friendships and romantic relationships.

Careerists tend to be quite satisfied with their college experience. They seldom change their major or career field as undergraduates. Similarly, 84 percent of the careerist valedictorians kept their original college majors until graduation. Like their Stanford counterparts, most graduated in four years. In the ten years after college, only two careerists changed their occupational fields: Monica, a Latina who abandoned her broadcasting ambition and settled on a nonprofessional job, and Lisa, a mathematics education major who became an actuary. The rare careerists who made shifts changed one vocationally oriented field for another.

Martin's life since college affirms his view of higher education as a direct pipeline to a good job. Careerist valedictorians got out of college exactly what they sought. Some found the prize sweeter than others, but most consider their bargain of hard work for vocational certainty a fair trade. As adults, careerists remain responsible, hard working, and self-sufficient. They are indeed the most predictably solid achievers among the Illinois valedictorians.

The Intellectual Path

Matthew went to college to explore a life of the mind. Without a specific career goal in view, he tried various liberal arts fields and settled on philosophy as an exciting intellectual endeavor. Matthew's approach to college was the opposite of Martin's; not surprisingly, the two young men had radically different undergraduate experiences. A similar intellectual interest, not utility, guided the academic and career choices of a quarter of Stanford undergraduates (Katchadourian and Boli, 1985). The Stanford team described these "intellectuals" as students who were open to new perspectives and directions, valued the liberal arts, and viewed academics in terms of intrinsic interest.

The Stanford men and women who focused on liberal arts earned the highest grades of any group and participated heavily in campus activities. Not surprisingly, most came from homes with highly educated, nontechnical professional fathers. The Stanford research team assumed that these more privileged students had less concern than other undergraduates with ensuring their financial security through a vocationally oriented college degree. Freed from pressures for upward mobility, sons and daughters of professionals were also more likely to benefit from intellectual models and traditions. They formed close relationships with faculty members who strongly influenced their ideas and career directions. Professionally related work experiences also affected their occupational choices.

As opposed to 25 percent of Stanford students, only 12 percent of valedictorians fell into the intellectual category. Male and female valedictorians were equally likely to be intellectuals; again in contrast with the Stanford group, where women were twice as likely as men to focus their college education on liberal arts learning. Eight of the ten valedictorian intellectuals came from the highest socioeconomic rank in the Illinois Valedictorian Project; all were white. Intellectuals were more likely than careerists to change their majors and career fields during college. Three out of ten moved away from their original career choice during the undergraduate years; four more changed fields after college.

The lower proportion of intellectuals among the valedictorians than among the Stanford students may result from two factors.

First, the valedictorians were much more diverse in their family and economic backgrounds than the relatively privileged Stanford student population. Few valedictorians considered attending elite non-Midwestern universities and few came from highly educated professional families. Second, the process of becoming valedictorian did not favor intellectuals. As their high school stories reveal, valedictorians reached the top of the class by accommodating family and school demands. Students who focus on following their own intellectual interests would be extremely unlikely to work hard at school subjects and tasks that they found intrinsically unengaging. Following one's own muse might result in high grades in some areas but seldom yields a perfect academic record.

Meredith: College as Intellectual Journey

Meredith considered private universities around the country where she could combine top-flight academics and music. Salutatorian of a superb public suburban high school, Meredith also won a National Merit finalist award and piano competitions. She had one younger brother, her father was an engineer, and her mother a homemaker and part-time secretary. She reported: "My parents never really forced me to work. They encouraged it—books all around and everything. But I never really felt pressure from them. I was one of the few who really enjoyed school. I felt weird because I really enjoyed learning things." She also described her family as quiet, saying that "in the evening, we all go off to our separate corners of the house and read." Although a self-described "bookstore freak," she stated music to be far the most important of her nonacademic activities. She had begun studying piano in kindergarten and by high school was also playing the oboe and singing in the chorus.

Valedictorians were sometimes taken aback by the initial interview for the project, expecting only questions about study techniques, upbringing, and school. When Meredith was asked if she had heroes or heroines, she laughed. "I like these questions! You know, I wish I could spend a lot of time thinking about them." Another indication of intellectual spark was Meredith's close relationship with a high school English teacher: "She started me writing in a journal and reading poetry and everything."

As she prepared to leave for college, Meredith had considered several different career fields. Engineering might be interesting, she said, but she had dropped the idea because she disliked physics. Psychology was a strong possibility, along with medicine. Meredith briefly considered forestry, since she loved the outdoors and her self-initiated project to learn how to identify trees. And music would certainly be a part of her college experience. "I think I'll like being in college. . . . When you're a freshman in college, there's a lot of things you have to figure out for yourself. So I'm looking forward to going there."

Meredith was placed on the waiting list at Yale and so chose instead to attend a prestigious private East Coast university known for science and for its renowned music school. When she spoke with us during her first year, we were surprised to find she was considering majoring in physics.

> That's really funny because . . . I said that I didn't like physics, [but] that is what I like the most now!. . . . I had a lot of ideas that I thought would be neat to do, but . . . I found first semester that my advanced calculus course was the most challenging one. So I thought, "Well, I'll take some more math, and I'll take physics next semester." And it turned out to be what I liked. There are a lot of people premed and majoring in biology to get into med school without really wanting to learn about biology in itself. And I found that with math and physics, there are more people who are interested in learning about the subject itself rather than just trying to use it or get over the hurdle.

Mathematics was deeply enjoyable, Meredith reported, because "there were interesting ideas: the way things were related and the way math works." Similarly, she was fascinated by popular and academic reading about new concepts of matter in quantum mechanics.

Along with her deepening interest in physics and mathematics, Meredith found that she was taken seriously as a pianist. Her piano teacher gave her extra lessons, taught her over the summer, and invited her to perform a recital. Meredith became more and more deeply involved in music, practicing between an hour and a half and three hours six days a week.

As a sophomore engrossed in her academic and music studies, Meredith felt no pressure to decide her future career. "I guess I stopped worrying about am I going to get as good a job as my father and things like that. Because if you keep worrying about that you don't have time to think about the things that are important to you and sort out what is inside. And I'm not saying that I'll probably get a bad job. I mean, if I apply myself with physics, I don't know what will really happen. I guess I tried to stop worrying about making money and stuff like that."

By her junior year, Meredith had played a recital and built a clavichord from a kit. She accompanied voice students, performed chamber music, and continued to be engrossed in her academic work. She began to explore Eastern religions, took up running, and became a vegetarian. A long-distance relationship with her high school boyfriend continued to be important to Meredith, although not part of her daily life during the academic year. Her boyfriend shared Meredith's interest in music and philosophy. She "had never been able to talk about things like that before. . . . Now, I'm finding it easier to think about things like that and pick them apart and continue thinking about them for days." Meredith was particularly interested in Jungian psychology, a topic she took up on her own.

Life after the first B did not arrive for Meredith until her junior year. As a first-year and sophomore student, she was pleased to make all A's in her courses but was not focused on working for grades. "A lot of [the work] isn't [for] the grades, I just want to know [the material] well. If you know it well, you are probably going to get good grades." Having declared mathematics and music as double majors, Meredith finished most of the physics major as well. A physics professor had taken an interest in her, she said, showing her around his laboratory and discussing possible research areas. Meredith's interest in physics decreased in her junior year, however.

I ended up sort of getting sick of physics. Because when I first started taking it, it was real neat. But then we got into the real heavy, mathematical, just-use-this-formula-and-keep-applying-it. So I got tired of it by the end of the year. So next year, I probably won't take any physics. Just finish up my math. And piano is still on. . . . I spent a lot of time studying physics, and if just a lay person asks me, "Well, what is this?" [and] I can't really explain . . . that makes me want to go back and figure it out some more. But as far as career and stuff, I don't see [physics] coming into play for a while, if ever.

Meredith's first B occurred in the physics course she disliked. Did it hurt? "Not really. It was good to know that I *could* get a B–. . . . I wasn't really interested in putting in extra effort so that I could have gotten an A."

By her senior year, Meredith was considering the future more concentratedly than before. Science technical writing was a real possibility for a job after college. "I realize that you have to think about the practical aspects of life—particularly, How can I earn a living when I get out of school? That brings me back to science and technical writing. That certainly is a way I can earn a living, and I think I would enjoy doing it too. . . . I enjoy the skill, the craft of interpretive writing in a technical way. I enjoy getting facts together and making a statement." Career prospects in music were the subject of many long talks with her piano teacher; pursuing a musical career was increasingly attractive to Meredith.

Everyone knows that out of every one hundred piano majors, ninety-nine of them aren't going to be concert artists. So every piano major reaches a point where she says, "What am I doing this for?" Look, if I could do anything that I would want to, I would probably want to be an accompanist, especially for singers, because I enjoy doing that and I'm good at it. Yet I've been sort of wondering, should I just forget everything and try it? Being really foolish thinking that way. But I've concluded that I should probably keep all my options open and this is one of them. . . . I'll probably have another long talk with my piano teacher when I go back. I'll say, "What am I going to do?" And he'll set me down, get me to just keep working ahead.

With a 3.87 grade point average, Meredith was elected to Phi Beta Kappa during her senior year. She felt ready to leave college. "School is too easy for me. I feel like not being in school will make me do more, work a little harder. Really focus in on what's important." Finding work as a computer research analyst after college,

Meredith was a highly paid, successful professional. She was never fascinated by computers, however, and not attracted to business. Six years after graduating from college, Meredith returned to graduate school for a doctorate in psychology. "My original intention in college was to major in psychology and then I got sidetracked into math and music. Really, the reason I got sidetracked, I think, was because Psych 101 was so horrible . . . it was a huge lecture class. I had never had anything like that before. But the interest in psychology has remained, and doing the work I do now, I like parts of it."

Meredith married an academic researcher in 1992 and gave birth to her first child in 1995. She hopes to combine a faculty career of teaching and scholarship with a full life of marriage, children, and music. "I think with psychology, I'm going to be able to finally really feel like I've challenged myself, that I really know something that hopefully I'll be able to apply that kind of supports my values—helping people and helping people find fulfillment themselves."

And the Career Follows

Meredith is not a typical high school valedictorian, but she is a classic intellectual. Intrinsic interest in arts and sciences motivated Meredith's choices from high school to college to career. From the first interview when she spoke of interests in Baroque music, identifying trees, and human psychology, it was clear that Meredith was a curious, engaged, self-motivated learner. Mastery, not grades, motivated her academics and music. David, a fellow intellectual, summed up the liberal arts approach to higher education:

> Sometimes I just have an enormous desire just to know everything, which obviously is impossible. I have a really strong desire to have a balance in education. Computers, for instance, a perfect example. I know absolutely nothing about computers, and I'm just dying to. I wouldn't want to be a computer nut but to be able to have a pretty good solid basic knowledge. But I just don't have the time with my other interests. And the thing is, when you see people that become computer nuts, you see to become like them would be twenty-four hours a day for the next five years, because that's what they've done. So there's no way you can ever catch up; there [are] always

people who know a lot more than you do, except in one or two fields. And that's frustrating. There are times when I just look at that bookcase and I just wish I knew everything that was in every one of those books; it's all so fascinating.

Meredith went to college with tentative ideas about what she would study. After enrolling in a wide variety of courses, she identified her intellectual passions and followed them. She continued to follow her interests and to seek intellectual challenges even as her focus shifted over time. Her ability to remain open to new possibilities was clear in her embrace of the previously disliked discipline of physics and her increasing seriousness about music in light of faculty encouragement. Meredith was equally able to discard areas that were no longer interesting, as she did when abandoning psychology after a disappointing introductory course and when deciding as a junior that the fun had gone out of physics.

Freeing herself from a direct connection between college major and career was also important for Meredith's college experience and eventual attainment. Meredith was aware of career issues, but confident that her skills and interests would lead to fulfilling work. As she had made her academic choices, she made a career choice on the basis of intellectual challenge rather than prestige or income. Work experience in marketing research also helped clarify her interests. In retrospect, the return to her early interest in psychology seems an inevitable integration of Meredith's interests and values. However, her eventual high-level attainment in the social sciences came about precisely because she resisted early career closure in science or performing arts.

Like their Stanford peers who oriented their college education toward liberal arts study, Meredith and other valedictorian intellectuals were exceptionally successful academically. This small valedictorian group also developed particularly close connections with faculty, as Meredith did with her piano teacher and—to a lesser extent—her physics professor. Similarly, Dale was handpicked to work in the studio of a prominent architecture professor.

He's kind of a groundbreaker. I mean he shakes the earth, and I like what he's doing, and it's amazing how things fall into place for me. . . . When you're in his class it's very free thinking, free willed—it's almost like talking to Aristotle. . . . It's like you're in Greece all over again. Then you go to the construction class, and [there] you do it exactly this way and this is what the line is supposed to look like, and it's a real contradiction. But it's exciting. It feels like I have a little bit more control over my education than I did before. You know, I'm very happy.

Like most of the ten valedictorian intellectuals and unlike the larger group, Meredith left her home state to attend a private elite institution. Intellectuals were the only valedictorians to choose the top tier of nationally selective, small liberal arts colleges. Her activities on campus, like those of other intellectuals, related to her academic and personal interests and clearly indicated the breadth of Meredith's development. The only area in which she diverges from the standard intellectual profile is her engineer father's technical profession. However, a classical music lover and voracious reader, her father apparently communicated to his daughter a view of life and work that centered on intellectual challenges and personal meanings. Meredith says of him, "most of his life he works. And why does he work? He works because he wants to raise a nice family and give us good things. . . . But you have to decide for yourself what's good and . . . what will mean the most to you. I'm the only one who can find that out for myself."

Striving for It All

The case of Marilyn represents a third undergraduate profile: the "striver." Marilyn always considered her studies as steps along an occupational path leading to professional work with animals. She also prized the intellectual excitement of scientific discovery, however, eventually coming to choose basic research over veterinary medicine. Unlike the predominantly vocational or liberal arts orientation of careerists and intellectuals, the orientation of strivers is a deep dedication to both vocational preparation and liberal arts learning. Just under a third of the valedictorian men and women were undergraduate strivers, almost the same percentage as the 1981 Stanford study cohort (Katchadourian and Boli, 1985).

Kevin: The Engineer Philosopher

U.S. novelists have been describing the likes of Kevin Grobach for a long time: white, ethnic, urban, proud of his parents, his neighborhood, his achievements, and who also has a strong sense of the life predicaments in which he is trapped. Kevin would never use the word "trapped" because he is an optimist and sees himself as being a fortunate human being with a lot of opportunities. Which indeed he has and which I believe he will make the most of. Kevin is, without a doubt, one of the solid ones. Yes, he is one of the solid ones; he knows who he is, he knows where he is, he knows where he's been, and he knows where he's going as best anyone can.

Terry Denny wrote these words in 1984, after an interview at Kevin's modest family home. An engineering major and an accountant's son could have been expected to lodge himself firmly in the careerist camp of college students. Instead, Kevin couched his commitment to engineering in terms of intellectual challenges and interpersonal connections. He read philosophy, psychology, and literature for college courses and for pleasure. He wrote poetry, essays, short stories, personal letters, and letters to the editor. Caring about both vocational development and intellectual engagement, Kevin fits the profile of a striver.

Kevin was the sixth child and first son of nine siblings. He has always been close to his parents, especially his mother. "She's always open, always ready to talk. That was probably one of the most influential forces—probably *the* most." Encouraged by his father as well, he pushed himself hard in both high school academics and athletics. "A lot of times in school and college and everything, I feel pressure. I'm afraid to fail or afraid to do badly—I don't know if it's put on by me or put on by my dad. Just to win at everything. It just seems like school, track, everything is the same: just the pressure I put on myself, the desire for perfection." As he approached college, Kevin knew that he had always succeeded when he worked hard. "Now I'm kind of scared. What if I do work hard and when I come down to the final point, I fail? I've never experienced that."

Applying to an Ivy League college never crossed Kevin's mind. "It's too far, and then things are expected of you." A Midwestern research university was prestigious, too, he said. Without much thought, Kevin applied to enter college as a business major. "Maybe the reason is that my dad is an accountant and always talking up the business field and all that, and I thought, 'Well, that might be pretty good.' Then I started reading over this one handout that the university gave out about how to help decide. My talents lie in science and math so I talked to a few deans over the summer and I kind of slowly changed over into engineering. Now I'm undecided in engineering. So, who knows?"

So far, Kevin's story differs only subtly from Martin's. Unlike Martin, Kevin was open to possible majors. He sought input from academic administrators and had difficulty envisioning himself in a specific career role. Still, his choice of major was clearly vocationally based. His dad would have "flipped," he said, if he had elected to concentrate in arts or humanities. And Kevin needed to support himself through college. An engineering co-op program, in which students alternate semesters of study and full-time engineering employment, allowed him to pay his way through college while receiving professional experience.

Like other valedictorians, Kevin faced an uneasy adjustment before finding that his hard work yielded mostly A's in college. After a C on his first chemistry test, Kevin gave up running and spent all his time studying.

> Then things started changing. I started playing racquetball, for one. I started budgeting my time more. The classes might have been getting more interesting. It might have been that my grades were starting to show after the first round of tests. What was hard about the first two weeks was no grades came in. No tests. I was still blind as to how I was doing. I was very uneasy. But after the first round of tests, I did pretty well. I settled down, then. . . . My grades started rising. To pull it off on my Chem final, I needed a really high score . . . to get an A in there, and I pulled it off. So, I just made it. I was really happy about that.

Kevin earned four A's and a high B in his first semester. By February of that year, he had made some close friends and was enjoying college: "I like it. It's new; it's different; it's fun."

Having found he could survive academically in college, Kevin began backing away from his former competitive intensity. "It just seems like I needed to prove to myself that I could do it. The second semester was pretty much the same pattern again, and then over the summer, I kind of relaxed. There was more free time. I . . . put everything in a better focus. You know, balance in the social, athletic, and academic life." Being recruited by engineering co-op employers was a self-confidence boost, as was his widening circle of male and female friends. "It was kind of like I was always on a high and feeling great, and so I made like three times as many friends. I know everyone on the whole floor and the whole hall. And it's not only knowing them. I'm willing to always spend time and talk to them and stuff." A final move away from his self-induced pressure came when Kevin observed himself competing intensely in a friendly game of football and vowed to stress enjoyment instead of winning.

Sophomore year, Kevin was ranked second in his economics class. He also chose to take art history, along with mathematics, physics, and engineering. Kevin enjoyed all his classes. "I not only like the material, I thought it was important to learn, and once you think it's important then you want to learn. In this last economics class I had, the guy was a really good teacher. He hit the important concepts, and he wanted to get you thinking like an economist, and he wanted you to integrate the different parts, put it together—some strategy or policy. That's where learning comes about that is unbelievable." Kevin served as an informal tutor in his residence hall, enjoying the process of making something clear and interesting to others. In teaching friends and his younger brother, Kevin tried to model his belief in centering on "fundamental concepts and fundamental thinking." He was open to peer as well as family and faculty influence. Living with roommates, he said, "opens up many more things. Your roommate always comes up with some ideas or some ways of viewing things or somewhere to go or just twice as many things than you can delve into."

Over the next few years, Kevin alternated semesters of engineering and on-campus study, reporting: "I like the challenges of work. I like knowing, believing, that I can become a good engineer. I like the fact that I am making money. I'm going ahead with what I like." He came to see his professional future in terms of developing interpersonal connections and communications: "Organizing the different parts. I enjoy that. I think I'd be good at it."

Disappointed that not all his university friends were faithful cor-
respondents, he nevertheless managed to sustain campus and work
friendships across his interrupted residence in both worlds. Kevin
chose co-op placements that involved the greatest challenge.

> Risk is where the fun is. Risk is where you learn or fail. And that's
> that. The steadiness, I don't really care for it. The main reason I
> took the job with [the] co-op is to keep an imbalance in my life. I
> had a couple of job offers, and I chose [the co-op] because it would
> keep me imbalanced; it would keep me off guard. Each time I
> would be somewhere different. I wouldn't know until the week
> before. I think that is good, just to get in those situations, see how
> to handle them. The more off balance, the more risks. The more
> you don't know about what's going to happen tomorrow, to a cer-
> tain degree, is good.

Kevin always enjoyed engineering classes and work, but several
times considered alternative careers. His growing extracurricular
involvement, including community service and political campaign
work, drew him strongly. "I want to do something socially important, something I would really learn from, something I would jump
into with enthusiasm." Along with reading, writing offered an
increasingly important outlet for Kevin. "I've been dabbling in writing. Writing journal entries, essays, letters, articles for newspapers.
I love to communicate and writing presents a great challenge for
me. My mom thinks I should be a journalist instead of an engineer.
Sometimes I feel the same way. I wonder how a logical, straight-
laced engineer can like writing rebellious essays probing life's
norms. My desire to learn and answer questions drives me to write
in hope for a reasonable solution."

Kevin persisted with engineering, but from the striver's dual
perspective of practicality and genuine interest. "There is a whole
technical field out there, a changing world that I want to be on top
of. There's a lot of interesting sidelights, literature and so-called
humanities, so the way I'm going, technically and professionally,
hopefully maintains social and very human type creative aspects."

Fourteen years after his high school laurels, Kevin is a married
electrical engineer achieving professional success through genuine
interest in his projects, his co-workers, and his company. "I think

I'm on the right track. I like the tremendous challenge in the industry. . . . And I know I can work with people and get something done pretty effectively, too." A supervisor who presents his group's projects in the perspective of larger company goals, Kevin also earned an M.B.A. to help him understand the marketing and business aspects of his industry.

Kevin maintains a wide circle of friends, stays active in recreational sports, and volunteers in community service activities. He remains close to his family, especially his mother. Clearly, he structured his college experience to ensure a clear career path. It was not as a careerist, however, that he responded in 1985 to the question of whether he considered himself an intellectual. "The word intellectual can have negative connotations. I do know that I love to read, reflect, and wonder about the world."

About Strivers

Careerism and intellectualism exist to differing degrees in every college student. Even the most dedicated undergraduate careerist finds some intellectual spark in ideas or courses. And it is a rare intellectual who ignores professional goals.

Kevin is a typical striver, according to definitions in the Stanford study. Not as intellectually deep as Meredith, Kevin was also not as narrowly career driven as Martin. Strivers normally come from less privileged backgrounds than intellectuals and seek upward mobility through college attendance. Kevin's father had attended college on a vocational track and the large family was never financially comfortable. Following his intellectual interests into a nonstandard career of journalism or a nonprofit human service job might have strained or even broken important relationships for this family-oriented young man. Again typical of strivers, Kevin spread himself thin trying to get the best out of intellectual interests and career preparation: "Sometimes I feel there's not enough time in a day to do all the things I want." The engineering co-op program literally disrupted his campus experience while time spent with friends, sports, and writing took him away from concentrated work in a specific discipline. It is perhaps because of this lack of focus that Kevin never became close to any faculty member. He played intermural sports, performed community service, volunteered for political campaigns, was an active church member, belonged to clubs, and served as an engineering honor society officer. "I joined so much stuff it was sickening." Kevin was influenced by multiple sources, another common facet of the striver's profile. His father, college deans, and course and work experiences all affected Kevin's decisions and self-view. Peers were also important reinforcers of both occupational and intellectual directions. Finally, like strivers in general, Kevin was well-adjusted, happy, and broad. There was no higher compliment, he claimed, than to be called "versatile." Kevin was an atypical striver in one way only. Stanford strivers were the least successful group academically. With a final grade point average of 3.6, Kevin was an excellent college student.

Valedictorians who were both intellectually and vocationally oriented were as likely as careerists to keep their original career field throughout college. They were slightly more open to occupational changes after college, though, with one in three eventually moving away from his or her initial choice. (Only one in five careerists had changed fields by 1994.) Four of the eight valedictorians with undergraduate double majors or careers were strivers. In each case, the first major was vocationally oriented and represented the career the valedictorian actually pursued; the second was a pure liberal arts discipline chosen for intellectual pleasure. A female chemist double majored in English before going on to a science Ph.D.; a physician added a B.A. degree in theology to her premedicine bachelor of science. An aerospace engineer received a second bachelor's in German and a journalist striver also majored in history. For these students, the very structure of their transcripts showed the dual emphasis on career preparation and liberal arts.

Disentangling Kevin's educational values from those of his family is an impossible task. It is unlikely that Kevin would have chosen a humanities major even without his father's expectations and his financial need, although he might not have continued with engineering. Imperative demands for security and upward mobility dominated the college choices of many might-have-been intellectuals; few ever seriously explored alternative academic paths. This was particularly true of students of color: African American, Asian, and Latina valedictorians fell into every category except intellectual. Michelle, an African American striver, was candid about her need to emerge from college with a secure, lucrative profession. "Going to school is definitely affected by the fact that I want to be able to take care of myself." About a third of Stanford minority students were strivers; nearly all minority valedictorians were careerist or unconnected undergraduates.

However successful in engineering, Kevin seems an unlikely candidate for eminence. When it comes to his occupation, he is interested but not passionate, hard working but not obsessed, imaginative but not mold breaking. Above all, he wants a balanced life with relationships at the center, followed by work attainment, and community and personal activities. Striving for breadth seems a likely recipe for happiness. Indeed, as Stanford undergraduate strivers also demonstrated, valedictorian strivers are particularly contented, well-adjusted men and women, and they continue to make choices that reflect their value for integrating interesting work within a balanced life. They continue to be happy adults. They seem to have fulfilled the prediction of the Stanford researchers, who concluded: "Strivers may be the salt of the earth, but they are unlikely to emerge as the seminal thinkers of their generation" (p. 181).

Unconnected Undergraduates

Before dropping out of university and then community college, Kate was neither strongly career motivated nor deeply intellectually engaged in her studies. Researchers placed just over a quarter of the Stanford class of 1981 in Kate's category, which they labeled unconnected. Unconnected students, they wrote, "fail to engage fully in their college education for no obvious reasons" (Katchadourian and Boli, 1985, p. 182). Concentrating on neither liberal arts learning nor vocational preparation, the unconnected group includes students who have difficulty settling on academic or career paths, who feel alienated from college life or larger social achievement values, and who have personal problems that divert them from educational involvement. Unconnected students are also men and women who never really wanted to go to college or who have strong competing interests to formal education or careers. Some appear to be potential careerists; others have unfulfilled intellectual interests. Like Kate, unconnected Stanford undergraduates were less satisfied with their college experiences and relatively uninvolved in college activities compared to their peers; unlike her, they also tended to be average or weak students.

Fourteen percent of valedictorians fit the unconnected designation, as opposed to twenty-eight percent of Stanford students. The eleven valedictorians without strong liberal arts or career connections form about the same size group as the intellectuals and a much smaller cluster than valedictorian strivers or careerists. The small number of unconnected valedictorians is no surprise. Top high school students came to college with a long history of caring about school achievement and identifying themselves through academic roles. The career pressures on students from middle-class and working-class families meant most of the academically talented group perceived a strong need to prepare themselves for lucrative work. Almost none of the valedictorians entered college alienated from schooling or from mainstream social definitions of achievement. Raised mostly in healthy families, the valedictorians were a remarkably psychologically well-adjusted group.

Why, then, were there any unconnected valedictorians? One possible answer lies in the gender split of the group. In sharp contrast to Stanford students, among whom unconnected men outnumbered women, valedictorians who fell into this category were much more likely to be female than male. Several of the unconnected women planned to emphasize family roles, including full-time childrearing, and did not expect to work outside the home during much of their adult lives. Without overwhelming intellectual interest in a liberal arts discipline, such students were also relatively uninterested in vocational preparation. One of the two unconnected males similarly believed that his undergraduate business education would be only marginally related to his desired profession of farming.

Other unengaged college students found themselves blocked from their desired career track or unable to settle on a major. Among this group are two of the seven valedictorians who earned less than a B college grade point average. Kerry, for instance, was deeply distressed when poor grades prevented her admission into nursing. More common were students who cast around for majors without ever finding a satisfying match. Only a third of unconnected Stanford seniors graduated in the same general career field they indicated as first-year students. Like the Illinois study group as a whole, unconnected valedictorians were more likely than their Stanford counterparts to remain in their initial career field. Even so, 55 percent of unconnected project members changed their career plans during college. Remarkably, by 1994, not one vale-dictorian who was an unconnected college student was employed in the field he or she chose when a first-year undergraduate.

Gail: Seeking a Niche

The project's first interview with Gail was proceeding in unre-markable fashion until the interviewer asked Gail how she liked her first year of college. For the first time in the conversation, shy small-town Gail sat straight up in her chair, looked the interviewer in the eye, and said emphatically: "*I don't like it!*" A story tumbled out of feeling lost and uncertain about academics, career, and her place on campus. "Everybody else knows what they're doing, knows what's going on. And here I am, I don't know what I'm doing half the time." Gail felt she was under a cloud of never-ending work and competition. She was already thinking about transferring.

> I'm not one to really like a lot of pressure, and I feel there's too much pressure here. Maybe I could learn just as much in a little different way without the high curves. A career is important to me but not that important. If I went somewhere else that was not as diffi-cult and it didn't have the pressure, . . . it's not going to hurt my career. My career goals are not such that I need a prestigious degree. But on the other hand, if I go somewhere else, is there going to be less pressure or am I going to demand just as much or more from myself? So that's what I'm trying to decide.

Gail had come to the university from a small town in central Illinois. The oldest and most serious student of three girls, she was the daughter of a building contractor who was a former teacher. Her mother was also a teacher, having returned to college for a degree when Gail was in elementary school.

Gail arrived at school with vague ideas about becoming a den-tist. She enrolled in the general studies division and began taking a potpourri of classes. Dropping chemistry was a major event in her first year—never before had she given up on an academic challenge. She had worked day and night on the course, but even though she was miserable, it had never crossed her mind to leave the course until her father suggested it. Leaving the premed "weed out" course behind was a great relief, but it also meant the end of her dentistry ambition. Choosing the next set of courses was traumatic: "I didn't know what to take. I had no idea and being in general studies, I was really confused. I didn't know what to do. It really got me down for a while because I didn't want to declare a major and I just wanted to take general classes all the time."

Gail's reaction to her first B's was mixed. In mathematics, she said, she did not mind a B because she anticipated a lower grade in such a challenging course. "I excuse myself. I had heard how horrible calculus was." A second B disturbed her greatly, however. "I think I deserved an A in that class, and that really disappointed me, and I was really upset about it. And another thing that really made me mad about the class was that I didn't learn anything. If I had learned something, if the teacher would have known what she was talking about and I would have gotten a B, that would have been a different story. But since I learned nothing and I knew more than she did, then I felt she had no right to judge me."

Gail enrolled in a course on career development that was very important to her. Through journal writing and other self-exploration assignments, she came to know herself better and to realize both the kinds of courses she most enjoyed and the need to find a better balance in her life between study and social activities. A general business major, she thought, would give her a good base for some kind of professional work with people. Maybe she could work in the personnel department of a company, Gail said, counseling employees on life-role balance and vocational decision making.

Sophomore year of college, Gail was trying to overcome her shyness and become more outgoing. Her major nonacademic activity was involvement in the Baptist Student Union. She would definitely work for several years after college, she said, although she expected to stay home with small children when she eventually had a family. She still considered transferring and was dissatisfied with her business major. "I don't really like being in business. I feel like I'm told so much what to take [rather than having] freedom. I guess with that, it doesn't matter what university you go to. I don't know." Organizational behavior research sounded interesting to Gail; she thought she might ask her graduate teaching assistant what that occupation involved. She decided against an internship that summer, returning home instead to work and spend time with her family.

By junior year, Gail had reached a certain peace with the university and her major. Although she continued to do well academically, she stopped studying so intensively and took one class for pass-fail credit instead of a grade. She added a volunteer job as a peer career counselor and two mornings of food service employment to her continuing church involvement. She still expected to work after college, she said, "but I wouldn't mind if I didn't work all my life. It's just not that important. I would like to be able to do some other things like, I don't know, get to know my neighbors, just be domestic for a while." Although the intensity of her disappointment about her major had faded, she still considered whether she could change fields and graduate on time.

> But I decided to just stick with business. I talk to people and have done a little bit of reading—not much. Just about how a liberal arts background is so good to help you think and give you a general background of different things. Like in my speech communications class, most of the people are speech majors or psychology majors and they seem to think more deeply or something. They tend to integrate several things more than I do, and it seems like in some of my classes I'm taught not to think broadly. And if organizational behavior is what I'm going to do, it's important that I really learn to integrate and to broaden and not be so narrow.

She still did not love the university, Gail said, but she had learned that with a different attitude, she could do what she wanted. "Not everything I want to do, of course, but I can do other things, and it's not as bad as I made it out to be." After the junior-year interview, Terry Denny wrote that Gail seemed much more comfortable with herself as a college student and as a person: "I am less concerned about her than I was a year ago. I felt she had the capability of working herself sick or worrying herself sick for not working."

Gail graduated in business administration with a 3.5 cumulative grade point average. After a frustrating job hunt, she applied to a company that was opening a new facility in her home town. "I thought, 'I don't want to live in this town; I don't want to work at this place.' . . . And I happened to get home just a little bit before they were going to close the applications, and I thought, 'what the heck!' I went in at 7:00 and filled out an application. They closed them at 8:00. Big deal. Anyway, they offered me a job—had 3,000 applicants and they hired about 120 people. So I got a job. At least it was full time and benefits, health care and all that." Gail began as a customer service representative, enjoying the challenge of opening a new facility and dealing with difficult customers. After a year, she was transferred to the accounting division where she spent several years in a position she described as "basically clerical" before being promoted to accounting manager in 1988. Gail finds it ironic that she ended up working in accounting. "Accounting really wasn't my field. I was just kind of in general business. And I really hated accounting."

Gail was considering a job switch when she met her husband, a fellow employee and lifelong town resident. The two married in 1988 and had their first child in 1992. Gail continues to work full time for the same company.

Missed Connections

A 1984 file note, written when Gail was a college junior, sums up the project view of her as an undergraduate: "Gail is not an intellectual but may very well be under-developed intellectually. That is, she has an eye and an appetite for the larger issues of life but is not in a curriculum that brings her into contact with people who can teach her how to think about such matters. She has a personal yen for learning more than business administration and engaging in some self-education beyond her college years."

There is ample evidence of Gail's intellectual side. Her excitement over the insights of the career development course, her envy of the social science majors' tendency to "think more deeply," and her chafing at the course restrictions of a business major all point to a college student who valued intellectual engagement. Yet Gail was clearly not an intellectual who perceived her college education in terms of liberal arts learning. She never considered letting her curiosity about ideas guide her academic choices, even when she told us she could see herself taking general studies courses forever.

It was as a frustrated careerist that Gail settled on business administration. She entered college seeking a career and even took a course specifically to determine her vocational direction. The career development course was a big success in opening Gail as a person but it failed to conjure the perfect occupation. Gail continued to work hard. Without deep genuine interest in many of her courses and without strong connection to a career goal, she found the requirements of a demanding university to be nightmarish pressures. By her junior year, she had retreated from the fray. She stopped seeking the perfect major, backed off from intensive studying, and made the best of the situation. After all, she told herself, work would not be a vitally important part of her life: "It's just not that important."

Gail's anxiety about school was shared by several other unconnected students. Valerie, for example, set up a series of tests for herself in which she tried experiences like study abroad, law office work, and a government internship. "I started thinking that since I don't know what I want to be when I grow up, I'd better not close any doors for myself now. I had to do everything perfectly so that when it came time when I had decided what I wanted to be, I'd be able to do it. I wasn't really able to enjoy school." Without a mentor or a strongly positive result from any one of these experiments, Valerie gave up on finding the perfect career field and defined herself instead in terms of her upcoming marriage and anticipated childrearing.

Unconnected students do not engage themselves deeply in liberal arts learning or in career preparation. No prototypical unconnected student exists, yet Gail shows many of the characteristics of this undergraduate type. Although she displayed intellectual tendencies, she never focused on intellectual engagement. Although she sought a career, she never found a satisfying major or occupational field. She was only minimally involved in extracurricular activities. Gail received academic counsel from no one. No faculty or family member helped her connect to an academic or career path; no job experience gave her a vision of what she could become. Like many unconnected students, she backed away from academic involvement and career planning, defining herself instead in terms of her future family role. She drifted into her post-college job.

Like the other unconnected valedictorians, Gail was not alienated from school when she arrived at the university. She was ready to work intellectually, and she was eager to find a fulfilling career. It is this profile that differentiates the unengaged valedictorians from their Stanford counterparts. And it is this profile that makes the story of the unconnected valedictorians so poignant.

Assessing College

How did the valedictorians do in college? They succeeded. Seventy-seven of eighty-one students completed college degrees. They earned a mean undergraduate grade point average of 3.60. Project men and women collected every honor higher education offers. They were socially active, gainfully employed, and involved in campus activities. They overcame normal adjustment challenges and accepted the first B with equanimity.

Like the attempt to weigh success on limited levels, simple outcome figures obscure the complexity of valedictorians' college accomplishments. From the choice of postsecondary institution to the undergraduate experience itself, valedictorians' educational achievements rested on the interplay between family background, personal values, and academic and career engagement. Students with identical grade point averages experienced college as deeply meaningful intellectual engagement in liberal arts or as highly specialized vocational training. Many students aimed broadly, although settling for less intensive involvement in both liberal arts learning and career preparation. A few found themselves unable to connect meaningfully with any undergraduate focus.

As might have been expected from their serious pursuit of high school success in the 1980s, three-quarters of the valedictorians focused their attention on the vocational purpose of higher education. Careerists were half of all valedictorians, concentrating chiefly on training for secure, well-paying occupations. Another quarter were strivers, seeking liberal arts learning along with career preparation. The final quarter of valedictorians, split about evenly between intellectual and unconnected students, found their educational focus in the pleasures of learning or nowhere at all.

As compared to Stanford students of the same era, the valedictorians were far more career oriented. They were also more stable in their choices of careers and majors, although goal changes varied across the four types. Careerists almost never veered from the vocational path they mapped before age twenty; a few strivers changed in college and a few more afterwards. Intellectuals, in contrast, changed academic majors and occupational goals relatively frequently, and unconnected students all abandoned their original college plans.

By the criterion of meeting personal ambitions, careerists were the most successful college students. A measure of breadth, however, puts strivers at the top. Apparently the happiest undergraduates, strivers were well-adjusted women and men whose search for balance continues into adulthood. What about the deep pleasure of intrinsic engagement and the quest for intellectual challenge? This axis of success places intellectuals at the apex, suggesting that intense intellectual involvement might generate greater achievement and perhaps deeper happiness than more shallow versatility. It is even possible to argue that some unconnected college students are among the most successful individuals in the Illinois Valedictorian Project. Although they were clearly unsatisfied undergraduates, some of this group have happily carried out life plans that conflicted with the heart of higher education. The former unconnected college students include two mothers working full time in the home who are among the most content valedictorians today. Alan, the farmer, was a business student who graduated with a 3.8 grade point average but felt little connection to his university. His family and religious faith currently anchor a life he finds deeply fulfilling. "I hate to sound self-satisfied, but I *am* self-satisfied. When I'm working on the farm, my children can work with me, and then you can have a relationship with your children through your work."

The Stanford study team predicted that undergraduates who stressed the liberal arts—strivers and intellectuals—would be more successful professionally than the highly channeled careerists or the disengaged unconnecteds. The "guess" of the Stanford researchers was "that the narrower Careerists tend to [end up] working for those of their peers who have broader visions and

more rounded educations . . . to end up toiling away as journey-
man practitioners of their trades, only rarely achieving true professional success and prominence" (Katchadourian and Boli, 1985,
p. 236). To some extent, this prediction was accurate for the valedictorians (interestingly, more accurate for the valedictorians than
for the Stanford researchers' own study cohort). Strivers and intellectuals appear in disproportionately high numbers among the
highest achievers in the Illinois Valedictorian Project. Intellectuals, in particular, hold the greatest promise for eminence of any
valedictorians. Intellectuals' endeavors in academic research and
in nonstandard fields like visual arts, writing, community organizing, and commodities trading provide more opportunities for
breakthrough achievements than careerists' business and technical fields or standard careers in education, health, or law.

However, many careerist valedictorians do seem likely to reach
the top of their professions, even if those career fields may be limited in themselves. Some vocationally oriented students, like Martin, are not particularly pleased with the reality of their realized
goals; others, however, are quite content with their professional
lives. And their approach to college appears to have little to do
with valedictorians' general life happiness or their success in establishing and maintaining fulfilling relationships.

Overall, the story of the valedictorians' undergraduate lives fails
to pinpoint the road to success. Again, success proves to be a slip-
pery concept. Beyond the unequivocal statement that high school
valedictorians perform magnificently in college academics, few
generalizations characterize the undergraduate experiences of academically talented students. Their varied approaches to higher
education illustrate the diversity valedictorians brought with them
into college and illuminate their increasingly divergent life paths.

Like other assessments of the life success of high school valedictorians, judging higher education outcomes does uncover cultural and individual visions of the purposes of a college education
and the nature of a good life. Different individuals, families, and
cultural groups prize varying degrees of security, self-expression,
challenge, balance, and intellectual life. Visions of the ideal life
course determine the choices of academically talented students
and their interpretations of their goals and accomplishments.

Chapter Five

Contingency Planning
Women and Careers

> *One thing that intrigued me at my high school was that*
> *such a disproportionate number of the top students were*
> *women at that age, and yet the further I go along, at each*
> *stage, there seem to be fewer and fewer women. I've never*
> *understood why that should be, and I've never understood*
> *where all those women went that were in classes with me in*
> *high school.*
> DAVID

In 1982, an astonishing pattern from project interviews forced gender differences in achievement to the center of the study. Terry Denny and I asked periodically how intelligent the students thought they were compared to others their age. That year, women's self-reports of their intelligence began a downward spiral. Women—but not men—showed a sharp decline in their self-estimated intelligence between high school and their sophomore year of college. As high school seniors, a fifth of the study women said they were far above average in intelligence. Only three

---

Note: Selected case material and analyses of female valedictorians in this chapter appeared in earlier versions in K. D. Arnold, "Undergraduate Aspirations and Career Outcomes of Academically Talented Women: A Discriminant Analysis," *Roeper Review,* 1993c, *15*(3), 169–175; and K. D. Arnold, "Academically Talented Women in the 1980s: The Illinois Valedictorian Project," in K. D. Hulbert and D. T. Schuster (eds.), *Women's Lives Through Time: Educated Women of the Twentieth Century* (San Francisco: Jossey-Bass, 1993a).

women characterized themselves as no smarter than average. As they left high school, male and female valedictorians estimated their own intelligence identically.

Almost two years later, we asked the question again. The big-fish-in-the-little-pond syndrome might predict that all high school students would lower their intellectual self-estimate in the more competitive college arena. And we already knew that many valedictorians attributed their achievements to effort instead of native ability. To our surprise, women—and women only—lowered their self-rankings after high school graduation. In their second year of college, over a quarter of the female high school valedictorians listed themselves as merely average in intelligence. Only two women reported themselves as far above average. In marked contrast, the percentage of men in the far-above-average category remained constant at about a fifth and men's overall self-ratings increased. By senior year of college, the picture had improved slightly. Only three women characterized themselves as average in intelligence in 1985. There was still a significant gender difference favoring males' intellectual self-estimate, however. As the valedictorians finished college, no woman said she was far above average in intelligence compared with her peers. The four women with straight A's, the future medical, law, and Ph.D. students, the Phi Beta Kappa honorees—not a single woman placed herself in the highest category of intelligence. Men, in sharp contrast, steadily increased their self-ratings. A full quarter of the male valedictorians left college reporting they were far above the average intelligence of their peers (see Table 6 for the full figures).

The finding that women but not men were decreasing in intellectual self-esteem was remarkable partly because it was the overwhelming group difference in the early project years. Most puzzling, though, was the discrepancy between women's achievements and their self-view. Women and men went to equally selective colleges and universities (although women were less likely to attend the most prestigious schools). Therefore, declining intelligence rankings cannot be explained by women's facing stiffer academic competition. Like their male peers, female valedictorians came to college with strong mathematics and science backgrounds. Twenty-four of the forty-six women chose college majors in the prestigious male-dominated fields of business, engineering, and science. Regardless of major, women's college grades were superb—even slightly higher than those of the men—and women were as successful as men in winning academic honors, merit-based scholarships, and undergraduate research and teaching assistantships.

Yet Meredith, a Phi Beta Kappa graduate in mathematics and music, told us she was deeply insecure about applying to graduate school: "I thought no one will want me." She described reaching for the telephone to request admissions applications and then pulling her hand away from the phone, unable to make the calls. With the help of a therapist, Meredith completed the admissions process: "Of course, everybody wanted me! I got fellowships everywhere, and I got in everywhere." By any observable account, valedictorian women were performing at the top of their college classes. So why were they discounting their intelligence more and more?

We came to believe that the mysterious gender difference in intellectual self-esteem had something to do with a second pattern that also appeared in the sophomore year. At age nineteen, the female valedictorians began talking about careers in light of motherhood. Six sophomore women left premedicine majors, their departure notable among a group that mostly stuck by their original choices. Two made the customary exit from the major after doing poorly in first-year chemistry. The other four, though, were among the top academic performers in the project. These high-achieving women, we found, were changing majors because they believed that becoming a doctor would keep them from becoming a fully engaged mother.

A premed major who changed to physical therapy and is currently a married mother and part-time physical therapist, told the project back then: "I'm interested in premed but not as much [as I once was]. I want to have a family where the woman is in the house more than a doctor would be able to be. You can't be a half-time doctor. You've got to put your whole self into it, and I don't know if I could do that and still put my whole self into my family. And it comes down to whether I want to choose between being a mother or being a doctor."

Another woman reported: "I've thought about it. Because it's tough. You know, wanting the balance with the career and the kids. I'd like to have kids, and I think it's important to their development to spend the first three or four years with their mother, but at the same time, if I did that, I mean—three or four years in chemistry— if you miss that, you can say goodbye to it for life." This chemistry major graduated in science and then switched to humanities. Currently, she is an academic researcher, married but without children.

A premed major who changed to psychology, said: "If I were a man I probably would go to med school and become a sports doctor. . . . Because I would never have to worry about being pregnant and staying home with children. It's not something you worry about as a man. As a woman, it is something I worry about, unless you say you don't want to have children. I want to have children. I want to stay home with them while they are younger, so I think maybe women that think like I do are thinking more practically." This woman is currently married, rearing three children, and not employed outside the home. In 1990, she told me, "I didn't back out of medicine because I couldn't do it or because I couldn't make it through med school. I would be a doctor now if I'd stuck with it. I just made a choice over life-styles."

Women in all majors raised concerns about the merging of family and career although none were married or engaged at age nineteen. There are "a few things I want," one woman told us. "I know I want to get married. I know I want to have kids. I know I want to have a career. I don't know how much weight I want to put on my career. I don't know how long I want to work. One thing that angers me is that as a woman I have to plan this." As we listened to women, we heard them configuring their future lives as occupational achievers and as wives and mothers. At this point, none of the actual contingencies of husband and children were known, much less controllable by the valedictorians. Yet women took a contingency approach, that is, they assumed their future careers would be strongly affected by family-related juggling of paid work, marriage, and childrearing roles (Almquist, Angrist, and Mickelson, 1980; Angrist and Almquist, 1975, 1993). Pressures to remain open to future family needs find women "groping for handles on the future they cannot predict, seeking sensible plans among hazardous contingencies. . . . This struggle to complete the puzzle while the big pieces are missing haunts . . . women" (Angrist and Almquist, 1975, p. 81).

Valedictorian women planned their work and family lives simultaneously, based on what they knew or what they thought they knew about the workplace and the home. Although male valedictorians also expected to marry and have children, men saw no reason to account for future families in career planning.

We followed up these unexpected findings in the next annual interview round with the "magical sex change question" (Arnold and Denny, 1984). We asked students to imagine their probable lives as a member of the opposite sex. Women had given some thought to this issue and had a lot to say. Most men found the question novel and difficult. As women, some men thought, their career advancement would be hindered by childrearing responsibilities or perhaps discrimination. One man facetiously offered that as a woman, he would still try to make it to the top and "be the president's secretary." A few women, in contrast, thought affirmative action would work in their favor in male-dominated career fields. However, valedictorians envisioned few differences as a member of the opposite sex except for anticipated family effects on the careers of women.

It was precisely this problem of combining career and family that dominated women's responses to the magical sex change question. Over and over, women said they thought life as a man would be easier because they would not have to worry about combining future motherhood with career participation. "Men have it easier because they don't have to worry about how to fit kids into a career" was a common female response. Many women said it would be more difficult to be a man because of pressures to succeed professionally and to support a family: "I'd never think to myself, 'I'm going to have to support a man someday and support my children someday.' I've always thought of myself in a supportive role." The most poignant response came from Diane, an immigrant's daughter, who said that if she were a man, "my father would have the son he always wanted. My sister and I are the epitome of what good children can be . . . but no matter what we do, I think my father is disappointed in us somehow, some way." Women gave instances in which they said it would be easier and in which it would be more difficult to be a man. Remarkably, no man thought it would be easier, in any way, to be female.

Four years into the Illinois Valedictorian Project, men and women had equivalent graduate school ambitions, college grades, and marriage expectations. With about 75 percent of the group planning graduate school, valedictorians' educational aspirations were much higher than those of undergraduate students in general ("Carnegie Survey of Undergraduates," 1984). And unlike their peers nationally in the mid 1980s, academically talented women were as likely as men to aspire to graduate study (Hafner, 1985). All the college seniors except one man said they planned to marry. With the exception at this point of this man and one woman, all of the valedictorians reported that it was at least somewhat likely they would become parents, and most men and women ranked marriage as relatively more important than career in their future lives. As they graduated from college, the valedictorians planned to marry in their middle twenties and to have two or three children beginning a few years later. Men and women placed equally high value on the use of their intellects and best talents in careers. They were equivalent in their moderate valuing of prestige, high income, and occupational security. Women were significantly more interested than men in the career values of working with people, helping others through careers, and finding work that allowed combining career and family.

Although male and female valedictorians expected similar futures of marriage, family, education, and career values, the gender difference that strongly confirmed the interview data was the finding that women planned very different career participation than men. As college seniors, two-thirds of the female valedictorians anticipated interrupting their professional careers or working part time, in every case to concentrate on childrearing, whereas all thirty-five men planned continuous full-time paid work until retirement. Significantly, female engineers, scientists, and business people were as likely as future teachers, nurses, and physical therapists to plan discontinuous employment. Only seven of the twenty-four women in male-dominated fields planned continuous full-time career involvement.

Diane, as a junior engineering major, set forth her plan for combining career and family.

I have a grand scheme of life. . . . Graduate at twenty-two. If I happen to meet somebody in college, date for about a year, marry a year or two after that. Preferably he would be older. Be married by twenty-four, even though I always said twenty-seven was plenty early to get married. I still think that. But if you think about it, if you get married at twenty-four you have three good years of single-life marriage together as a couple and at twenty-seven start having children. You're still really young and able to enjoy your children's life more, I think. Be more active in it. Have two to three kids by thirty-two, I guess. . . . I would like to be able to quit work from the time I give birth to the time they're in kindergarten. And then go back. . . . Be retired at fifty and be worth a few million.

At thirty-two, Diane still wanted to leave work to raise a family, but she had not yet married. Ambivalent about her engineering specialty since the first year of college, she had earned an M.B.A. and moved from the technical area to the financial division of the large company where she had been employed since college. Although she had always dreamed of running her own business, she never seriously pursued this option. Expecting to leave the labor force for childrearing affected Diane's career identity and her vocational choices. Her career might have looked different if she had expected continuous professional employment. Because of its reliance on marriage and childbearing in the twenties, Diane's "grand scheme of life" rested on contingencies she could not control.

In their early twenties, women's reports of the work they expected to be doing in their thirties differed from men's in several ways. Many women listed childrearing or homemaking in addition to paid employment, some said they would be working in the labor force *or* in the home, and several specified part-time employment. Yvonne, one of the most outstanding students in the study, reported her career ambition as "either working as a physician or mother and homemaker." (Yvonne is now an unmarried physician but is still unsure whether she will continue practicing medicine once she has children.) No man mentioned any consideration of family expectations or work schedule in listing his aspirations. Male career planning focused firmly on future occupational roles.

Women's professional expectations were also more vague than those of most male valedictorians. Men tended to report an occupation, level, and professional setting. Women did not. For example, a female accounting major listed her future career field as "accountant" while a male in the same field wrote, "controller, senior executive in private industry." Another woman listed her career ambition as "trying to run my own company in whatever looks promising" while another man planned "my own marketing consulting firm."

By the end of college, the dramatic difference between men and women who were high school standouts was not undergraduate academic achievement or graduate school aspirations. Both males and females continued to earn superb grades, win high honors, and plan graduate study. Women chose difficult curricula and prestigious occupations as often as their male counterparts. In many ways, female and male valedictorians were far more similar than different. Still, more women than men held unfocused career goals. Only women as a group lowered their intellectual self-esteem during college and only women placed future parenthood at the heart of career planning.

Becky noticed the disappearing women well before David did. Girls must just not like engineering, she thought, as she noticed the dwindling number of female classmates by sophomore year.

> In engineering, I don't know if it's male chauvinism, but it's male-oriented because a lot of the girls are getting weeded out, and I don't know why. It seems a lot of them must have dropped out. I took physics 101, 102, and 103, a required sequence for engineering. And in 101, my class had a lot of girls in it, and in 102, my class had a lot of girls in it but a little bit less, and in 103, I'm one of two girls in the class out of thirty. I couldn't believe it. . . . I walked in and they're all guys. We do have a lady professor this time. I never had one of those. . . . I think a lot of girls go into it, but they don't really know what they want to do. Some girls just don't really like engineering and they get out of it. I really like it, and I don't see anything else.

Women's vagueness about their futures as engineers and the lack of female models are clues Becky provides in answer to David's implied query, Where did all those women go?

Whether contingency planning around future family expectations diminishes women's actual career attainment has become one of the central questions of the Illinois Valedictorian Project.

We are already certain, though, that it is only young women who consider what kind of career they want within the constellation of their life roles. "Before women decide *what* occupation or career to pursue, they must decide whether or not and to what degree they wish to make outside employment a focus of their lives. Men, in contrast, are rarely allowed to consider the '*whether*' and begin instead with the '*what*,' thus getting an earlier start in the process" (Betz and Fitzgerald, 1987, p. 10). Unlike a group of gifted 1970s college women (Angrist and Almquist, 1975, 1993), the female valedictorians did not seek to delay career decisions until the pieces of marriage and family were in place. Instead, these academically talented women made commitments in anticipation of quickly establishing an enduring marriage with children and a husband able and willing to support a family with his salary alone.

Not All Women Disappear

Not every project woman modified her career plans because she believed high-level employment and full-time mothering could never go together. Female African American valedictorians, for example, do not fit this pattern. Black women, as Chapter Six describes, carefully ensured they could survive on their own. And some white women ignored family contingencies and assumed they would fit in marriage and children when they happened. Beth, for instance, chose doctoral study in science rather than medical school because she wished to combine her interpersonal interests in teaching with the intellectual challenges of chemistry. "My parents were pushing me to go to medical school—I think pushing is the right word. My mom particularly was saying that having an M.D. would give me more career flexibility to take time off to have a family and still be able to go back and find some paying work once the kids were older. I don't know if it's true or not, but that was her point. I thought it was pretty dumb to make a decision based on these nonexistent children." If she did have children, Beth said, maybe her husband "would spend more time with the kids than I would and the kids would turn out wonderful." Significantly, Beth questioned her mother's claim that only some careers accommodate mothering and that the woman would take primary responsibility for childrearing. Most female valedictorians took these notions, authorized by their mothers and peers, as given. When Diane, as a sophomore, considered a future without marriage, it was with the sly pleasure of confounding her mother. "Don't tell my mother this—it'll curl her hair but good—but even if I wouldn't end up marrying anybody, I could still see having a good life. I want to do a lot of things besides getting married. . . . Besides, [it is never certain] that a woman is going to get married and have a family." It was rare for a white woman in this study to acknowledge that she might not marry when she chose or enjoy the financial option of reducing her paid work.

Side by side with the bright women who lowered their career aspirations for future families, some female valedictorians continued to aspire to the highest level of professions. In the fifth year of the study, therefore, we turned our attention to career differences among valedictorian women (Arnold 1993a; 1993c). A series of qualitative and statistical analyses revealed two distinct groups of women among the former high school valedictorians. One group of the recent college graduates aspired to the highest professional levels, the other chose distinctly lower-level careers. To reiterate: *high* and *low* represent social prestige rankings of occupations, not personal worth or life success. The division of women into occupational groups was modeled on comparisons among males in the Terman longitudinal study of high-IQ individuals (Oden, 1968). Contrary to previous research and popular wisdom about status attainment (social mobility), the female high and average aspirers were equivalent in ability, intellectual self-esteem, and family socioeconomic status (Arnold, 1993c). They attended similarly prestigious colleges, were equally interested in graduate study, and were highly interested in using their best talents in careers.

What separated female valedictorians five years after high school was work and family values. One group planned more continuous careers than the other. If the high-level career achievers did expect to reduce their paid work to accommodate future childrearing, they planned to work part time, while lower-aspiring women, professionally speaking, planned to leave the labor force entirely when their children were small. High-aspiring women also planned later marriage and childbearing than their less ambitious peers.

Expectations for the sequence and extent of labor force participation, we found, explained most of the difference in talented women's career aspirations. In their early twenties, nearly all the women were still setting their aspirations in terms of expected, not actual, family involvement. Among the women, only Kate married in the first four years after high school; she and one unmarried valedictorian were the only mothers by 1986. Six other women married in the year after college graduation.

The highest-aspiring women differed from their equally talented peers chiefly in their expectations for continuous careers. Other factors separated the two groups as well. Top-career aspirers had more undergraduate experience in their chosen fields, including professionally related paid and unpaid internships, research and teaching assistantships, and jobs. High-aspiring women desired careers that helped others but were not necessarily "people oriented." A single background factor differentiated the groups: mothers of the highly aspiring women were more highly educated than mothers of the less-aspiring female valedictorians.

Overall, then, expected career continuity, professionally related experience, and mother's education separated the two female vocational groups very accurately. The same factors were absolutely useless in explaining men's vocational patterns. Instead of falling into distinct groups, men's aspired and actual career levels form a continuous, bell-shaped curve. Differences in career levels of male valedictorians have to do with ability, college quality, intellectual self-esteem, and the desire for prestigious, challenging careers—the kinds of factors that common sense and sociological theory tell us should make a difference in career outcomes.

How did women's plans turn out? The valedictorian story is not yet over, but the fifth-year pattern seems to be holding at the fourteen-year mark (Arnold, 1993c). Today, at age thirty-one, three-quarters of valedictorian women who held high aspirations as college students are indeed working and studying at the highest professional levels. Senior-year aspirations strongly predict career outcomes a decade beyond college. Approximately 40 percent of the female valedictorians are clearly top-career achievers. These study women are physicians, attorneys, professors, scientists, and business executives. Another group includes valedictorians in middle-ranked occupations like nursing, physical therapy, and precollege teaching. Finally, a third group comprises women working at nonprofessional jobs that do not require a college degree or rearing children full time. In terms of the entire valedictorian group, women are still found disproportionately at both the high and the low ends of the career spectrum.

How did expectations about family and career actually affect women's occupational status? The latest count shows 67 percent of the female valedictorians are married and two-thirds of these women are parents. Although, in college, the high-aspiring group planned later marriage and later childbirth than less highly aspiring women, it turned out that both groups married at the same rate and at the same ages. Some of the top-career achievers married earlier than they anticipated and many of the lower-aspiring women married later or remained unmarried through their early thirties. Here, the plan was not carried out. It appears that *expecting* delayed marriage is a more powerful predictor of career attainment than the actual age at which women marry. The highest-achieving women have, however, carried out their plans to postpone childbearing.

The interweaving of career aspirations, family expectations, and undergraduate professional experiences comes to life in the stories of individual woman. Allie appeared briefly in Chapter Two as the number two graduate in the Catholic girls' school where Kate was valedictorian. Allie's story portrays many of the gender-linked themes in the Illinois Valedictorian Project.

Allie

Allie is a white woman from a working-class family in a small industrial city. Her parents, an electrician and a secretary, never attended college. Allie's only sibling, a younger brother, was an average student. Their home was not one with a lot of books or discussions of science or world events. She credits her parents for her academic achievement, though, because of their strong values for hard work and doing your best. By the first grade, Allie already knew she was a good student. She read independently and did well in all her classes, but she always enjoyed math and science classes the most. Academic achievement had become a way of life by high school. "High school came easily for me, it really did. I worked. I was socially active. I went to sports events. I never really gave up anything that I can think of."

In high school, Allie had a teacher for physics and chemistry who was trained as a chemical engineer. He encouraged Allie to consider medical applications of physics. He also encouraged her to attend a Big Ten university engineering open house. Allie was happy to have a day off from school to travel to the event. She was impressed by the nuclear engineering exhibits and representatives, later saying, "I guess I applied in nuclear engineering more or less on a whim." Allie found that college was not as effortless as high school. After receiving a D in her first semester of college calculus, she changed her study habits and became more serious about her classes. She had an active social life but no serious long-term romantic involvements in high school or college.

Her first two years of college, Allie was unsure whether she wanted to remain in engineering. She considered law school. Her sophomore year, she reported: "I'm just now getting into my field. I've been talking with people that are in graduate school now. People that have gone out to work and come back. Even professors."

Allie's advisor recommended a class in bioengineering her sophomore year, for which Allie lacked the prerequisite. When Allie expressed strong doubts about her preparation, her advisor insisted she could handle the work. He physically accompanied Allie down the hall to the office of the professor of the course so she could ask his permission to take it without the prerequisite. The instructor agreed, provided that Allie stay in close touch with him during the semester. Allie not only did well in the class, she got to know that faculty member fairly well.

At this point, Allie still did not know if she wanted physics or engineering, work or graduate school. She continued to consider the possibility of law school. Her sophomore year, she had this to say about her career:

> Maybe I won't even like the field when I get there. I really don't know. Maybe I won't want to cope with it. After I get done, maybe I'll want to say, "forget it; I want a family." [Maybe I'll stay] home. Throw it all away. I don't know. At this point I hope not because I really enjoy what I'm doing right now. But I don't really know what the industry's going to be like at all. So I guess right now, ideally, I'd want to work because I think I would be unhappy if I didn't have that stimulation. Maybe there would be something I could do at home. . . .

The professor whose bioengineering course she had taken recommended Allie for a research assistantship in a laboratory. Allie took the job, but she had doubts about her ability. "When I was approached for the job, it took a lot of convincing. I didn't want it. I was afraid this professor was assuming my physics background is a lot better than it is." In the lab, Allie found that she was able to do the work. She got to know more graduate students and faculty in nuclear engineering. She started being known around the department as the "medical engineering person." She began spending time socially with graduate students. That summer, following her junior year, Allie followed a professor's recommendation and took a summer job at a national laboratory.

Again, Allie initially doubted her ability. She confessed: "At first I was mortified. I just couldn't believe what they expected me to do in eleven weeks. It was two new computer systems and I hadn't done any programming since my sophomore year, but I think it was probably the best experience I ever had because now I know I can do it. Throw something at me. I'll live through it and work it out."

The laboratory job helped Allie believe that she was exceptionally competent—something people around her had been telling her for the past three years. The experience also allowed her to envision herself in a high-level position. "It wasn't what I expected it to be. . . . Fantastic people [are] up there doing fantastic work. But they are people, and they have a lot of good times, and they are not gods or anything. I think wherever I end up I'd be okay." She returned to this idea later in the interview: "I thought there were a lot of people who knew everything about everything. This *is* a national lab, these people *are* Ph.D.'s. And they are just people. And they make mistakes."

Her senior year in college, Allie was offered a research project in radiation technology in a hospital. She was now considering which Ph.D. program would be best in her specialty. She spoke knowledgeably about the work of potential doctoral research supervisors around the country. She had dropped the idea of law school and was totally involved in her science. In the project interview that year, Allie responded to the quotation read to her from two years before in which she had said she might give up a career for a family. "At this point, the career comes first. Last spring, I did a lot of things with graduate students. That and my national lab job have probably strengthened my conviction. There really was never any pressure put on in high school. It just happened, more or less. Now I see there is potential, and I think it's silly to waste it, so I want to be good at what I'm doing." As a college senior, Allie said she would deal with marriage and family decisions as they came up. The ultimate for her, she said, was "always being challenged. I can never perceive myself as being in a situation where I would stop learning."

Allie was one of only three women in her graduating class. Early in the study, she had told us, "there are a couple of professors who are biased, that don't like girls around." She was aware of being among a small minority of females in her field but was never preoccupied with being a woman in science. "Sometimes that bothers me because I'm being singled out because I'm a woman and not because I'm good at what I do. But I think that is helping me too. Being a woman is opening a lot of doors, and then once I get in, I can prove myself. I don't feel any different than women outside math and science, but I don't think I'm that much different from the men in nuclear engineering either."

Allie today is a postdoctoral fellow in cancer radiobiology, having earned her doctorate at one of the top research universities in the country. Her self-confidence as a scientist and her knowledge of career management in her field are considerable. Despite success in publishing her dissertation work, Allie is deeply concerned about the funding climate and politics of academic science. And she still has some ambivalence about the dedication required of a research scientist. In a 1994 written survey, she provided the latest version of her ultimate life:

1. Being overwhelmingly successful in my career (or at least well funded)
2. Having a happy home-life with well adjusted children
3. Having lots of time to do needlework
4. Being a good caring and moral person

Allie is among the most successful project women in her early career. Her current achievements are based on belief in her ability, fascination with her subject, and work and research experiences in her field. Allie arrived in college with a vague interest in medicine and physics and with a strong background in mathematics and science. Recognition from others, interaction with practicing scientists, and involvement in undergraduate research immeasurably strengthened her commitment, identity, and career knowledge as a scientist.

What Kind of Career?

Compared to men, women have an extra task in their vocational development: they have to decide the place of career involvement among other important future roles. This what-kind-of-career stage coincides with the undergraduate years, when students are under considerable pressure to consider their vocational direction. Keenly aware that she is expected to marry and become a mother, the college woman believes she has a choice about professional career. Meredith put it this way: "If you're a man, you have to have a job. If you're a woman, you can have a job, but you don't have to. Even my advisor in college said to me, 'Well, you know, you're a woman. If things don't work out, you can always get married.' [He said it] kind of jokingly, but I don't think it was really a joke." The complexity of the weaving of roles becomes considerable when women are unable to control whether the major roles of marriage and motherhood will even be readily available to them at particular times in the future. Accompanying this uncertainty—and in some senses caused by it—is another kind of veil over the future. Not only does a haze shroud a future picture of somehow combining paid work with family roles, even an academic star has great difficulty envisioning herself as a career standout.

Clear ambitions and commitment to achievement goals rest on our ability to see ourselves in those roles. As girls and young women, females can see their way to being good students—they are already experienced in academic achievement and their supporters are often female teachers. And they can imagine themselves doing more of the same in college—continuing to be top performers. It is in imagining career ends that women have difficulty. Not only do they have difficulty imagining exactly how career and family will be combined, vocational ends themselves are unclear.

Allie was a successful science student, but it was not at all certain that she would ever consider herself a scientist. In common with other valedictorian women, she distinguished sharply between academic and career identity. Theresa, as a college senior, said, "Going to graduate school scares me to death. Because, I mean, I like math but I'm not, like, a Mathematician." Another valedictorian, Meg, said after graduation that "I don't see myself as a scientist. I see myself as somebody who has succeeded in a science curriculum in college." As a college junior, Rachel said, "I just really can't see myself as a research chemist. None of my friends are chemists. I consider myself an academic chemist. I've always done well in my chemistry classes. But to actually go into a lab and [have people] say, 'Okay, run this reaction,' I really can't see myself— . . . . Maybe I'm just playing at being a scientist."

Companions and Guides

"None of my friends are chemists." It was not through privileged social class or sheer intellectual passion that Allie succeeded in science. Allie's talent was developed because—and only because—she finally connected to the field of science through personal interactions with scientists. There were two ways in which these connections were vital. First, Allie came to see herself clearly as a practicing scientist as she worked successfully in group research teams and at a prominent government laboratory. A public identity as the "medical engineering person" also bolstered her professional self-view (Bloom, 1985). Before these experiences, as she said in her sophomore year, she "didn't know what the industry was going to be like at all." Second, Allie's consistent doubting of her abilities was overcome by faculty encouraging, supporting, and *pushing* her. Her advisor dragged her to the office of the professor whose class she doubted she could handle. That professor employed her in his lab—again despite her misgivings—where Allie saw graduate students and department faculty doing science and leading their lives. Beth, whose college trajectory in chemistry was similar to Allie's, also got close to faculty and graduate students. "I see that they have interesting lives . . . and I feel like I have a number of role models for fitting children into a complete life."

The national laboratory summer job was a breakthrough for Allie. Until then, the small-town electrician's daughter was sure the limits of her achievement were always just about to become visible to others. She resisted opportunities initially because she feared she lacked the knowledge or skills to meet high-level challenges. After a summer in which she interacted with professional scientists and easily mastered a challenging assignment, Allie knew enough about herself to understand, at long last, that she was capable of holding her own with the best.

"I Just Needed to See What I Could Do"

Even the best students cannot aspire to what they cannot imagine (Markus and Nurius, 1986). Simply envisioning going to college was an issue for a few of the rural white and urban minority students.

> I was always the little-time type. For a while I wasn't even going to go on to college. I was just going to get married and have kids and work here. . . . I had a boyfriend here, and I didn't want to leave. And finally I left, and I just loved it, and I felt like I was really doing something and was really accomplishing something, and I felt like once I got done, I would really be able to do things. And I think now, when I truthfully think about it, if I would have stayed here and gotten married and been a secretary or worked in a grocery store or something, I don't think I would be happy [or feeling that] I was really doing anything for myself or for others. And those are important jobs, too, but I just think that I . . . want to do more. And I don't really know when all that change came about. I think it was just after I'd been to school. I just needed to see what I could do.

Lynn, a rural salutatorian, spoke these words when she was a college sophomore, a year after telling us she did not plan to have children. In 1994, Lynn was a certified public accountant, married with one child. She enjoyed her career and her steady advancement in a financial services firm but was aware of some discrimination in her company and the growing desire to spend more time away from work. "I wouldn't want to be a CEO. That would become your life, and then you'd have these other pieces of life that would have to be sacrificed, and to me, those pieces are the more important pieces. Anyhow, your ideas change, huh?" The ultimate for her now was "to be a full-time homemaker with no money worries." Going to college had opened a new world for Lynn. For the first time, she saw she "could really do things" she had never before imagined. She did eventually decide to take time out for childrearing, but her early career aspirations and achievement were unaffected by future contingency planning.

As an undergraduate, Beth lived in a chemistry fraternity with mostly graduate students and worked in two professors' laboratories. By junior year, she was hooked on science.

> To go into the lab and do chemical procedures in crystallography, it almost feels like you're doing an art form. It's like you're playing the piano or something. You learn how to do it well by watching other people and by practicing and you finally get it right. You get a good resolution profile or whatever, and boy, oh boy. It's almost aesthetically pleasing. . . . In high school, I thought that science courses were [the] more real, more serious courses. They were definitely meatier for me intellectually, and I like that thought, and they were so damn hard. They just took me on an emotional roller coaster: I'm succeeding, I'm failing, I'm succeeding, I'm failing. And I just loved that chemistry was that hard for me and yet I always came out okay. And it was so fun when there was something that I considered that difficult, that substantial, and I was getting good at it.

For Beth, opportunities to try laboratory research and teaching introduced her to work she came to love. Stepping into new achievement arenas was equally vital for Allie. Working alongside practicing scientists, whom she came to know professionally and socially, allowed Allie to envision herself clearly in a high-level career. Her public labeling as a biomedical engineer strengthened her developing self-view as a future scientist. That is, Allie deepened her professional identity when professors and supervisors recognized her as competent, singled her out for opportunities, and treated her as a future colleague. Finally, Allie aimed for the top after participating in testing situations that strengthened her confidence in her professional promise. Allie was a very good student, but her career socialization had almost nothing to do with getting A's in college classes.

Null Climate; Chilly Climate

More than half of the women in the Illinois Valedictorian Project never encountered testing opportunities in college that allowed them to understand how professionally talented they really were. Most were, therefore, unable to see themselves clearly in high-level careers. Although they continued to earn stellar grades in demanding college courses, women without female models, faculty mentors, or contact with practicing professionals rarely developed a strong career identity. For women, top grades in college did not translate directly into high intellectual self-esteem and big career aspirations. Ambitious Diane, who was interested in undergraduate research and eventually opening her own company, was unsure how to accomplish her goals. "I wondered, how do you get involved in that [research]? I would love to do some kind of research, you know, and I see some undergraduates doing research, and nobody has ever approached me. I guess you have to go out and do the looking yourself. . . . I can't see starting my own firm. How do you start with something like that? Where?"

Diane's path of chemical engineering seemed to her incongruous. "Can you imagine a middle-aged forty-year-old woman being a chemical engineer? I just can't picture it for some reason. I don't know. God, I must be a sexist. I guess I have a gender gap problem. Because when [the teacher asks] all the little kids . . . what their parents do—'Yeah, my Ma is a chemical engineer'—that just sounds so bizarre." Without knowing any adult women in her field, Diane could not see herself as an future career achiever. Nothing outside her imagination suggested how professional and family roles might fit together.

From time to time, valedictorians told us stories of sex discrimination. A few encountered professors who said females did not belong in mathematics and science. A handful spoke of being belittled or sexually harassed on the job. Like Meg, some women wrestled with feelings of inferiority they attributed to being female: "As a female am I not as worthwhile? I think I grew up thinking that was the case. So it's something that I really had to deal with. I think I maybe will always have to. I struggle with the idea of staying home with kids if we want to have kids. . . . I fear that I will feel less important even though I think that nurturing children or nurturing any person is a wonderful thing to do and a very important thing to do."

As it does in Meg's words, the lesser social status associated with female-dominated professions and full-time childrearing came through in the valedictorians' views of themselves as achievers. Hope, for instance, was appalled to find she had internalized the idea that female-dominated fields were less rigorous and prestigious. "I went into a master's program in theology, and the first day I was there, I . . . went to orientation . . . and there were probably twenty people in the room, eighteen of whom were women. My first thought was, 'Oh my God, this is all women; this must not be a very difficult program.' My second thought was, 'Oh my God, I don't believe I just thought that.'"

For the most part, women reported relatively few instances of discrimination in their college years. Instead, they faced what has been called a "null academic environment," in which they were treated equally with men but not given the experiences they needed to translate their academic success into career ambition (Freeman, 1975). Like women, the majority of undergraduate men never found a mentor; both sexes experienced college faculty as generally unsupportive beyond the classroom. For men, academic achievement seemed to be enough for continued ambition. For women, however, personal sponsorship into testing opportunities was necessary for high career aspirations. Role models, guides, and sponsors all connected women to nonacademic opportunities where their success and enjoyment of professional challenge made career futures seem real. Once a woman envisioned a high goal and saw herself as capable of attaining it, guides and professional contacts helped her understand how to negotiate big-time career paths.

Some of the high-aspiring women enjoyed strong mentoring relationships with undergraduate faculty that abruptly ceased in graduate school. Although close to college faculty, Beth never found a mentor in her chemistry doctoral program. "When I get to thinking that science is completely nonsexist, when I start having those delusions, I start thinking, 'Who is your role model in your department? Who, in the end, do you want to be like?' And then I start to get annoyed because there's not a woman professor in my department. It's fifteen men. . . . Part of mentoring, to me anyway, is about what it would be like to be that person—'Oh, whoops, I can't. I'm a woman.' It's just that at a real sort of basic level, it's harder to identify."

As a doctoral student in mathematics, Theresa said she had never felt a personal connection with her graduate program faculty.

> This is my fourth year here and it's really hard. . . . I had a wonderful group of friends at [undergraduate school] who were faculty members and fellow students, and I had an excellent relationship with my adviser, an excellent relationship with other members of the faculty. And of course you come here, and now you've come to a much better university, with much better faculty members, with many more graduate students, and so now you're just nobody in this sea of faces once again. It's very hard to deal with that when you're used to being at the top of what you're doing and important to the people around you, and you come here and they really don't give a darn what happens to you. I mean they give you a certain set of requirements that you meet and if you pass them on time, they seem to like you. . . . I came from a place that was so open and loving, and to come here, it's kind of a shock.

Hope, who had been so surprised to find herself in a female-dominated masters program, was a minority again in her prestigious doctoral program. For the first time, the Phi Beta Kappa graduate felt silenced in class.

> The seminar style is like mud wrestling, the guys get in and "grrr, grrr." The first year and a half I was here I literally could not speak in seminars. I had been an incredibly verbal person for the first twenty-three years of my life, and I came here, and I was physically shut down because on one level I'm not a combative person, although I've become a more combative person than I was, and on another level I would speak and my voice would sound like some thin, squeaky unauthoritative thing with all these bass powerful voices, and so even if I was saying something intelligent, it didn't sound like that.

Hope was aware that she was not one of the students her powerful advisor mentored. Nor was she adept at the academic politics and self-promotion she increasingly sensed around her, although she did learn "by watching people succeed at what I wanted. People getting money or getting positions, having relationships with people that I would really like to have with them. Watching how they did it. I kind of know it now, but I still don't do it really well." By the time she reached her dissertation, Hope was still unconnected. "Nobody has really taught me how to do a dissertation. I'm just kind of floating it. It's not as fun as I thought it would be." In graduate school, high school valedictorians continued to excel academically. Even at the doctoral level, though, women felt a strong need for mentors, interpersonally supportive environments, and help in negotiating academic politics and career management.

Lacking guidance for envisioning and negotiating elite career paths, and facing uncontrollable family contingencies, many top female academic achievers stepped off the fast track during college. Those who remained experienced out-of-classroom opportunities in which they deepened their professional identity and knowledge through interactions with faculty, peers, graduate students, and professionals. Professors of high-aspiring women did more than assign A's for superior classroom work. They served as models, guides, and sponsors. They went beyond encouragement to push students like Allie into places where women doubted their ability to compete. Academically talented women flourished in these challenging work settings, where they learned what they could be and observed how to negotiate paths to top-level careers.

Many women who had developed strong career identities through undergraduate faculty relationships and professional experiences faced a null academic environment for the first time in graduate school. Although these female graduate students found the loss of personal faculty connections distressing, they were able to persevere. The damage to women's career attainment by graduate faculty neglect, however, is unknown.

Putting the Picture Together

Intellectual self-esteem and family-centered career planning: how do the two come together? For academically talented women, not scholastic achievement but expectations about family roles predict vocational outcomes at age thirty-one. We believe that the tangle caused by simultaneous career and life-role planning, at a point when vital pieces are unknown, affects women's intellectual self-esteem. We are certain it affects their career aspirations. Before college, boys and girls measure their intelligence according to success in the achievement arena of school. In college, however, a shift occurs. As they approach the end of school, students begin developing an achievement identity linked to postacademic attainment. In fact, one of the developmental tasks of college is to change one's achievement identity from being an adolescent scholastic performer to being an adult career achiever (Chickering and Reisser, 1993). It is precisely this transition that is more difficult and more complicated for women than for men. And it is precisely this difficulty in setting and pursuing high career goals that diminishes women's view of their own competence in relation to others their age. Outstanding classroom performance becomes a less and less believable source of self-worth as the world around young women moves from valuing school success to valuing career attainment.

When women increasingly become unable to see themselves in socially valued adult achievement roles, their intellectual self-esteem declines. Signals from professors, parents, and peers may reinforce the view that women are not being taken seriously as future career achievers. More important, however, is the confusion surrounding life-role planning. Without a clear idea of what it would be like to be a scientist or professor or business executive, talented women also lack clear models for joining motherhood to major careers. As undergraduates, then, female valedictorians make potentially life-defining choices without practical knowledge of the realistic demands of high-level careers, without models of how to manage career and family involvement, and without the ability to envision the career component of their adult lives.

It is quite realistic to suspect that intensive work and career involvement will be difficult to balance. As Meredith said: "Say you're a lawyer and you're working sixteen hours a day, then you're not going to be the kind of mother that your mother was. You're a human being, and you have constraints, and you can't do everything. You can be a mother, but you're going to have to make compromises there. And you can be a lawyer, but you're going to have to make compromises there, too. I think it's better to realize the compromises in advance than to try to live up to both of those [models] and get a bleeding ulcer."

The search for balance between actual life roles is another story, told in Chapter Nine. To a great extent, women are correct in foreseeing barriers in current occupational and family structures. Still, the first decade of the Illinois Valedictorian Project featured women's lowering of their occupational aspirations in *anticipation* of having difficulty combining motherhood and career. For most female valedictorians, college did little to mitigate their confusion, almost nothing to address their extra stage of career development. When some women experienced more than the null academic environment, however, they became convinced that significant career achievement would be fulfilling and attainable. The beneficial career effects of faculty interactions and professionally testing experiences held true whether a woman approached college as a careerist (like Lynn), an intellectual (like Beth), or a striver (like Allie). Unconnected students, by definition, failed to become socialized into majors and careers through faculty and professional connections. It is perhaps because top grades do not necessarily lead to career focus for women that the group of unconnected valedictorians is overwhelmingly female.

An Expanded View of Intellectual Self-Esteem

We periodically asked valedictorians to reflect on Illinois Valedictorian Project findings such as the female decline in intellectual self-esteem, but we did not normally share with them our interpretations of project data. It was in Gloria Steinem's book on self-esteem (1992) that Beth came across the project results on gender differences in intellectual self-esteem and read the interpretation that an unsupportive college environment caused undergraduate women to lower their estimates of their own intelligence. Beth articulated an important interpretation in this 1993 electronic mail message to me:

> Pretty intriguing numbers. They're obviously saying "something" about gender differences and self-image. Here's what feels wrong about it to me, though. Although I have no specific recollection of responding to that question in interviews, I am pretty confident

that I am one of those women who was less likely to assess myself as being "far above average" in intellect as I got older and progressed further in the educational system. Frankly, I consider that more a sign of maturity and wisdom than of low self-esteem. What I find more alarming is that the men's percentages don't change at all. When I was in high school, I was very competitive. It was important to me that I "beat out" Bruce as valedictorian. Intellectual achievement was one of my only sources of self-worth then, and most of my friends were intellectual achievers, too. I think I thought of myself and most of the people I knew best then as some sort of "prime genetic stock" intellectually. Cards we were dealt. Yeah, I seemed to have been dealt a pretty good hand. "Far above average" on the intellect scale.

I don't think of myself that way now, and I have higher self-esteem, even higher "intellectual" self-esteem. I think that a rigid hierarchical scale of intellect is something that I would have started rejecting, certainly by the time I graduated college and maybe even after sophomore year. I think that I tend to perform well in certain kinds of ways that are valued in standardized tests and competitive educational systems, but that there are all kinds of ways of being smart and the kinds of achievement that I've been rewarded for don't even begin to include them all. Part of the imperative to teach comes from NOT thinking that I'm any smarter than anyone else, from being absolutely convinced that I can communicate my intellectual insights to anyone who's made the internal commitment to learn something from me.

I tried to share these ideas with my friend, Andrew. Andrew snorted and said, "Beth, I am far above average in intellect and so are you!" I was flabbergasted that he didn't get my point (since we do connect intellectually on so many other issues), and I caught myself thinking (admittedly disdainfully), "Well, there's a typical male response!"

So I just find myself questioning Steinem's implicit assumption that the male trend was "healthy" whereas the female trend was "unhealthy."

The lowering of women's intellectual self-esteem rankings might reflect a growing sensitivity to other people and to other modes of knowing, Beth's response implies. A lower self-ranking could demonstrate a rejection of simplistic, hierarchical definitions of ability and an increasing appreciation of the multiple intelligences of others (Gardner, 1983). Women might report lower intelligence ratings because they were broadening the value they placed on others.

This overlapping interpretation fills in the puzzle of women's intellectual self-esteem trends in two ways. First, it provides a potential explanation for the drop in intelligence estimates of women who did not plan career around future family roles. A highly career-centered woman who also wishes to marry and have children, Beth removed motherhood from her career-planning considerations. "If I were a man, I wouldn't be so anxious to put off getting married. Just because you get slapped with kids and then social roles—it's your responsibility." Possibly Beth and other high-aspiring women freed themselves from constraints in their planning by questioning major tenets to which other women held fast. Unlike most female valedictorians, Beth disbelieved that only some careers accommodate childrearing. Unlike most, she questioned whether the woman must always be the primary child care giver. Women like Beth who pursued career paths without regard to expected family contingencies might reflect in their intelligence ratings a growing sensitivity to the experience of others and an increasingly less hierarchical view of intelligence.

Second, the idea that the drop in intelligence self-ratings is a product of a developing appreciation of others relates to the contingency planning predominant among female valedictorians. A broadened definition of life achievement as anchored in relationships might reflect undergraduate women's growing value of interpersonal measures of success. "Some of us are making decisions for family," Jane declared, implying that climbing a career ladder is a less valid measure of achievement.

From School to Postschool Success

The relationship between contingency planning and intellectual self-esteem potentially involves interactions between individual valuing of relational spheres and societal measurement of adult success as occupational attainment. As the valedictorians told their stories, two pronounced gender differences occurred at the same point in time. Women—and only women—lowered their intellectual self-esteem between high school graduation and sophomore year of college. And it was female valedictorians only who considered children and careers as inextricably linked. A good portion of these superbly qualified women lowered their career aspirations explicitly to accommodate future childrearing. Future family expectations interfered not at all with men's career planning, and college enhanced men's intellectual self-esteem.

In the valedictorian's world, status depends on occupational attainment. As women lowered their career aspirations in favor of future parenthood, they began pursuing achievement paths that society values very little. Because grades were no longer the adult currency of attainment, college women who chose not to aspire to stellar careers were no longer able to consider themselves as the best of their age group. No longer were women at the peak of what school rewards. Without the top-career aspirations that anchor high status, women no longer reported they were far above their average peers. Evidence is plentiful that female valedictorians' decline in intellectual self-esteem relates to family-driven career planning: the strength and rarity of the gender difference in intelligence ranking and its incongruity with academic performance; the simultaneous appearance of the self-esteem decline and family/career conflict; and the lack of identity resolution in the role society values most highly.

In short, we believe that women lower their career aspirations because they cannot see a workable future in which they act both as high-level professionals and fully involved mothers. Without clear promise as career achievers, women think their status goes down, and they begin to label themselves as less exceptional in relation to their peers. At the same time, women might also devalue academic intelligence as they come to define their adult selves within both private and public roles. As in Allie's case, academic performance is almost incidental to the larger drama of life-role planning.

David, the valedictorian who wondered aloud where all the academically talented women had gone, was a third-generation Ivy League graduate with professional parents. His speculation about women's careers not only reveals the indirect link between academic achievement and careers for women but also demonstrates his own experience in which grades translated directly into career ambition and professional attainment.

My theory is, I guess, that women were expected to, or no one minded for them to, do very well in high school in terms of grades in high school math and things like that, but that didn't immediately, directly, translate into career ambition. Whereas for me, one just seems like a perfectly logical outgrowth of the other. You do your best in a high school class, and you get an A. You do your best in a college class, and you get an A. You get admitted to law school, and you do your best, and you get an A, and then based on that, you get a job as a law clerk, and you work very hard and do a good job in that and make a reputation for yourself, *and it all kind of naturally follows.*

I assume that it must be the case for some people that the fact that you got an A in Miss Stevenson's English class really bears no connection to how ambitious you are for yourself in your career. . . . I can see, when I'm frustrated in my current job, a small amount of appeal—even though I know I could never really do this—but there is a certain idea that a job, even for someone with a lot of talent, is basically a way to support yourself and that the ideal job is something that is relatively nontaxing, goes from nine to five, and then you go home. Particularly if your life were centered around being home, if you were married, have children, and this nine-to-five job pays enough—I could see how your attitude would be very, very different than if you were looking to really pursue an ambitious career.

For David and for most of the men in the valedictorian study, career achievement "kind of naturally follows" academic attainment. For academically talented women, in contrast, school success does not guarantee occupational success. Even the best female college students need people who will support them, encourage them, and—most important—who will connect them to opportunities. Women whose gifts are not developed in these ways aspire and achieve less than their equally able peers. Valedictorians who are fortunate enough to enter the interpersonal net of talent development carry their remarkable academic accomplishments into the top ranks of professional careers. It is these women who remain on the paths to eminence, but it is their sisters who continually pose the question of whether career eminence signifies life success.

Chapter Six

Hidden Lessons

Race, Class, and Tacit Knowledge

*For there is no creature whose inward being is so strong
that it is not greatly determined by what lies outside it.*
GEORGE ELIOT, *MIDDLEMARCH* ([1871–1872] 1977, P.
577)

In 1992, thirty-year-old Monica met me at the door of her small
rented house in a tidy working-class urban neighborhood. A
warmly friendly and strikingly attractive Mexican American woman,
she spoke accentless English. Monica fairly glistened when she
introduced her two-year-old son, Luis. She was teaching him in two
languages, Monica said proudly, and showed me his room full of
children's books. On her one day off a week, mother and son traveled to city parks, museums, and children's events. "He's so smart!"

Along with her son and husband, her mother was central to
Monica's life: "I feel bad because I left my mom when I got married." Even after she had her own family, Monica remained
immersed in the daily lives of her parents, brothers, and sister. "My
mom, I'd do anything for her. She just took a trip to Mexico to see
my grandma, and I took a week's vacation and painted her
kitchen. . . . That was my vacation this year." Raising five children
while working long hours as a seamstress had been immensely difficult, Monica knew: "I saw how hard my mom worked, and I didn't
want to disappoint her." She cherished her mother's pride in her
academic achievement. Her mother consistently urged Monica to
go to college instead of marrying immediately after high school.

With her mother's support, Monica became the first person in her family to attend college. At age twenty-four, she was married in the church of her first communion, confirmation, and high school graduation. By the time of her marriage, to a Mexican American carpenter, only a semester remained to her degree. Her graduation had already been delayed because of financial concerns and employment demands. Before the wedding, Monica's mother made her new son-in-law promise that Monica would finish college.

Monica had come to the United States from Mexico, knowing no English, when she was five. Both her parents worked full time, although her father, a butcher, was sometimes unable to work because of poor health. By the time Monica was eighteen, she had graduated as valedictorian of an urban Catholic high school in a class of seventy-six Latina and African American girls. Monica downplayed her high school achievement: "I just think I lucked out. I mean, we were a small school . . . must have been the talented or the smart girls went to better schools. . . . So I was one of the mediocre ones." Regardless of her self-assessment, Monica loved her high school: "It really was like a family. It honestly was."

Remaining at home until she married was taken for granted; Monica considered only local universities. She chose a college that an acquaintance told her was the best in the city for telecommunications, a career in which she aspired to be "a Latin person making a statement." Monica earned A's and B's in her college courses. During her first years of college, she worked part time in a hospital rehabilitation center, contributing much of her earnings to her parents and siblings. She also completed two internships at broadcasting stations, including coordinating a program for cable television. "I absolutely loved it," she reported. She did not find a mentor at her internship sites or at the college, however. Despite her excellent academic performance, Monica never got to know any faculty outside the classroom. "All the teachers work in the business, and they don't have time to help you out." The college offered no career guidance or even oversight of internship experiences.

In her third year of college, Monica attempted to work full time and continue as a full-time student. She began dating her future husband. A niece chaperoned their dates. For the next few years, she worked full time and attended college part time. When

Luis was born, a few years after her marriage, Monica was twelve credit hours away from graduation. She left school, temporarily she said, as she and her husband each worked two nonprofessional jobs. Monica still firmly intended to finish college. She was proud of her younger brother, whom Monica had helped become the first college graduate in the family. "I take care of my whole family. I'm the one who is taking care of the money, taking care of the house, remembering the bills, remembering everything. Plan parties. I do everything. Very stressful. But I keep it inside. . . . I worry a lot. I do too much for too many people. I mean, I do too much for my family. . . . I never say no to my sister, my brothers, anybody in my family."

Monica's husband, who had not attended college, did not actively urge Monica to reenroll. With two jobs and responsibilities for her extended family and infant son, time and money were problems. "God, I'd love to graduate. . . . School is so expensive— I don't know how people do it. . . . Some people do it. Maybe there's a trick, I don't know. There's got to be a way." When Monica did return to her college to make arrangements to complete the remaining semester for graduation, she approached a college counselor to arrange a part-time schedule for her remaining twelve credits. "I couldn't understand. I mean, I want to go back and graduate there; it's a very good school. And I asked [the counselor] to explain it to me, and the way she explained it to me, she said you're better off taking six credits. If not, you're going to lose credits. And I did not understand it. And I came home and I was depressed. . . . It didn't make any sense to me. Is that the way they do it? That's why I haven't gone back."

Not only was Monica unable to afford tuition for six credits at a time, she discovered that the college had lost the paperwork for her internships and given her F's. "That's like six credit hours. That's a lot of money. And you know what? I had really good grades there; I had A's and B's. And to see those little F's there, that hurt. That really hurt." When I urged her to follow up on the credit requirements and internship grades, Monica said that too much time had elapsed; she would just continue to "run around in circles." Even if she had gotten to know any professors, she said, there had been considerable faculty turnover and changes in requirements since she left the college. With finances making reenrollment increasingly difficult, Monica attempted another route into a media career. Taking a pay cut, she accepted a clerical job at a broadcasting station.

> I told them I'd like to move up. I told them what I was studying. They said no problem. I wanted to go upstairs to production, and [the boss] said, 'well, within six months you go upstairs and you'll be doing what you want to do.' And when I started talking to the girls there in the office, they said once he has you here, he's not going to let you move. One girl had been there for about four years, and she wanted to move to a different department, in production, and he did not want to let her go. And that's it.

Monica left the station after one week, utterly discouraged about her future in broadcasting. By 1992, she was working full time at only one job, as a bookkeeper in a wholesale/retail store. The job did not pay well, she said, "and I hate working with numbers. That's always been my weak point. And that's what I'm doing. It doesn't make any sense to me." Although Monica worked six days a week, she was free on Sundays for the first time since Luis was born. She delighted in her bright, active child. "I'm really trying to teach him English and Spanish. I've gotten him his first library card. I'm teaching him. There are a lot of things that I can take advantage of that probably my mom didn't have the opportunity to." Returning to school had become a dim possibility. "The problem is time. I just finally got some time to be with my son. When he's ready to go to school, maybe I'll try to figure out a way to go back. It's not like a priority, although it is with my mom. When I got married, she said, 'You better graduate.'. . . [But] school is so expensive. I wouldn't know what school to go to. I really wouldn't. I don't know what I'd major in. They've changed everything. Now you need credits in places you didn't before."

Even if she graduated, Monica did not intend to continue in broadcasting. "I went in there bright-eyed and bushy-tailed, but it was terrible. I liked the learning process, the whole going to school, going to classes, and learning. But getting into the field and all the politics of getting jobs—it's who you know, not what you know."

Fourteen years after high school, Monica's ultimate goal was spending time with her own family and her mother, and somehow helping others through volunteer or paid work. "I'd like to get involved in something. I don't know what. I think there is something I need to do. I don't know where. I think a lot of Latin people are getting a raw deal. They need someone to speak for them. And there's no one there yet." As for college, "I don't think I'll go back to school. I haven't gotten the bad taste out of my mouth yet."

There Must Be a Reason

Monica is a strikingly beautiful woman with above-average intelligence, far above average interpersonal skills, and a kind of determination and stick-to-itiveness that should have paid off with a diploma. But work, work, work and school, school, school and work, work, work do not necessarily produce a college degree.

Threads of gender, culture, and class are interwoven in Monica's story. Brought up in an urban Mexican American community, Monica strongly identifies with the close family connections of her culture. Leaving home before marriage is unacceptable for a conventionally reared Mexican girl. Although remaining with her family limited her college choices, Monica genuinely desired to live with her parents. During college and after she married, Monica continued to place her extended family at the center of her life. She organized family events, offered emotional support to her mother, contributed financially to her parents and brothers, and looked to relatives for a traditional introduction to her future husband. Three years before Monica married, Terry Denny wrote of her:

> Monica is a sound, solid person. She is an incurable domestic but it is not based solely or even principally on her need to create her own nest. Rather, her utter devotion to her mother lies behind her interest in taking care of a house, in being around the house, and in contributing to the maintenance of a home. Her culture bombards her with the appropriateness and importance of getting married and having children—but she resists the message. She does want to marry and have children (perhaps adopt them) but she also wants to finish school and to try her hand in the television world. No small measure of her strength comes from her mother who apparently has supported her for some time against the conventional wisdom of getting married and having children at a young age. The pool of marriageable men is a small one for Monica. That

is, most of the Mexican American men do not go on to school. The places her life takes her are not that numerous (neighborhood church, family, Friday night bars, homes of a few married female friends), so it's hard to see how she is going to meet a man with her intelligence, education, kindness—a good match. Whatever she does and wherever she goes, her immediate family and her extended family will control her destiny.

Seven years later, these words faithfully describe Monica while leaving out the vital role of higher education in determining her fate. Monica's family indeed defines her life, but family members never sought to block her ambitions. With the strong support of her mother, Monica attended college and prepared for a career. In defiance of cultural stereotypes, she anticipated professional work along with future marriage and childrearing. Monica's inability to reach her educational and occupational goals had nothing to do with talent or effort—she was a highly successful college student. Financial constraints played a large role in her departure from college. Part-time enrollment and full-time employment delayed Monica's graduation and limited her involvement in college life. Helping her family financially also strained her resources. Once she married a man who did not value college as highly as she, additional financial sacrifice became even less feasible. Monica chose to spend her time with family and to help support them financially. Above all, Monica values close family ties.

Monica also values achievement goals and in no way chose to be marginalized in college. College was the opposite of her family-like Catholic high school. Without rancor and without attributing her treatment to being minority, female, or poor, she reported being ignored by faculty and obstructed by the college administration. As a working commuter student, she also remained outside informal peer groups in her major. Lacking guidance and support from faculty and internship supervisors or access to a peer reference group, Monica never amassed the tacit knowledge to turn her motivation and ability into a broadcast communications career.

Tacit knowledge is information that is not formally taught but is necessary for the successful management of education and careers (Polanyi, 1966; Sternberg, 1985; Wagner and Sternberg, 1986). Direct guidance on how to choose a college and major, for instance, does not normally occur in the high school or postsecondary curriculum. Students learn about possibilities through family members, acquaintances, teachers, and counselors.

Monica, like many first-generation college students, found few sources of sophisticated advice. As a working-class student whose education required considerable family sacrifice, Monica knew that college needed to result in reasonably lucrative work for her. Unlike more privileged students from professional families, though, Monica had little idea of the full range of possible careers and almost no conception of how liberal arts study might relate to adult employment. She chose broadcasting as an exciting field in which she could use her talents and serve her community. Her interest in academic life focused almost exclusively on advancing her career in television. It is doubtful whether she realized the difficulty of establishing herself in such a competitive field or understood how her skills might be transferred to other pursuits. Facing a dead end in communications, Monica was unsure how to choose another major or college. When college equals vocational preparation, any decision about future education requires a firm professional direction.

"Her naïveté with respect to higher education is astounding," Denny wrote in 1990. "Here she is some twelve credit hours away from a degree, goes in for counseling and advice, gets handed some mumbo jumbo double talk and accepts it! And if she feels guilty about anything, she feels guilty about not finishing college because of the money that her mom put into it for her." Cultural custom kept Monica from aggressively challenging unjust failing grades or questioning the decree that she must take more than one course at a time. Poor tacit knowledge played an even more central role in these cases, since Monica did not know how to pursue such issues within the college structure. No one offered to intercede or to support her through the process of resolving obstacles to graduation. (Both Terry Denny and I offered assistance and advice, but our interactions with her were too few and too long after her decision to leave college to be useful to her.) Without any sense of entitlement, Monica did not believe a challenge could succeed. In her world, individuals do not prevail over school systems or employers.

Without the advice of mentors, concerned faculty, or experienced broadcast professionals, Monica found herself unable to overcome the barriers in her path. Two successful internships, which showed Monica she could thrive in her chosen field, came to nothing because she was unsure how to capitalize on her experience and negotiate a career path. The enthusiasm and professional identity the internships provided were negated by the failing grades Monica received when the college lost the verifying paperwork. Although she possessed the ability and motivation to succeed in the competitive world of telecommunications, Monica was left with a distaste for her chosen profession and for higher education. She turned her considerable energies to her extended family and to her son's education, sadly interpreting her path in the framework of her religious faith: "There must be a reason why I didn't go into what I wanted. I sure did hate it after a while. I was very disappointed. So there must be a reason things happen. Maybe there's something else for me. I don't know what it is yet."

When Talent Is Not Enough

Monica kept her promises. She made sacrifices for her education, worked hard in college, and maintained her fundamental commitment to family. It was higher education that failed to keep its promise to Monica, turning aside the potential professional contribution of this talented woman. Many of the themes in Monica's story are echoed in the experiences of other Mexican American and African American valedictorians. Monica's experience is also the story of some first-generation, working-class white men and women. For these students, no linear relationship existed between ability, motivation, and professional outcomes. Complex interactions of gender, culture, race, and class refute the existence of a straightforward meritocracy.

The valedictorian project's three Mexican American women, five African American men and women, and one Asian American man formed a diverse group in terms of culture, family background, and college life. For instance, although Luz grew up in a community and school very much like Monica's, she struggled to win permission to attend college from parents who believed that higher education was unnecessary for a girl. Jonas's father was college educated and his mother was a high school valedictorian (however, Jonas was orphaned by the beginning of high school).

Eric, also African American, had only one high school graduate in his large family, an older brother who was chronically unemployed. Eric said, "I believe if I were to graduate from a university, I'd be the only one in my entire family and extended family also that has done that." The word "if" underlines the paucity of role models and family supporters for Eric's college ambition. Xhou's father and mother were also poorly educated (only to the sixth grade), but these immigrant parents clearly expected their son to attend college. Xhou also anticipated marrying a Chinese woman known to his family. These expectations were fulfilled: Xhou became an engineer, married as his family expected, and earned a master's degree after college.

Mexican American women faced strong cultural expectations for full-time homemaking, whereas African American women worked to ensure they could support themselves financially. Students of color differed in how strongly they believed in their talent, from Monica's belief that she could be valedictorian only at a weak school to Luz's fierce statement that "I will always try to strive for something higher because I know I did it once. I have to keep doing it. I'm not going to drop dead. Just because I was successful once, I want to be successful again."

Gender, culture, and class strongly affected white students in the group as well, of course. For example, the college years of a Mormon valedictorian were shaped by his attendance at a religiously sponsored university and by his two-year missionary stint. The daughter of an Armenian immigrant was allowed to live on campus during the week but expected to return home each weekend. A working-class Catholic man chose a career that would allow him to remain in his home town to live near his family and help with their financial struggles. Beth's professional parents were intellectuals who supported her liberal arts exploration and who communicated their love of language and ideas to their daughter. Moreover, many first-generation college students reported poor tacit understanding of education and career management and lack of mentoring by college faculty.

Academically talented students of color struggled with unique obstacles, however, that differentiated them from white valedictorians. Despite their diversity, virtually all Latina and African American students met hostile college or workplace environments.

Without disregarding their differences, it is therefore valuable to consider minority groups together in another "overlapping reading" of project data. All the students of color in the Illinois Valedictorian Project came from lower-income homes in urban minority communities in Chicago and East St. Louis, Illinois. All began college at predominantly white colleges and universities, although one student, Eric, eventually transferred to a historically black college. Like Monica, all of these students faced challenges in financing college. Like her, they followed relatively narrow vocational tracks within higher education. All but one reported being marginalized in their predominantly white institutions, and most told of racism in their college or work lives. Finally, poor tacit knowledge kept African American and Latina students from considering a full range of educational and career options and from skillfully negotiating high-level achievement paths. (Of course, the project sample is too small for the experiences to be generalized to all students of color, or even to all high-achieving African American and Latino men and women.)

Taken together, these factors accounted for lower educational and career achievement of students of color as compared to white valedictorians. Monica and Jonas were two of the four project valedictorians without college degrees. African American and Latina valedictorian college graduates took an average of almost six years to earn undergraduate degrees. The shortest time to graduation for a student of color was four and a half years; three-quarters of white students completed college in four straight years. In contrast to the larger valedictorian group, African Americans and Mexican Americans were overrepresented among college transfers; half changed colleges. Only Xhou and one African American woman earned master's degrees. In contrast, well over half of the Anglo valedictorians received graduate degrees and 30 percent hold terminal degrees. Fourteen years after high school, students of color were more likely than other valedictorians to be underemployed, and they were more often dissatisfied with their occupations.

Michelle: Limiting Tracks

"Really, in high school they were pushing engineering. That's all they really pushed. If you were strong and took all of the math classes and science classes, they pushed engineering. So really, we weren't exposed to much of anything else. Then I went to the Minority Introduction to Engineering program. So that seemed kind of interesting. . . . Mainly, I didn't know of anything else to be." Michelle worked hard in high school to make sure she would be prepared for college. She received considerable recognition and support from teachers and enjoyed a summer in a special engineering program for academically talented high school minority students. Firsthand knowledge of the lives of poorly educated African American women in her community spurred Michelle's determination to pursue a secure, well-paying profession. "Going to school is definitely affected by the fact that I want to be able to take care of myself. If I didn't have to worry about paying for things, I might make different choices. I can't really say because I've never had that." Michelle chose her university "mostly for the money—for the financial aid." She had not intended to apply there, but her counselor was impressed with the school's minority engineering program and encouraged Michelle to attend. "I just filled out the papers and stuff because he asked me to."

Michelle excelled in her undergraduate engineering classes. She did not become close to any faculty members but did get to know the administrator of the minority engineering program and the department secretary. An instructor nominated her for a merit scholarship, which she won. She was active in both predominantly white and minority engineering organizations. The black student organization was central to Michelle's social and academic sense of belonging at the university. "I felt more isolated because I was black than because I was a woman . . . [but] I knew a lot of other people like me." Despite her success and involvement, Michelle expressed persistent doubts about engineering. As a junior, she told us: "In high school I didn't know what I wanted to do. . . . They were pushing engineering, and it seemed like the best option, but I still wasn't sure. And now that I'm in it, I still feel the same." The summer jobs she got through the university showed Michelle she could perform in a professional setting but failed to resolve her ambivalence about engineering.

To reduce her heavy course load and allow time for activities, Michelle took an extra semester to graduate. After college, she took a job at a public utility company near home where she had worked during the summer. For the first time, she found herself without the peer and organizational support she had enjoyed since high school. Working with construction crews and supervisors was frequently frustrating and discouraging. "It might just be personality differences. It may be because I'm black. It may be because I'm female. And it could be because I'm young and have a degree. I don't know." Her enthusiasm and career orientation slowly diminished as Michelle found herself five years later "still doing the same thing I was doing when I started." She continued to take pride in her ability to get along with people and her willingness to work hard. She began an M.B.A. program at night, hoping to move into a setting where she could work with people and do work "that matters." She also became active in community service in her city.

In 1994, three years after completing her M.B.A., Michelle was still with the utilities company and still unhappy with her work. She never received the guidance or testing opportunities that might have helped her implement her longstanding dream of owning a business. "When I was in high school and college, there was a lot of attention, but somehow this just seems kind of a letdown. But it's more. I guess I owe to these people who thought so highly of me to get further than where I am now. Not necessarily in a corporation, but something that is going to make a difference, like having my own business, eventually being able to hire black people."

Throughout her stellar academic career, Michelle was convinced she could reach her goals through hard work and ability. A decade beyond college, she was less confident than in college, writing in 1994 that "life is difficult and complicated and will always be." She was not intentionally marginalized at work, Michelle claimed. "I'm different, and it's easier not to deal with it than to figure out what is it—this person had all this promise and enthusiasm and talent, and now they don't seem to be showing that. What is it? Something is different. Something has happened. [My supervisor] probably doesn't know that, of course; he doesn't even know that I had that enthusiasm before." The ultimate for Michelle now is to find a husband and start a family. She also hopes "to figure out what I do best and then have someone pay me to do that. . . . To really feel as though I am truly the master of my destiny."

Switching Guards

Following deliberate exposure and encouragement to enter engineering, Michelle entered a very specific undergraduate track at the university her guidance counselor suggested. She acquiesced to engineering because she viewed college as career preparation and because she knew no other options. Although Michelle was unique among minority valedictorians for her high satisfaction and involvement in a predominantly white university, she faced considerable isolation and racism in her postcollege professional life. Getting out of engineering proved to be more difficult than getting in. Although she had always rationalized her undergraduate major as a flexible entrance to other fields, Michelle never understood how to exercise those options. The rich opportunities and sponsors she encountered in engineering education disappeared as Michelle considered a switch to business. Financial needs and professional isolation worked against a career change for this talented African American woman. Even assessing the degree of risk in leaving engineering was impossible for Michelle without the guidance and sponsorship of a career mentor. Clearly, Michelle entered a professional field without comprehending the full range of occupational choices or the intricacies of career management. Higher education did not fill in this missing knowledge.

Twelve years after high school, Luz echoed Michelle. "Because I didn't know any better, I didn't realize another career would probably be better for me than engineering. I mean, I might have the skills, but it's not something I really enjoy." Luz, like Michelle and Monica, was ready to make a career change but unsure how to go about it. "If I knew what career I'd really enjoy, I'd go for it, because I know if I really put my mind to something, I'll accomplish it. But right now, I'm not sure." In an attempt to explore possibilities, Luz took some graduate engineering classes. She earned A's but never found an adviser among her colleagues or professors. Like Michelle, she remained at a public utilities company in a job she disliked and, also like Michelle, experienced isolation in the field and at the office.

Michelle, like Monica, had limited her college search. Virtually all of the African American and Latina valedictorians made college and major choices on the basis of casual or limited input. Eric, for instance, felt he "blew it coming out of high school" because he was unaware he could apply for scholarships at colleges around the country. Luz attributed her sketchy knowledge of college possibilities to money, noting that her parents could neither advise her on institutions nor travel to explore different campuses. "It's not so much being a minority as it is that most minorities don't have the financial backing to take them along their career paths as smoothly as those who do have that kind of financial base."

The three Latina women were also restricted geographically, as their immigrant parents expected daughters to remain home until marriage. Luisa's career prospects were dramatically affected when she moved with her parents to the Southwest after her sophomore year as an accountancy major at a major university. After a year away from school to establish residency in the new state, Luisa resumed her studies at the local comprehensive college. She graduated from the lower-ranked institution as the top accountancy student in her class but was unable to find professional work in the town. Abandoning the idea of taking the CPA examination, she took a job as a bookkeeper at an area business, a job she still holds. "Every decision I make must involve my parents," Luisa told us. "They have always relied on me for everything. I am the only child. They cannot speak English. It must be this way. They are in my thoughts all the time in every important decision I make. This will not change."

It is difficult to fault those who placed minority valedictorians on narrow achievement tracks. Some were well-meaning high school teachers and counselors who sought to protect students from risk by entering them in clear, secure career paths. Some were educators eager to increase the numbers of women and minorities in technical fields. In addition, there were the students' internal freely chosen obligations to family, culture, and home. Without the tacit knowledge to understand career alternatives, plan professional routes, or map switching points, talented students were stuck with their original, limited tracks. Genuine financial constraints along with hazy conceptions of options kept minority valedictorians from effectively releasing their talents and energies in new directions.

College Outsiders

Jonas followed his gripping valedictory address by "floating" at the edges of two colleges. Salutatorian Eric "never really got a sensing there at the university." Luz phoned professors who told her they had no time to talk: "I can't find any support or any interest. . . . If I see that somebody is interested in me or somebody is concerned about how I'm doing, you know, that pushes you to go ahead. I'm really trying hard, and I see no motivation coming from anywhere." Nearly all of the top students of color struggled at the margins of predominantly white colleges and universities, unconnected to the central social and academic systems of their institutions.

The case of Barbara, an African American engineering major, offered the most extreme example of exclusion—and racism—in the valedictorians' undergraduate years. A solid engineering student at one of the top universities in the country, Barbara was excluded from white study groups, once told by a professor that she was stupid, and ignored by a graduate teaching assistant who refused to call on her during review sessions. Several key engineering professors, she said, showed biases against both women and minorities in "the way they talked to you, the amount of effort they put in trying to help you. I mean, it was there." Barbara was left on her own. "I was always very studious and I was always trying very hard. There were a lot of times when I did poorly on tests, where I just made a C because that was the only thing I could teach myself."

When Barbara developed abdominal pains in her sophomore year, university doctors suggested she change her major to something easier and referred her to a psychologist. Although she only half believed the stomach aches were her own fault, Barbara avoided going back to the health center "to be told how silly I was." When she finally became unable to attend classes, she returned to the clinic, where she was rushed into surgery for acute appendicitis. Among the valedictorians, only Barbara attributed her negative college experience to racism. "In a lot of ways, I feel that this was done to me because I was both black and female." Barbara left school but soon returned to college because she saw no other alternative for making herself economically self-sufficient. Her enthusiasm for the university and for engineering had given way to a grim determination to survive to the degree.

Barbara credited the "unbreakable" network among African American engineering students for the only support she received on campus and as the reason she made it through college. Luz also found her only source of support in the minority student organization on campus. "And a good thing they were there. . . . I look for Hispanics and I met Hispanics. I feel more at ease with them; I don't know why. Most of the time I'm talking half in English, half in Spanish. Friends don't have to be Hispanics, because I had a black friend and a Chinese friend. But I've never had a white friend." Luz volunteered in the office of the organization because she was so grateful for the help she had received there. Professors weren't interested in students, she said. "They just go and lecture. They don't care."

Among the African American and Latina valedictorians, Michelle had by far the best college experience at a predominantly white university and Barbara, Michelle's salutatorian, the worst. Between these extremes, other talented minority students described various degrees of disconnection from the hearts of their institutions. Like Monica's, their hard work and good grades never resulted in personal attention by faculty or involvement with a professional reference group of peers, graduate students, or practitioners. Some, like Luz, were rebuffed when they sought help or advice from professors; others, like Monica, never perceived openings to ask. Commuting and employment exacerbated the exclusion of some students of color from the center of college life, but even full-time residential students like Barbara were pushed inexorably to the margins of undergraduate academic and social life. Clinging to others like them provided the light gravity that kept Barbara and Luz in college. Lacking even these ties, Monica and Jonas floated away from higher education.

What Goes Without Saying

Monica, Michelle, and the other minority students in the Illinois Valedictorian Project possessed stores of tacit knowledge they never learned in school. They knew about city life and caring for your own. They knew about culture and differences. They knew about economic uncertainty and the struggle to live a life of dignity and respect. Talented students of color learned these lessons from the people they knew; they accumulated information through direct experience in inner-city life. Although such practical knowledge remained unrecognized and largely unusable in formal higher education, the tacit knowledge of African American and Latina valedictorians also comprised extensive information about doing well in school. Like any top student, academically talented minority students knew how to study, take tests, and please teachers. They were skilled in translating hard work into academic success.

Knowledge about doing well in school accompanied these students to college and helped them succeed in postsecondary academics. Such tacit understandings fell short in assuring top college achievement, however. Outstanding students of color arrived on campus without the web of white middle-class family and school structures that provided Anglo students with practical knowledge in such areas as college choice strategies and career planning. Students of color were unaware of the full range of occupational possibilities. They were never taught how to demand and receive attention in a mostly white environment, how to hold out for the right job, how to choose a graduate school, or how to change occupations.

Individuals accumulate tacit knowledge through a process of direct experience and personal interactions (Bloom, 1985). The interactive nature of talent development, apparent in the valedictorians' high school years, ceased during college for nearly all minority men and women. Ignored by faculty, outside the central college intellectual and social structures, African Americans and Latinas at predominantly white institutions never had the opportunity to develop subtle skills of translating intrinsic academic interests into clearly formulated career goals and effectively managed educational and professional activities.

Without access to insiders, students of color were left to teach themselves. Barbara completed every class problem set and attended every review session to learn what she could from the questions of the white students who were called upon. Luz added a second major in computer science and an extra year of college on the casual advice of a summer job interviewer. Gaps in tacit knowledge held tangible consequences. Karla, the third African

American woman in the valedictorian project, successfully completed a prelaw major at a prestigious university but received no assistance in entering law school. By college graduation, she had never spoken with professors, savvy peers, or law students about her chosen field. She knew no practicing attorneys. A strong belief in her own ability, founded on an exemplary academic record, encouraged Karla to follow her dream of a career in entertainment law. Her uninformed approach to law school practically guaranteed her failure. Karla chose a local, low-ranked institution so that she could live at home and work full time during law school. No one counseled Karla to apply for fellowships nationally or to finance her professional degree through loans. Her law school was not one of the few in the country that prepares entertainment lawyers. She had never been told of the connection between first-year grades, *Law Review* election, and career prospects. After an exhausting year of full-time work and full-time law study, Karla's grades were mediocre, and she was dismayed at the mismatch between her expectations and the realities of being a law student. She dropped out and took a well-paying insurance industry job requiring considerable travel. Karla dislikes her job but remains in the position because of the money, the security, and the inability to frame alternatives.

Like Monica and Jonas, Karla knew she was talented. Like them, she aspired to a glamorous career partly because she knew she had the talent and drive to succeed and partly because all prestigious professional paths appeared equally hazy and unreal. Tacit knowledge about law school, law practice, and entertainment law might have helped Karla succeed in her chosen profession; wider practical information might also have led to a different occupational choice. In any case, stellar classroom performance in high school and college did not equip Karla with the advisors or knowledge to escape her lucrative but disliked job. Similarly, Monica and Jonas each aspired to communications degrees with superior academic skills but without the practical understanding of how to build broadcasting careers. Most valedictorians of color who managed to implement their original career plans were no better off, finding themselves unable to escape narrow tracks they might not have chosen with wider comprehension of occupational possibilities.

Eric: When It Works

Among the African American and Latina valedictorians, the story of Eric differs markedly from the rest. Eric seemed an unlikely candidate for success. The salutatorian from Jonas's high school, Eric's commencement address was short and unremarkable. More telling, his family valued formal education very little. A middle child in a large family, Eric was the only one who studied amidst what he described as the "uproar" of his crowded home life. The only older brother who had finished high school was out of work; no other immediate relative had finished high school. Some of his siblings resented Eric for his hard work and academic accomplishments, claiming he got extra privileges and thought he was above them. He was not treated as special, Eric insisted. He worked after school for lunch money and bus fare to school. Like Monica, he also contributed money for family bills.

Eric could never say why he was so different from the rest of his brothers and sisters. Possibly his school orientation came from living with his grandmother for a time as a child or from an early love of reading. His teachers encouraged him from his early elementary years, telling him "to keep working, to keep working." He did keep working, developing strong habits of persistence and the ability to detach himself from chaotic surroundings in order to concentrate deeply on his studies.

After leaving high school as the number-two-ranked student, Eric entered a local predominantly white university to study engineering. He never realized he could apply for scholarships nationwide, he said. Besides, he wanted to remain near his family, "to help with the struggle." The university required all professional students to spend two years in general studies before entering their specialized field. Eric found himself unable to begin engineering courses. Worse, his grades were slipping below the competitive entry requirements for the major. Eric dropped out of college, unable to cope with family problems and still dig himself out of his academic hole. "I never really got my feet on the ground as far as studies. Seems like ever since high school, my family was always getting up and moving seemed like every two to three months. Family problems, such as no one to pay the bills, that's one of the reasons why I chose to stay in the area at first, to try to help out my family with bills. . . . I just thought there was the obligation. A personal thing. The family was so close, [I] had a lot of younger brothers and sisters, trying to help them as I went along."

So far, the story is familiar. Eric had never left the margins of the university, never made a personal connection with a faculty member, never understood how to reach or modify his professional goal. At this point, however, Eric's life began to travel a different path. "After a while I just sat back and promised myself that, 'Eric, what you're doing is really hurting yourself more than helping the family to go along. You're still not doing well in school; the family's going to survive whether [you're] there or not.' And that's what happened. I decided to go."

Like other minority valedictorians, Eric planned for the future with extremely limited practical knowledge of financial aid opportunities, colleges, and fields of study. As he considered transferring, his memory returned to a popular high school administrator who used to sing his college song in the school hallways. Eric applied to this administrator's alma mater, a historically black college in the South. He was accepted into an engineering program that he could finance (like Kevin, as described in Chapter Four) through a co-op, alternating semesters of on-campus study and full-time engineering employment.

From the moment Eric arrived on campus, his college experience was transformed. For the first time, he became involved in campus extracurricular activities and social life. "I got a start in what I considered college life, getting comfortable in school." For the first time, his professors actively encouraged him. They spent time with Eric to make certain he made up deficiencies from his earlier college work and assured him that he would do well if he worked hard to master the fundamental concepts in introductory courses. They worked out a program to enable him to complete the program in four rather than the normal five years. Even though Eric's first year was still shaky academically because of continuing family problems, he received "a lot of respect from my instructors because they knew how good a student I was or how good a student I could be."

Eric entered the engineering curriculum immediately, "doing something I always wanted to do." He socialized and studied with other engineering majors, growing in confidence as other students sought him out for academic assistance. In his semesters of employ-ment, Eric applied the academic skills he had mastered, became acquainted with practicing engineers, and developed an identity as a competent professional. Shortly before graduation, he mar-ried a fellow student. The couple moved back to Eric's home city, where he had accepted an excellent engineering position. He and his wife adopted her young half-brothers and sister and invited one of Eric's brothers to live with them for a time "to get his attention" and turn him toward education as "the road to take." Eric became an active volunteer in the African American community. He enjoyed his work as a mechanical engineer and planned a future M.B.A. to help him move up in management.

Eric was unique among the African American and Latina undergraduates. Guided by professors, peers, and practicing engi-neers, he entered fully into the academic and social heart of his second college and became socialized into the professional world. Eric and Michelle were the only two students of color with positive college experiences. It is surely no accident that Eric attended a historically black college and that Michelle's predominantly white university featured a strong minority engineering program.

Eric's graduation from college occurred nine years after he left high school. "Graduation at [the college] is probably one of the highlights of my life. . . . [I]t's something I had waited for, and I had worked hard for it. And to look out when I was going up to get my diploma and look up and see the two most important people in my life, my wife and my mother sitting in the audience, was one of those rushes of moments that you probably never forget. The expression on their faces—they are as happy for me as I am for myself."

The Best Minority Students

Eric's story starts out like those of the college dropouts and dissat-isfied workers. Like them, Eric entered college without the finan-cial backing and untaught practical knowledge that more privileged youth took for granted. Like the others, he began higher education as an academically capable, motivated, hardworking stu-dent. He also longed to remain close to his family and to help with their struggles. Enmeshed in financial and family problems and unable to make a real connection to the university, Eric drifted away from education. His comeback required genuine access to the core of a college where his considerable ability and drive were recognized and nurtured through an interpersonal process of talent development. Eric flourished under these conditions, becoming an exceptional adult contributor to his family, profession, and community.

Eric's initial experience at a predominantly white university mirrored the entire college lives of the most academically talented African American and Latina students. College bonds weakened for students who lived off campus, took outside employment, and maintained active family commitments. Unskilled in navigating the university, these students were unlikely to enter the personal networks where insiders traded the practical information they desperately needed. Racism and active exclusion completed the push to the margins of higher education. Minority men and women continued intensive academic effort, earning good or even excellent grades but not realizing that the achievement arena was in the process of shifting beyond the classroom.

Women of color in male-dominated college majors suffered particularly from the effects of marginalization, according to project findings. Unlike white women, the biggest issue for minority female undergraduates was not what kind of career to plan within the constellation of family and work roles. African American women anticipated full-time continuous professions and prized economic self-sufficiency; Latina valedictorians also planned high-level careers. These talented women took career orientation for granted, but the steps to achieving their goals remained secreted in locked or unknown rooms. Professional trials, so vital for raising the ambitions of Anglo women, were a mixed blessing for women of color. Because they were still different, still professionally naïve, and still subject to exclusion, minority women were unable to find models and mentors at internship and job sites. Professional opportunities failed to provide personal contacts for tacit occupational knowledge. Although Monica learned through her internships that she loved her chosen field, she lacked the contacts to capitalize on her experience. When career-related work convinced women like Michelle that they would prefer a different occupation, they could not shift tracks.

Eric eventually succeeded brilliantly because he gained access to a network of faculty, peers, and professionals. Through them, Eric learned the practical information he needed, and just as importantly, translated his adolescent achievement into a strongly positive personal and professional identity. Class-related tacit knowledge, not financial disadvantage alone, circumscribed Eric's horizons until he found a college that truly let him in.

For minority students, as for women and working-class white valedictorians, superior college grades did not lead smoothly to high-level satisfying work. College educations that ignored the gap between academics and career preparation proved insufficient to assure the fulfillment of promise among even top students of color. The tacit knowledge of planning and negotiating a professional career path was not easily accessible to first-generation, nontraditional college students. Talented minority students were excluded from the sources of vital untaught information by isolation, by racism, and by the failure of colleges to involve them at the core of the institution. Despite their superior ability, motivation, and academic preparation, these serious learners succumbed to that abandonment in college (Monica, Barbara, Jonas), during the transition from college to work (Luisa, Karla), or in early careers (Michelle, Luz). The omission of active assistance shaped the adult achievement levels of African American and Mexican American valedictorians fourteen years after high school.

Entering higher education, getting good grades, majoring in science and engineering, and graduating college seem like success. The African American and Latina members of the Illinois Valedictorian Project *have* succeeded; each is an educated, competent, contributing member of a multicultural community. A close look at the actual college experiences of these exceptional men and women, however, reveals the struggles and wounds of the undergraduate years. Lowered academic achievement is perhaps the most benign effect of higher education's failure to nurture the promise of the highest ranking African American and Latina high school students. More disturbing are drops in self-confidence and the disappearance of the enthusiasm and energy students carried from high school. Her job supervisor never knew how enthusiastic she used to be, Michelle said, and her black engineer friends feel the same.

They've gone to a company and been there four, five, six years, whatever, gone back to school or they've taken other jobs. Just don't really care. Their career wasn't as important to them as it was when they were an undergrad. I know I'm discouraged. . . . They say if you're a minority, if you're a woman, you have to work twice as hard to be just as good, and I really do feel that way. . . . I already know about having to understand where people are coming from, having to recognize that there are cultural differences, and being able to get around that. I already know that because I had to do that. . . . I'm not the one that has to deal with it. But people who deal with me are going to have to change.

Eric's story demonstrates how higher education can develop the talents of a promising first-generation college student, overcoming limitations of poverty and enabling cultural commitments to family and community. Like the rest of the students of color in the valedictorian project, Eric brought to higher education the traits that led him to the top of his high school class: hard work, persistence, intellectual ability, belief in his talent, and the old-fashioned American dream of rising through merit. These blessings were not enough at a white university; his eventual success stands as a testament to a historically black college. Monica, in contrast, found no way into her college or profession despite her deep desire for higher education and her willingness to direct her considerable talents toward continued achievement and social mobility. Her unsuccessful educational path demonstrates how predominantly white colleges and universities waste the promise of even the top African American and Latino students.

Chapter Seven

Channels of Success

From College to Career

*Eminent creators typically crystallize their interests, and
become in some way involved in their future careers in
childhood or early adolescence.*
R. OCHSE, *BEFORE THE GATES OF EXCELLENCE* (1990,
P. 94)

*I have always wanted to write vocational theory all over
again; not about how you choose what you are going to do,
but about how you give up all the other selves you are not
going to be.*
WILLIAM PERRY, JR., "SHARING IN THE COSTS OF
GROWTH," IN *ENCOURAGING DEVELOPMENT IN COLLEGE
STUDENTS* (1978, P. 271)

How academic standouts pass from school to career greatly determines whether they stay on the fast track—or even in the running—for extraordinary adult achievement. The top student in the
class carries into postsecondary education strong academic ability,
exceptional work motivation, and vigorous ambition. Valedictorians have reached the academic peak by excelling at the range of
subjects and tasks that constitute the occupation of "school." By
the time they leave college or graduate school, these star generalists are expected to have channeled their talents into specific
career tracks.

According to vocational psychologists, career outcomes depend on a satisfactory meeting of personal traits and occupational opportunities (Holland, 1985; Osipow, 1973). Individuals search for a match between the world of work and their abilities, interests, skills, and values. College-bound youths, the story goes, accomplish this developmental task during the "moratorium" of the undergraduate years, when they narrow their career direction as one facet of establishing identity (Chickering and Reisser, 1993; Erikson, 1959, 1968). Critics have charged that this widely accepted conception of career development overstates both the freedom of the individual to choose and the potential of most jobs for human fulfillment (Warnath, 1975). It also assumes that young people have somehow acquired a reasonably complete, realistic picture of the occupational world and that the career "map" will remain relatively stable (Gottfredson, 1981; K. D. Hulbert, personal communication, November 18, 1994).

Valedictorians' young adult lives support both sides of the debate. Indisputably, academically talented high school students devoted considerable attention to career preparation and vocational decision making during college. Many were motivated to become high school valedictorian in order to reach the top rung of the early career ladder. Secondary school honors, they said bluntly, led to good colleges, which led to good careers; these life-defining opportunities were the only lasting legacy of high school prizes. Motivated by pragmatism and the 1980s preoccupation with well-paid business and technical professions, careerist and striver college students viewed higher education precisely as a time to make firm career decisions and prepare themselves for work. An enjoyment of writing, a desire to help others, or an ability to learn mathematics easily were qualities readily projected onto college majors and career objectives. Without exception, valedictorians aspired to adult employment they considered worthwhile and fulfilling.

Nevertheless, curbs to an unrestricted matching of talented individual to fulfilling career are also indisputable. The cases of female and minority valedictorians, for example, demonstrate how gender, social class, and ethnicity circumscribed the possibilities students envisioned (Astin, 1984; Gottfredson, 1981) and effectively blocked some channels to which they aspired. Some valedictorians who followed clear channels to their chosen career found their professional grooves turning into deep ruts. Such stories raise the important question of whether strongly defined career paths are liberating or confining for academically able college students.

Channels to Eminence

The trajectory of eminent creative achievers differs from the vocational psychologists' view of career development as a late adolescent process associated with identity crystallization (Ochse, 1990). Historical and contemporary eminent achievers typically "fall in love" with a particular talent domain in childhood or early adolescence (Feldman, 1986), focusing strongly on that single area instead of multiple pursuits (Bloom, 1985; Ochse, 1990). Powerful early interest evolves into lifelong, intensive, even obsessive involvement in the talent area. Combined with prodigious work and persistence, this motivational profile yields significant creative achievements in fields like science or the arts. Exceptional adult achievers often recall formal schooling as a disliked distraction or even an impediment to learning and production in their specialty (Goertzel, Goertzel, and Goertzel, 1978). The few who enjoyed school and were high academic achievers were able to concentrate their schoolwork on high-level and independent learning in their area of interest (Ochse, 1990).

Clearly, this profile of eminent creative achievers is at odds with the major body of findings on high school valedictorians. (Which may suggest, as a reviewer of a draft of this book pointed out, that eminent creative individuals are different in kind and not just in degree from "the rest of us," including those of us who do extremely well in school. That is, achievement so extraordinary that it transforms a domain would probably not be predictable on the basis of grades or other standard achievement indicators.) Top-ranked secondary school students used their strong work ethic to pursue multiple academic and extracurricular interests. None was obsessed with a single talent area to which he or she subordinated school and social involvement. Most followed the values of their families and their historical era to pinpoint a career that would use their academic skills and yield secure, lucrative employment. As a rule, valedictorians relegated their early interests to hobbies, second majors, or regretted dead ends. The serious athletes among the valedictorians never pursued sports occupations. Most of the high school musicians hung up their instruments during college. Journalists ended their newspaper work in high school or college. The many students with international interests learned languages, and some studied abroad, but no one has thus far made an international career. Monica, Jonas, and Karla were unsuccessful in implementing careers in the entertainment industry.

Only a very few high school valedictorians attempted to carry intensive childhood interests directly into college majors and careers. Among this handful are the three students who majored in studio art, architecture, and creative writing. Of these arts majors, only the architect, Dale, is currently earning his living in the field of his college major. Deborah, the sole community activist in the group, brought her early spiritual and political values into a career, and a few of the scientists, like Beth, have long been fascinated by their areas. The small group of students who approached college as intellectuals includes most of the valedictorians who can trace their career fields to intensive childhood interests. Significantly, it is these men and women who remain the most likely project candidates for extraordinary career attainment.

Focus or Traps?

Premature career focus, according to vocational psychologists, can result in identity foreclosure and truncated achievement (Marcia, 1966). Unhappy careerists stuck in technical professions they chose at age seventeen seem to illustrate the need for undergraduate exploration. Researchers of eminence, on the other hand, point to enduring childhood interests as the typical precursor of exceptional adult accomplishment. And although some of the most outstanding adults in the Illinois Valedictorian Project have incorporated their childhood dreams into careers, they have delayed narrowing their vocational focus. Is it really necessary for well-rounded academic achievers to constrict their interests into a specific vocational channel? Is there an optimal time to commit to a path? What happens when talented people find they cannot implement their chosen vocation or discover their early choice is a poor match for their adult selves? What kinds of channels seem to produce occupational success and career satisfaction?

Individual stories illustrate the variety of ways in which clear pathways to career attainment can provide focus for some high achievers and traps for others. The cases fall into several categories in which valedictorians follow early dreams smoothly, leave or remain in early channels they later find stifling, juggle multiple talents, or find desired channels blocked.

Darren: Smooth Passages

Darren, unlike Monica and Jonas, moved smoothly from a high school interest in the arts to a career in television that "perfectly fits my expectations." His story of increasing career definition and deepening tacit knowledge demonstrates how college can turn high academic achievers into professional attainers.

Darren grew up in a tiny rural town, valedictorian of a class of thirty-three. Twenty-five of his classmates had gone to school together for twelve years; three were Darren's cousins. By the time he graduated, Darren had played in the band, sung in the chorus, and performed the lead in the senior class musical. He was also an active church musician. An avid television watcher, he was fascinated by a speech communications course during his last semester of high school.

> I've always been sort of a ham; well, not really enough to get into a lot of the theater and everything, but I've been interested in the humanities type of thing. And . . . you don't really get that in a small town [school]. So my senior year, they finally got a speech course, and it was just a semester-long thing, but the lady who taught was just super. I mean, she was one of those people who has done everything. She has been in front of the camera, she's been involved with radio, and she is really the one who got me interested. Before then, I had thought about it, but since I had no background, I thought, 'There is no way that I really have any business trying to get into this.' But I got the boost from that, from my last semester of high school, and I took off from there.

Darren kept in touch with his high school teacher after leaving for a regional state university. In his first year, he enjoyed several speech communications courses he took as part of his search for the perfect major. He worked part time in the speech office, where he got to know department professors. By the end of the year, he was nearly certain he would major in mass communications.

Darren's high school teacher recommended him for a radio station internship during his first summer home from college. He was not offered the job, painting houses and working on the family farm instead. With a friend, Darren returned to college early to compete for a slot at the university cable television station. He had heard the station was hiring, he said, and he was willing to take the forty-hour training course in hopes of landing a job. Darren was hired, working on two cable television shows during his sophomore year. He was now committed to a communications major.

A big-time career in broadcasting felt wrong to Darren. He would rather not work in a high-pressure situation, he said, spend most of his time at a job, or live in a big city. Job security was also a consistently high priority. Besides, "right now it's not feasible as far as my own confidence is concerned." He was enthusiastic about a different career path, one that would accommodate his desire for more regular hours and a rural life of marriage and children: "I'm more into corporate communication and the production of training films and things like that. Where you can have a little more flexibility. . . . I guess I'd have to start in the commercial TV game, maybe. But that's not what's in my future."

He had learned about industrial broadcasting from his high school speech teacher on a visit to his old high school, Darren said. The teacher "had visited a station at [a company in Illinois] and said that it was real nice. And I thought, 'Well, why do they need a station?' So I checked into it a little more and found out that a lot of companies have their own studios, and the idea of that kind of appealed to me. . . . Something that's not being broadcast for millions of people, [it's] just being created for a specified group. So I thought that was a little more where I wanted to go."

With a corporate job in mind, Darren began taking courses in industrial psychology and public relations. Familiarity with personnel issues and external communications, he thought, would serve him well in making training or publicity films. He also saw corporate human resources as a fallback career. By Darren's third year in college, many of his closest friends were fellow broadcasting majors, including a graduate who was employed at a major regional television station. Darren continued to keep in touch with his high school teacher: "She tries to help me all she can." A professor offered him a graduate assistantship, not realizing Darren was only a junior. Perhaps most important was Darren's work at the university television station, where he had taken on increasing responsibility.

As he approached graduation, Darren had built an impressive network of professional contacts.

For all the valedictorians and salutatorians who supposedly want to get places on their own because that's what we've got over other people, when people come along and tell [us] that "oh, I got this job because my Uncle Max knew Fred's neighbor who has this opening," that sort of gets to [me]. So I always sort of rebelled against that; but the more you look at it and the more you see it, you know people are going to hire people they know a little more about.

So I had . . . an interviewing class, and they stressed that a lot in there. We had to do two papers with three interview sources. So I decided that I would take advantage of that, and I did one paper on . . . what employers look for in college graduates who have no experience, and I talked to somebody in personnel at Mutual Insurance, and I talked to somebody in personnel at Murphy Printing, which prints a lot of magazines, and then I talked to my industrial psychology professor, because I'm a psychology minor, and we talked a lot about that. And I got business cards from them. . . . Our next paper was a career paper, so then I took that opportunity to find out more about corporate communication, and I contacted a man, through somebody I know here at home, a guy who is head of the TV sales training at Caterpillar in Peoria, and he was really nice. And then from the man in personnel that I met at Mutual Insurance I got the name of the man who is in charge of the TV station [at Mutual], and I talked to him. And then I interviewed my [high school teacher]. She had done some sales training for United Airlines in California. So I got a few things there.

Because his college offered no courses in industrial broadcasting, Darren found a professor with experience in the field and arranged an independent study in corporate communication. He prepared a résumé tape as his study project, a professional audition tape of his video work from the television station and department studio, and he reported: "Right now, I'm satisfied with where I'm going. And I know enough about the area where I don't have a lot of uncertainty clouding my decision. So I feel pretty good."

Darren's values consistently featured creative work that was both secure and enjoyable. Even more important to him, however, was personal time with his extended family and hoped-for wife and children. In 1982, at age nineteen, he reported his ultimate ambition as living in a middle-sized town as a married father, enjoying his work. In 1984 he declared that "what it all boils down to is that I just want to be happy. I want to enjoy what I'm doing, and I don't want to ever dread having to go and do what I've chosen to do."

By the time he graduated from college, Darren was a skillful, confident broadcaster with deep practical knowledge of the industrial television world and professional contacts throughout the state. He took his dream job, a position at a corporate broadcasting studio in a middle-sized town forty miles from his parents' farm. He began moving up from production assistant to writer/producer of nonbroadcast television programs, the precise ambition he had reported in 1986. Four years after college, he married an elementary school teacher. That year, he reported his ultimate as "a healthy happy family and work that makes it a pleasure to get up in the morning." The couple had a daughter in 1990 and a son in 1993. "As much as I like my job, my personal life is still priority number one," Darren said in 1993.

Darren was not a particularly privileged or sophisticated high school graduate nor did he attend a prestigious university. His high school mentor opened the possibility of broadcasting for Darren and continued to assist him in finding opportunities and acquiring practical knowledge. Excellent academic performance in college courses gave Darren a final cumulative grade point average of 3.80. More important than academic achievement, however, was Darren's practical experience working in the departmental office, producing real broadcasts at the university television station, and conducting informational interviews with practicing professionals in his intended field. Long before leaving college, Darren had clarified his values for creative work within a family-centered life. His four undergraduate years constituted a steady progression of increasing technical and career management knowledge. By the time he graduated, Darren had decided what he wanted and knew how to reach his clearly envisioned goal.

Smooth Variations

Darren found a fulfilling career that fit his artistic and personal values through a series of experiences that deepened his knowledge about himself and the world of broadcast communications. Other valedictorians traveled similar pathways of increasing career definition. By 1994, two-thirds of the study group were happy with their work in the labor force or as full-time homemakers. Thirty-four valedictorians (42 percent of the total group) had reached their current satisfying work through relatively smooth passages from education to career. Some, like Darren, reached career decisions after a short period of exploration in the first two years of college. The structure of most colleges supports this decision sequence, with initial core liberal arts courses followed by a commitment to a specific major in the junior and senior years. The five attorneys, for instance, all arrived in college with an interest in law, which they crystallized after exploring various liberal arts fields. Lisa entered college intending to teach high school mathematics; her interest in applied mathematics and a business career resulted in a smooth change to actuarial science. Lisa, like Darren, used the early undergraduate years to explore career possibilities within her interest area; like him, she chose a specialty she learned about in college.

Not all smooth career paths followed Darren's and Lisa's sequence. Half of the valedictorians who followed clear paths into satisfying jobs remained in fields they chose before entering college. Again the structure of college interacted with career decisions. Many schools, including the University of Illinois, require students to enter directly into such specialized programs as engineering, business, and nursing. Other majors, like chemistry, require early commitments because of their heavy, sequential course load. Students who decide on such fields after two years of liberal arts exploration find themselves out of step for course requirements and four-year graduation. The two nurses and four physical therapists who entered narrowly channeled college programs are all satisfied with their work; early specializers in engineering, business, and medicine report mixed career satisfaction.

Marlene is a good example of a careerist who made an early vocational decision she has never regretted. As a high school senior, Marlene knew she wanted a respected, secure, people-oriented career in which she helped others. She also aspired to a balanced life of part-time work and rearing children. Marlene fulfilled her aspirations exactly, applying directly to a professional program in physical therapy, which led to fulfilling work in her chosen field. Extensive clinical work built Marlene's professional skills, confidence, and tacit career knowledge over her undergraduate years. She married her longtime boyfriend four months after college graduation, working full time as a physical therapist and then part time after the birth of her second child. Several other project mothers with untroubled career paths have reduced their labor force involvement or would like to do so. Some, like Marlene, have always known that career would take second place to family. Others, including a few men, have gradually subordinated professional ambition to personal and family time.

A third pattern of smooth career development resembled Darren's sequence of exploration and deepening commitment but took place over a longer period of time. Bill, for example, resisted his father's pressure to become a doctor. Instead, he majored in English with the expectation of a future business career. As an undergraduate, Bill started two successful enterprises, a university note-taking service and a corporate souvenir business. He also worked with a venture capitalist. After college, he narrowed his career direction from multiple interests in nonprofit organizations and entrepreneurship by working at different kinds of positions and completing an M.B.A. degree. Bill now works as an executive at a small high-tech firm, preparing himself to head his own company. His long-term plan, he said in 1994, calls for early retirement so he can devote himself to travel and to part-time work in the nonprofit sector. Bill, like many of the highest level professionals in the Illinois Valedictorian Project, set out on a broad path that allowed him to explore professional fields during the undergraduate years and beyond. By the time they made career and graduate school commitments, these valedictorians knew themselves well, possessed considerable practical occupational information, and drew on a variety of relevant academic and employment experiences.

In summary, slightly under half of the valedictorians found smooth paths to careers they enjoyed. Some, like Darren, discovered their channels during the first few years of college and deepened their commitment and qualifications through a series of work experiences and personal interactions with faculty and practitioners in their fields. Others, like Marlene, were fortunate enough to enter prescribed vocational grooves that suited them well. Finally, some of the highest achieving valedictorians, like Bill, followed an extended but unified sequence of career exploration, work experience, and vocational commitment.

Rachel: The Wrong Groove

Following a clear, smooth channel does not necessarily lead to a satisfying professional life. Rachel, one of the most academically talented of the project valedictorians, persisted for a decade in a track that never felt exactly right. After two years of high school chemistry with an admired teacher, Rachel automatically signed up for chemistry at her private, religiously affiliated college. Perhaps she would follow her mother's recommendation and become a doctor, Rachel thought. In any case, she aimed for a career that would be secure and reasonably lucrative, "a job that isn't risky." She indulged herself in English courses, enjoying literature and expository writing but never seriously considering a career in the humanities. "English is a hobby. . . . But that doesn't even seem like school to me. I've taken some literature courses. You know, it's the kind of stuff I do on my own."

Rachel excelled in chemistry, enjoying the problem solving and rigor of the field. From her first year, chemistry professors took notice of her ability and encouraged her to major in the area. After discovering in sophomore biology that she disliked dissecting animals, Rachel committed to a chemistry major. All of the department faculty gave special attention to Rachel and her best friend Sophie (also a project member). "My chemistry professor kind of took us under his wing." By junior year, Rachel was teaching an organic chemistry laboratory, tutoring, and proctoring department examinations. She conducted research with a faculty member. She was a member of the American Chemical Society, which awarded her two scholarships. At least one of her science professors had become a friend. "I'm getting a lot of personal attention, especially in my department," she reported.

Yet despite her growing involvement in chemistry, Rachel did not define herself primarily as a scientist. Literature classes continued to draw her, along with cello lessons and playing in the college orchestra. She prided herself on being well rounded and people oriented, qualities she saw as different from those of most male chemistry majors.

> It seems like all the guys that are chemistry majors take it more seriously. Whereas I'm always trying to prove that I'm fun and I'm not a chemistry "squid," as they call it. I'm always trying to be nonacademic. Trying to get the best of both worlds. . . . I don't ever get any enjoyment out of chemistry as such. I enjoy teaching the labs and that kind of thing, but—I don't know—I can't see myself being a research chemist. Having this burning desire to want to find out one eternal question, you know. That's just not me. I'm not that. I'm more—light.

As senior year arrived, Rachel had decided that a faculty position would allow her a more people-oriented professional life than an industrial laboratory job. Either way, she needed her doctorate. Graduate school in English was out of the question, she said, because humanities students were rarely subsidized, whereas she could "definitely get paid to go to grad school for chemistry." She would look around for a job after graduation, Rachel said. "I'm not real hot to go on to grad school because I know it's going to be rough. I don't know if I'll enjoy it. I don't know. If I were ever to do it, I should do it now. While I still am current. But I'll see."

Her last year of college, Rachel won a major award for travel to an international science meeting. She was elected to Phi Beta Kappa, having maintained straight A's through four years of college. Rachel's chemistry adviser was "kind of pushing" her into graduate school. He urged her to attend his doctoral institution, one of the best chemistry departments in the country. When he arranged with his own Ph.D. adviser to offer Rachel a full doctoral fellowship, she decided to go directly into graduate study.

"It was again [the pattern in] my life, where I just let people point the way."

As she left college, Rachel was apprehensive about her future social and academic life in graduate school. "My friends here are all from music or English. I don't consider myself the scientific character. And I'm wondering if I'll fit in. I'm afraid that I won't like them or they won't like me. And that's kind of a drag. Because I really want to make good friends there. But I will really never be out of the chemistry department. I'm hoping there are some regular people there." Rachel was even more concerned about her ability to succeed academically in a top chemistry graduate program. She was an excellent academic chemist, she reasoned, but not really a talented scientist. "I'm wondering if I'm one of the overachievers. What's everybody else like? I don't feel like I've done anything important. And I really feel, going to graduate school, like I don't know anything. And when is everyone going to find out? I've just been playing the games, you know. And just doing well playing the games."

These worries, not surprisingly, were unfounded. Rachel found friends in the chemistry department and elsewhere. She was a strong but not outstanding doctoral student, publishing two articles with her major professor's laboratory team. She described chemistry as "elegant," "abstract," and "artistic," but enjoyed the field "on paper" more than in the laboratory. "I just don't like doing the lab work. It's messy and it's dirty and it's dangerous and it's difficult. . . . For me, it's drudgery." Although she performed well academically, Rachel was "always afraid. I always felt really stupid and like I was a real fraud a lot of the time. . . . No, I was never confident. Professionally, I always felt that everybody knew a lot more than me."

After her first two years, Rachel seriously considered taking an industrial chemistry position and leaving school with a master's degree. A strong performance on her comprehensive oral examination seemed like "an omen" that she should stay in school. She continued toward the Ph.D. and soon began dating a graduate student in her laboratory group. When they married, Rachel was finishing her dissertation, and he was two years away from the degree. Her major professor offered her a postdoctoral position to continue working in his lab while her husband finished school. The offer threw Rachel into a crisis because she realized that she dreaded resuming the work of the past six years. She was well aware there would be limits on her future in chemistry if she stopped working in a lab and lost track of the professional literature. She was reluctant to abandon the effort she had put into science. At the same time, she asked herself: "Do I want to stay doing a job that I don't like just that so when we leave I can get another job I don't like?. . . . But that is what I was trained for."

Her sharp distaste for resuming laboratory work coincided with a job offer from a national science-test developer. After agonizing about the decision, Rachel took the writing position. She deeply enjoyed science writing, which took her back to her original love of reading and writing. "What I do is sit around and write and edit, which I really like to do." She hoped to make a career writing about science, although she did not rule out teaching chemistry to nonscientists at a community college level. Rachel was unsure how to build a career as a writer but eager to discover more about this professional path. "In a way, it's like my career is coming apart, but I'm coming together. It's funny, because I don't have this high-powered career goal right now, but I'm slowly sliding into my niche." Exploring a new career was made possible, Rachel acknowledged, by marriage to a future well-paid chemist who looked forward to the career track she had abandoned.

In 1994, Rachel was home full time with her first child while her husband worked full time as a chemist. She had done some teaching to nursing students but was unsure when she would return to the labor force or how her career might develop. Looking back on her path to the doctorate, Rachel attributes her choice of chemistry to the encouragement and special attention of her undergraduate professors.

> It's been tough because chemistry, looking back, really wasn't my favorite subject in the world. . . . I don't really know why I did it. But once I got here [to graduate school], I had to finish because I couldn't quit. It was just the way it was. I was able to do it, through all those times that I should have gone to graduate school in English, which was what I really wanted to do. But I couldn't have, probably, supported myself, and if I did [go to graduate school in English], it would have been so hard. I didn't want my parents to

support me anymore, but I knew I wanted to get an advanced degree. This just fell into my lap.

Rachel had not been a stellar doctoral student, she said, because she was not passionate about chemistry. "At some point, no matter how talented you are, you have to put in the time and have the passion for it."

Suffocating Channels

"The only thing that's kept me going is this stupid refusal to quit," Rachel told us. She proceeded down a clear road, encouraged by professors and sponsored into research and teaching opportunities in chemistry. Well before college graduation she had entered a network of professional contacts and been anointed as a future top-ranked scientist. Like Darren, Rachel had the experiences she needed for sophisticated tacit knowledge in her field. Unlike him, she resisted full socialization into her profession. Rachel was not attracted to chemists as friends and rarely enjoyed her work in science. She continued because she was capable of success in a profession that promised the security and financial independence she craved. Without knowing how to build a career around her genuine interests, she responded to the strong enthusiasm of her science mentors and "just let people point the way." If she had not been such a talented chemistry student, Rachel might have paid more attention to her lukewarm attraction to science. Her capability to succeed in a difficult academic field became a source of pressure to capitalize on her talent; interpersonal attention by adults she respected also kept Rachel on the wrong path. The forces directing Rachel toward science were largely absent in humanities. Successful also in literature study, Rachel discounted English as an indulgent hobby pursued for fun on her own time. No English professors took her under their wing or showed her how she could make a solid career in the humanities. She never gained the confidence or tacit knowledge to understand that her outstanding academic ability would lead to fellowships in literature doctoral programs. Instead, Rachel traveled the chemistry path to the academic end, coming to grips with the reality of her career only as she completed her lengthy training and faced her first professional position. In her early thirties, Rachel faced the career exploration many of her academically talented peers completed ten years earlier.

Rachel persisted all the way to a doctorate in a field that never deeply engaged her. She did leave research science at that point, though, a courageous act for a young woman who had always followed the marked path. Other valedictorians have not yet managed to depart deep career channels they now perceive as stifling. Michelle, the African American engineer featured in Chapter Six, was "pushed" into her field and, like Rachel, stayed because she was talented and reasonably successful there. As a single woman without family financial backing, Michelle cannot explore a new occupation while a spouse or parent supports her; more importantly, she has little idea how to switch from being an engineer to owning her own business.

Half of the valedictorians who have reported significant career dissatisfaction followed relatively smooth channels to their current occupations. Among these fourteen unhappy workers are half of the project's engineers. A first-generation college student of immigrant parents, Diane chose engineering precisely because it offered a clear pathway to a well-paying, "glamorous high-tech job." She did not expect to find intrinsic enjoyment in her undergraduate studies or occupation, subscribing to her father's motto that "You can't have a good time and work too." College was her job, done well when resulting in lucrative work. Performing her student job under these circumstances made Diane's undergraduate days tense and difficult, especially during her first two years. "I've been home so often. I haven't been up at school because I couldn't stand the feeling I'm getting. I'd go to classes and then I could hardly wait to get away, to leave campus. . . . I wonder if I should go back to school at all." At her father's insistence, Diane continued in college, getting some work experience in her field but never getting close to any faculty or performing undergraduate research. She "wasn't too keen" about her student engineering jobs but pushed her interest in business aside as a future dream. Diane looked past graduation as the beginning of her real life. "My life cannot go on until I get past these next couple of years. But the minute I can get past the next couple of years, then I should be able to start relaxing and enjoying my life a little bit." Unfortunately, Diane enjoyed her professional engineering work as little as her undergraduate major. While earning an M.B.A. at night, she began moving away from technical work at her large company, finally ending up in the management side of the company. Her 1994 goal for the next five years was "just keep plugging away."

Diane at least managed to change her professional specialty. Another valedictorian engineer, the man who listed his desired pseudonym as Dittohead or Cobra Jet, still unhappily performs the job he took after college in his home town. Two years after college, he had a stomach ulcer, "caused by a stressful work situation compounded by a nagging, nontrusting new supervisor." In 1988, he responded to a questionnaire by writing that his ultimate goal was "cruising a faraway highway, good tunes up loud, in a restored muscle car, while catching admiring stares." The same year Paul, an accountant in a prestigious firm, wrote that his ultimate was "winning the lottery, quitting my job, driving down to the Keys, and not coming back." Another businessman, Al, felt trapped in his disliked career at age thirty-two, "becoming a slave to the economics of the life-style which we have developed." The most surprising part of the nineties, Al said, was "always knowing what I wanted in life and reaching a point where many areas, primarily professionally, are uncertain to me."

Nick: Bumpy Paths

Just as smooth channels can lead to either satisfaction or suffocation, rough career routes do not necessarily mean an unhappy work life. Rachel began finding her niche only after abandoning a clear career trajectory. Some valedictorians, like Diane, were able to maneuver themselves into more fulfilling specialties within the same company or profession. Accountant Martin (the careerist profiled in Chapter Four) was miserable at a public accountancy firm but happier as a company financial officer. For other valedictorians, work happiness depended on sharp turns and deliberate departures from straightforward career paths. Nineteen of the happily employed project members followed decidedly jagged career trajectories. Unhappy workers are split evenly between smooth and rough channels, although the valedictorians who work as nonprofessionals followed decidedly bumpy paths.

The story of Nick illustrates the difficulties in leaving a clear path. From the time he was in high school, Nick was motivated by the desire to be upwardly mobile and to maintain his close family ties. The oldest of four children in a lower-middle-class family, Nick was close to his grandparents and brothers as well as his parents. His mother, a high school graduate, worked as a secretary. Nick's father had attended a regional college and worked as a salesman and small businessman. He was unemployed during some of Nick's college years.

In addition to earning top grades at his Catholic high school, Nick was an outstanding athlete. Sports—baseball, football, and basketball—ranked a "close second" to academics in his life. In addition to his own participation in sports, Nick helped his father coach an elementary school sports team and coached during college breaks in addition. He also worked during the school year and summers at a variety of jobs including construction.

Security and helping others were vital to Nick. He was deeply aware of his family's financial struggle and hoped to be able to help his parents and brothers financially when he left college. In Nick's family, "every generation gets to be a little better off. My grandfather graduated from high school, worked at a factory. He told his son, 'I don't want you working in a factory.' My father worked for somebody he really didn't like for years and put in a lot of time, and he said [to me], 'Don't get stuck in something—you're smart enough. Do something.' . . . Now here I am . . ." Having money was futile unless you used it to help others, Nick said. In particular, he dreamed of being able to set his father up in a business and to assist his brothers in completing college.

Nick funded his studies at a Catholic university through a combination of scholarships, loans, and year-round employment. He continued involvement in athletics at an intramural level and worked as a peer counselor in the residence halls. Nick studied hard. In his first year of college, he observed that sometimes he was motivated not so much by wanting to do well but by not wanting to fail. "A lot of my studying was trying to get a scholarship . . . and also because, to be totally frank, I didn't have any money to do anything. I would go the library on Saturdays because . . . I couldn't afford to go out." He never considered taking time off from college to work, Nick said, because of "my dad's ego. . . . Because that would have meant he couldn't provide for me."

Nick majored in accountancy. Economic necessity drove his decision, although he maintained throughout college that he might become a teacher in the future. "It's hard to say. If I follow my dream, I'll be a high school history teacher and coach." As a junior, Nick explored the possibility of a double major in education and accounting. When he found that this path would require a fifth year of undergraduate studies, he gave up the idea "due to financial constraints."

Regardless of his decision to continue in accountancy and his awareness of the relatively low social prestige associated with teaching, Nick continued to be attracted to education. "I think education is a very important field, and that's why I want to get into it. Because I feel like we can do better, and I feel like I can help." In addition to economic disincentives and a desire to experience the nonacademic world, Nick felt he had to defend his growing interest in teaching. "Just opening my mind up to teaching as a vocation has been a big step. I mean, people want you to be successful and that kind of stuff. I don't tell very many people because most of the time the reaction you'll get is, 'Oh, why do you want to waste your time teaching?'"

Nick earned a cumulative college grade point average of 3.78. He became a certified public accountant and worked for six years at one of the premier accounting firms in the country. His highly paid work involved long hours and considerable travel. Nick enjoyed his first opportunities to travel, particularly a two-year stint on the West Coast. He was able to realize his dream of helping his family financially. He found public accountancy stressful and generally unfulfilling, however, and he missed living near his family. In 1988, he wrote: "I don't like my job and work. Too many hours, consequently my personal life is the pits. . . . Part of my problem is I have no plan." For Nick, the ultimate is "to be happy. I realize this is vague, but given how unhappy I am, I long to be at peace with the world and myself. I'm sure that happiness will involve being part of a family I love and who love me."

Being laid off from his accountant's job was a turning point for Nick: "The feeling of being expendable and unwanted was tough."

Nick later considered losing his job a positive factor that pushed him into teaching. Without seeking another accountancy position, he returned home and entered a university program leading to certification as a high school history teacher. While attending classes at night, he taught history at the Catholic high school where he had been valedictorian.

Nick was thrilled with his career change. "I'm much more happy. It's been a much more rewarding year. I think I've probably touched more people and been touched by more people than in the six years I was out of school." Nick had mixed feelings about his study of education. On the one hand, "it felt great to be learning something I wanted to learn. . . . Wanting to be there was a big plus." On the other hand, as in college, Nick was concerned about the cost of his education. He also found the rigidity of the teacher education program particularly distressing. Although he was teaching full time in the Catholic school, Nick's teacher certification program would not allow him to use this experience or to remain in a paid position in the school in order to fulfill his student teaching requirement. Without such flexibility, Nick said, he would have great difficulty funding the remainder of his degree. Nick was also dismayed that "there is no consideration for life experience," adult learner status, or current professional situation in meeting requirements for graduation. "I am trying to get my certification without quitting my job. I don't see the sense in quitting a job to work at the same job for nothing, in order to get a piece of paper that says I can do the job that I am already doing!"

In 1994, Nick was fighting university and state bureaucracies to earn his certification and deeply enjoying his full-time teaching. "I have found my career," he wrote. "I am excited about my job every day. . . . I like to talk about school. That, along with the fact that I read history literature and watch television programs that deal with this area, tells me that I am in the right field. I sure as heck never did that with accounting." Along with teaching, Nick was coaching junior varsity girls' softball. Money continued to be an irritation, although not a deterrent to a teaching career. "The good teachers don't teach for the money, but you do need to make enough to survive and raise a family." Aware of social disrespect for teaching, Nick was firm in his vocation: "I'm very proud to be a teacher."

Nick's story shows the importance of family socioeconomic status in career decisions and underlines the disincentives for a talented young man to enter teaching. During college, the relatively low salary and prestige associated with teaching kept him from pursuing his strong interest in the field. Nick returned to his early goal because of his service values, commitment to education, and family orientation. As compared to accountancy, teaching permitted Nick to pursue a profession in which he could be of direct service to others, look forward to a better balance of work and family time, and have geographic stability and proximity to his family.

Changing Paths

In his first career as an accountant, Nick found himself precisely where he had aimed during college: in a lucrative, prestigious professional career. Like all valedictorians, he was used to accomplishing his goals and working hard to succeed. These qualities both helped and hindered Nick and other outstanding students in changing career direction. On the one hand, strong motivation and a history of success bolstered Nick's confidence in his ability to switch occupations. On the other hand, even though he had never enjoyed accounting, six years of success along with his need for financial security pressed Nick to remain in that first occupation.

Nick and other valedictorians initially settled on poor career matches for several reasons. First, the need for financial security was genuine in the context of many students' family background and the precarious economy of the early and mid-1980s. Second, Nick was interested in two professional fields that required commitments early in the college years. The demands of his business major precluded time for liberal arts exploration and identity clarification. After two years of college, it was already too late to add an education major without remaining in school an extra year. Some valedictorians never allowed themselves the luxury of exploration, believing they had to commit to solid prescribed paths immediately. For many fields, they were correct about the necessity for early choice. Third, Nick lacked deep tacit knowledge about the realities of accountancy when he chose his field. In fact, he learned about the career only after graduating and beginning practice.

Nick, along with almost one in four valedictorians, changed occupations in the decade after college. He was able to find a more satisfactory second choice because he already held a strong alternative area of interest and because he possessed significant practical knowledge about the profession of schoolteacher. Nick needed the personal will to make a major change but acknowledged the effect of a setback in his first occupation in motivating him to follow his dream. Seeing his layoff as a positive opportunity for change was a healthy psychological reaction to that first major setback of his life. Less explicitly recognized by Nick were other opportunities that enabled a career switch: parents who supported his decision and offered him a place to live; a private school teaching job that paid his tuition and allowed him to begin his new career; and the absence of financial pressures from a family of his own. That responsibility to support a family is sufficient to stop Al from leaving business and following Nick into high school teaching and coaching. Michelle has no financial backing to leave engineering in order to pursue the risky path of opening her own business. Luz deeply desires to leave engineering but can identify no strong alternative interest.

Like Nick, most star students who would like to change occupation channels face the dilemma of disliking work that they nevertheless perform extremely well. Always responsible, top students wonder if it is worth the upheaval to leave a career that might not be perfect but is progressing well. Even Nick faced serious disincentives to entering teaching. The risk in leaving a well-paid, prestigious profession was real for Nick and for other security-minded valedictorians. Trying to begin a profession later than usual raises distinct difficulties; Nick's nontraditional route to teaching may yet prevent him from becoming certified to teach in public schools. The risks and disruptions of major changes are enough to dissuade occupational switches by some men and women with family and financial responsibilities. Other valedictorians are kept in unsatisfactory occupations by the same lack of tacit knowledge that propelled them onto limited paths in college.

Despite the pressures keeping them in ill-matched occupations, a quarter of Illinois Valedictorian Project members changed career paths and found satisfying work. Among this group are the six mothers who work full time in the home. Five of these women changed their occupational direction in college or their early careers; the sixth, Emma, earned her Ph.D. but does not plan to practice in her field of chemical engineering. Another group of successful changers is made up of students who juggled more than one interest during college or even into early careers. Hope, for example, graduated Phi Beta Kappa in chemistry but chose to continue with graduate study in theology. Meredith worked in science writing and computer technology before deciding to return to an earlier interest in psychology. Valedictorians were generally successful in entering new career channels because of their outstanding ability, impeccable educational credentials, and strong values for achievement and hard work. Unlike most eminent creative achievers, they were not wedded to a single intensive talent domain. With pragmatic adaptability, valedictorians recast themselves from superb generalists to career specialists. The most successful often resisted such narrowing as long as possible, but none found themselves prized in the labor force for the multiple talents that led them to the top of the academic ladder.

Blocked Paths

Whether bumpy or smooth, the channel to a satisfying adult occupation has thus far eluded about a third of the valedictorians. Besides unhappy workers who feel trapped in the fields they chose as late adolescents, this group includes thirteen valedictorians who never found a path at all. Gail, the unconnected small-town student described in Chapter Four, cast about for a career path until settling uncomfortably in general business. Her undirected job search and disconnection from faculty or professional mentors landed her between the clerical and paraprofessional rungs, performing work she views as a job not a career. Monica and Jonas left college because they saw no way to channel their academic accomplishments into communications careers; both work at nonprofessional jobs.

Eight of the project members, including Gail, Jonas, and Monica, hold job, rather than career, orientations. They work for money only, in positions outside progressive professional paths. Because they are capable, responsible, hard workers, the eight are successful at their jobs. Gail has been promoted within her company. Jonas worked his way up to supervisor at his delivery firm. Monica has been given considerable responsibility for finances and personnel at the store where she works. But these students have ceased defining themselves in terms of public work achievements.

Seven of the eight students in this group were married parents by their middle twenties but most departed from career channels before establishing families. Not marriage and children but unconnected college experiences account for the group's lowered occupational attainment and muddled career channels. From lower-middle-class and working-class-families, these students display the now-familiar profile of hazy career knowledge and near total lack of guidance in negotiating the stepping stones between school and postschool achievement.

Of the eighty-one project members, two valedictorians only have purposely avoided defined professional channels. William, the son of factory laborers, defines himself as an artist and a socialist. Ideologically opposed to participating in mainstream occupational structures, he works at temporary jobs like substitute teaching in order to support himself as a writer. Barry decided after college not to pursue a career in international relations. Instead, he eventually took a job as a bank teller, repeatedly turning down promotions into customer relations and management. In 1990, he described his decision to "drop out of the path."

> I was never wanting to start, because I knew if I started I'd be "it," just like I was in high school. You know, if I was going to get straight A's, I was going to get straight A's from the first day of my freshman year. I was going to get good grades at the university, be able to get into a position where I could get that good job. I was going to do it all the way. So when there was a certain time there, at my university studies, that I knew I had to commit all the way, I never did it. I never wanted to start. I never wanted to go through with it. . . . There was no moral sixties-ish justification to drop out to find myself or to explore nonestablished ways of doing things. I basically just dropped out, dropped out of the path. As I said, there was no glorious reason. I would probably say that it was fear. Fear of committing to something—to life, to life itself. Because once I chose something, I would be on one path. I always wanted to have multi-paths ahead of me. I can do that now.

Deeply influenced by Zen texts he encountered in his college studies of Japanese language and culture, Barry determined to step off the public achievement path and determine his own, personal goals. In 1994, he wrote that he had no plans for the next five years but was struggling with the realization "that the mundane routine of day-to-day life was not as wholly satisfying as I had anticipated. (Where is the book *Zen and the Art of Clerical Work?*) The free time I have so purposely strived to create has not been fully utilized by myself to my satisfaction."

William and Barry are highly unusual among the valedictorians in rejecting mainstream occupational achievement paths. Their peers who also lacked professional trajectories aspired to high-level career channels but floundered amid hazy alternatives and hidden vocational knowledge.

Evaluating Channels of Success

Becoming a successful, contented career achiever was far from automatic for the best Illinois high school students of 1981. Darren's passage represents the textbook case of late adolescent vocational development. To identify and reach his goal of satisfying creative work within a family-centered lifestyle, Darren needed mentors, nonacademic professional experiences, and time for identity exploration. Under these rich conditions of talent development, Darren flourished as he moved smoothly from academic to postacademic success. Committing to a channel midway through undergraduate study fit the higher education structure perfectly and equipped Darren for satisfying work immediately after college. It is worth noting, however, that Darren entered a communications track with negligible potential for creative eminence.

Rachel demonstrates the challenges of multiple talents and the dangers of choosing a vocational path before developing a strong, internally centered identity. The seductiveness of visible pathways to prestigious careers and the paradoxical limitations of broad success potential are also morals of Rachel's story. When tacit knowledge, work experience, and interpersonal support are present only for selected pathways, students like Rachel cannot freely match their interests with career channels. Having dropped out of research science after the Ph.D., she now faces a search among ambiguous vocational tracks outside the educational institutions where structured exploration and mentoring occurred for students like Darren. Leaving the labor force entirely for childrearing is both a result of her movement away from a clear vocational path and a complicating factor in implementing a new direction. Rachel's potential remains high but her career outcome is unclear.

Nick stands for the many careerists who never entered the talent development network of undergraduate support and experience. Choosing a technical focus because of his financial need and poor tacit career knowledge, Nick's narrow vision led him deep into a rut. Superb college grades were enough to propel Nick into a top accounting job, but not sufficient to socialize him into a profession that fit his deepest values. Switching channels is possible, as Nick's story shows, particularly for strong students with powerful alternative interests and with the credentials and habits of success. Changing paths is not without costs, however, and cannot occur without support and tacit career management knowledge. Without these conditions, even top academic achievers cast about ineffectively, remain unhappily in disliked professions, or step off professional tracks entirely.

So do clear occupational channels aid or trap superb students? Commitment to a career path is both narrowing and necessary; the issue is when and how young adults make vocational commitments. Clearly, committing to a narrow vocational channel at the very beginning of college can lead to feeling trapped in deep ruts in adulthood. Such narrow pathways result in success and contentment only if they represent strong continuing interests or if they turn out, through chance or occupational flexibility, to correspond with a valedictorian's adult self. Some students were fortunate enough to choose narrow channels well; more changed occupations or settled for unfulfilling careers.

It was not a random group that traveled unhappy paths or failed to find vocational channels. Students of color and first-generation college students were disproportionately careerists and were particularly at risk during the transition from school to work. Nonacademic knowledge of career alternatives and how to reach them was notably lacking in valedictorians who picked very narrow career grooves and hung on for dear life. And women's paths too often depended on an incomplete understanding of possible work and family configurations (discussed in Chapter Five). The same disconnection from talent development networks prevented such students from knowing how to choose and enter new paths. The stories of successful channels, stifling ruts, and missed paths all point to the same conclusion: the successful passage from school to postschool achievement requires an interpersonal process of increasing self-understanding, career socialization, and tacit knowledge. This central achievement project occurs mostly outside of the college classroom and cannot be accomplished by an individual alone. Leaving school at the top is insufficient for guaranteed passage through top occupational channels.

Valedictorians' trajectories bear little resemblance to the early intensive specialization of eminent creative achievers. Academically capable men and women almost never follow a single-minded interest from childhood into careers. Top-grade earners demonstrate their talent within a system that prizes breadth; superb students are practiced at succeeding even in arenas they find unappealing. Valedictorians possess the ability, motivation, and credentials to prosper in a wide range of occupations. But being able to do almost anything is not always a blessing. Top students can easily find themselves dutifully performing in careers they do not particularly enjoy. The happiest have found adult achievement arenas that do engage them, occasionally through the luck of good early choices, sometimes by leaving worn paths, and most often through exploring themselves and careers with the help of guides and sponsors. The eighty-one men and women of the Illinois Valedictorian Project are still writing their stories. As they near their mid-thirties, valedictorians with the best shot at stellar careers appear to be those who resisted narrow channels in favor of a process of extended exploration, deepening self-knowledge, guided vocational understanding, and gradual career focusing.

Chapter Eight

Delights and Troubles
Becoming an Adult

> *It was hard. Being away and relating to people. Being on your own.*
> ELIZABETH (1983)

> *Finals were terrible. Janie really messed up my mind during finals.*
> CHRISTOPHER (1985)

> *Through my studies at Bible School and travel in Europe, I have realized the joy and freedom of living life totally in God our Creator.*
> CHARLOTTE (1986)

> *I especially need the money since Dad lost his job at the bank and hasn't found a new one yet.*
> JEFF (1984)

> *The big news in my life is my perpetual honeymoon with Mark. We got married June 9 and, miraculously, every day we are happier than the last.*
> VALERIE (1986)

> *Once again, relations with my father have broken off—we haven't spoken for four months now.*
> ROBBY (1986)

*My ultimate would be to never have to worry about what I
ate and how many calories it had.*
BRIDGET (1988)

Even in 1988, extreme prejudice exists.
MICHELLE (1988)

*I was very surprised at the bond I feel with my
children. . . . I didn't realize that I would have the kind or
depth of love that I have for them. (Not that they cannot
bring out the worst in me at times, also!)*
ALAN (1988)

*The one thing that I've found is that maturity doesn't
necessarily come with age. It's like we're all a bunch of five-
year-olds running around in big bodies.*
MAUREEN (1990)

*We got the word that they were going to lay off 120 people.
And I was one of those people.*
GUY (1990)

*My job by its nature is stressful. Often I have a pit in my
stomach that will not go away.*
DAVID (1994)

It's time to make some dreams come true.
CLARE (1994)

A student taught us how to ask one of our questions. "What are you
struggling with these days?" I asked her. "What do you find difficult in your life?" "Oh," she responded, "you mean, what are the
hard things?" The "hard things" became one of the few questions
valedictorians answered at every interview. It took ten years before
we learned how to ask the opposite question: "What is your greatest delight?" From discussions and survey questions of satisfaction,
"bests," and life beyond classes and work, we deduced the students'
joys over those ten years.

The valedictorians experienced the joys and sorrows of normal development. These academic achievers' changing preoccupations over the years evoke psychologist Daniel Levinson's model (1978) of age-related adult stages. Even though Levinson's model was developed on the basis of research with an all-male population and even though its application to a wider group should be undertaken cautiously, its general framework does correspond closely to the early adult patterns of the female and the male valedictorians. The period Levinson labels the "novice phase of early adulthood" occurs between the ages of seventeen and thirty-three, corresponding almost exactly with the current time period of the Illinois Valedictorian Project. The novice phase involves leaving adolescence and making a place in adult society. Young people form a picture of themselves as adults during these years, including forming a life-style and vocational "Dream" of what they hope to become. Beginning to implement the Dream with the help of mentors, establishing a career path, and forming intimate relationships and family structures are all tasks of the twenties and early thirties, according to Levinson.

The novice period begins with the "early adult transition," when young people start moving out of their adolescent world and exploring possibilities for adulthood. Crossing this boundary means developing a personal identity: asking "Who am I?" is a central activity between ages eighteen and twenty-two.

Beginning at approximately age twenty-two, when many leave college, young people enter the adult world. Levinson sees this stage as a time of exploring and testing initial choices about work and relationships. At the same time, young adults make initial commitments—to occupations, jobs, life-styles, romantic partners, and family. By the end of this period, around age twenty-eight, a provisional life structure is in place.

The final stage of entering adulthood is the "age-thirty transition." Occurring roughly between ages twenty-eight and thirty-three, this period is a sometimes turbulent time of appraising the commitments of the postcollege years. Faced with the long-term implications of their initial choices, young adults now seek to develop an adequate, stable life structure for the future. Reexamining their lives around age thirty, individuals either strengthen their commitments to their previous choices or find new directions for their personal and achievement lives.

Project members appeared to follow Levinson's young adult trajectory. As valedictorians began defining themselves apart from their families and high school selves, the threshold between adolescence and adulthood both frightened and exhilarated them. In college, they grappled with issues of social competence, autonomy, identity, and purpose. The boundaries of experimentation and exploration were circumscribed for some "good kids" who never sought a break with the past. Others chafed at the limits they had previously accepted, breaking out of old roles in college or even beyond.

After college, former high school valedictorians worked simultaneously on establishing themselves vocationally and developing intimate relationships. Their focus and timetables varied. Some students finished their education, married, and were parents by their middle twenties. Others were still completing graduate training and looking for mates in their middle thirties. A few never sought traditional paths of professional achievement, heterosexual marriage, or childrearing.

By the time they entered their early thirties, most valedictorians did indeed reconsider their earlier commitments. Many modified or changed their career paths during these years while others confirmed their provisional choices. "Life [now] is more focused— work and family—and less exploratory," Kevin wrote at age thirty-two.

As a group, valedictorians have always led well-rounded, socially integrated, "normal" lives. Better-than-average have been their families' stability, their own accomplishments, and their coping abilities. Just as the stereotypes of the one-sided academic grind or the obsessed genius are myths for high school valedictorians, also false is the conception of academic achievers as troubled individuals effective only in school. With rare exceptions, valedictorians are notably healthy, successful, content, psychologically well-adjusted adults. None has had a trouble-free path, and some have faced serious life difficulties, but they have generally been able to cope with challenges, a hallmark of their academic careers that has held true outside school.

The valedictorians' ability to cope with usual (normative) life stresses and unusually serious (non-normative) problems probably relates to their longstanding habits of academic and personal effectiveness, including control over reaching their objectives; commitment to self, values, and goals; and ability to see changes and external demands as challenges—a constellation of traits that Kobasa (1979) and Maddi and Kobasa (1984) call the "hardy personality." (The valedictorian interview transcripts were not analyzed in terms of coping strategies or defense mechanisms [Vaillant, 1977]. However, the study group does appear to conform to a model of coping in which stressful situations elicit appropriate use of tolerance [including denial]; consideration of the problem in a new, more positive light; and actions to change the environment [Lazarus and Folkman, 1991].)

Following valedictorians over time reveals the normal highs and lows and the typical life stages of young adults. In short, the hard and the delightful things in academic achievers' lives are not too different from anyone else's, although valedictorians seem less often trapped by their misfortunes. This parallels Lewis Terman's findings for his high-IQ longitudinal study group. Members of this group were likewise characterized by developmental patterns that were generally healthy, well adjusted, and not terribly different from those of less-gifted same-age peers (Terman, 1925; Terman and Oden, 1947, 1959.)

High School Plus Four

Being away from home is hard.
CAROL (1983)

The thing that I struggle most with is trying to live my life the way that God wants me to live it.
MELISSA (1982)

I don't mean to sound conceited or anything, but I guess nothing's come that hard, or at least yet.
ANN (1982)

Sometimes I get really high on myself; sometimes I just get really down and I don't have enough confidence in

> *myself. . . . I think life really fluctuates a great deal; it*
> *does from day to day, from hour to hour at times.*
> MAUREEN (1983)

> *That's the only thing that gets irritating, how everything is*
> *put off till later.*
> DAN (1983)

> *I didn't enjoy myself last year. All I did was study, which*
> *is ridiculous, and now all I'm doing is enjoying myself*
> *and I'm not studying. So I've got to find a balance pretty*
> *soon.*
> HOPE (1983)

> *If I got anything out of college, it's growing up. The*
> *process. Different things come your way that you wouldn't*
> *get anywhere else, and you've got to take them and learn*
> *from them.*
> HANNAH (1983)

> *I think I've become more relaxed and at ease. . . . I think I*
> *can tell people now more what I think and how I feel.*
> CAROL (1984)

During the first four years of the Illinois Valedictorian Project, the valedictorians' lives were dominated by the personal and achievement tasks of college. While doing well academically and finding a vocational channel were sources of both anxiety and satisfaction for individual valedictorians, leaving home and family, finding friends, and falling in—and out of—love frequently took equal or top billing among undergraduate concerns. Valedictorians poured energy into exploring who they were and what they stood for, an enterprise that continued beyond college but reached its zenith there. Still, the achievement tasks of college predominated, as students pointed to their school and early work lives as the big news of 1985. That year, as most received undergraduate degrees, 65 percent of the valedictorians reported jobs or graduate school as their primary preoccupation. Another 20 percent pointed to both public and personal news as important. Only 15 percent listed solely personal issues, ranging from travel and being on one's own, to parents' health and—for three students—the birth of first children. Overall, then, at age twenty-two, valedictorians' delights included college graduation and undergraduate honors, finding first professional jobs, getting into graduate school, and becoming financially independent of parents. On the personal front, students were preoccupied with dating and a few with marriage and childbirth. Men and women relished experiences of personal growth ranging from developing autonomy to becoming more socially comfortable. Recreational pursuits like sports, travel, extracurricular college activities, and hobbies took their place among the best parts of valedictorians' young adult lives. Religious activities and spiritual growth were important anchors for many undergraduates.

Troubles had also arisen by the time most of the group graduated from college. Previous chapters told stories of unhappy searches for career tracks, financial hardships, confusion about juggling future work and family, and experiences of marginalization and discrimination. Four years after high school, some students were grappling with difficult romantic relationships, money problems, and occasionally rough adjustments to work and graduate school. Two dozen were still undergraduates, including a handful who were struggling hard to remain in college. A few had faced sharper troubles, including unwanted pregnancies, serious automobile accidents, grandparents' deaths, and parents' illness or divorce. A small group of undergraduates suffered physical symptoms of depression or stress.

High School Plus Seven

I'm still not sure where next month's rent will come from.
CHRISTOPHER (1986)

All my life I've gone about things with passion—I put my heart and soul into things I enjoyed such as school and sports. I just don't think I can put my heart and soul into accounting.
NICK (1986)

*I think that most everybody either sleeps with people or
thinks about it a lot.*
Beth (1986)

*We've grown a lot together, teaching each other about life
and getting along in a demanding world, and leading the
"Let's Have Fun" parade down many avenues in the city.*
Kevin (1988)

A $72,000 family income doesn't go as far as I thought!
Robby (1988)

*Competition at law school makes me realize I'm no longer
a "big fish," just one of the masses.*
Dan (1988)

*Currently (pick one or more): (a) gun shy, (b) too busy, (c)
too unsettled, (d) all of the above, to date seriously.*
Gordon (1988)

*I think that I have become more in touch with myself. I
know myself better now than two years ago.*
Angela (1988)

*While writing my thesis I realized what I was capable of
achieving when I put 100 percent effort into a project. It
was probably the most difficult thing I have done in my
life but it was a great feeling when it was done!*
Sally (1988)

Recall that 65 percent of the valedictorians in 1985 pointed to work
and school as their major life events. By 1988, the landscape had
shifted. Three years after college, 65 percent stressed personal
delights and difficulties as the most significant news in their lives.
A quarter pointed to both personal and public achievements, leaving only 10 percent saying the best part of postcollege life was professional or graduate school life. Seven years after graduating as the
best high school seniors, academic achievers found their greatest

delights in love, marriage, and friendships. Becoming parents, establishing financial independence, traveling, and buying homes were other frequently reported highlights. For those who considered jobs or graduate school among their greatest satisfactions, most pointed to markers of recognition and to the pleasures of stretching to accomplish difficult tasks. Although much less frequently than in college, a few men and women identified personal development as their greatest joy in the three years after college. At this stage, fewer valedictorians than in college said religion was the best part of life; only a handful of students continued to place Christianity at the very top of their priorities.

By 1988, valedictorians also had plenty to say about the worst experiences of life since college. Difficult romantic relationships or no relationship at all headed the list of troubles. Although only 10 percent pointed to work and graduate school as the focus of their greatest delights, a full third reported job or school as the worst part of life. The transition out of college posed challenges for many. Some had problems finding jobs; others disliked their professional work or chafed at long hours or heavy business travel. Some top students who continued their education found themselves neglected by graduate school faculty, burdened by intensified academic competition, or struggling to establish an effective line of research. Three left graduate school; others, like chemistry student Rachel, seriously considered quitting.

Many valedictorians in their mid-twenties lost grandparents and a few developed health problems of their own. Some, including ill-paid graduate students, continued to struggle with serious financial problems. Again, a few valedictorians faced troubles beyond these normal trials. The first project divorce occurred in 1986. Two students were victims of violent crimes. Two others struggled with psychiatric conditions that emerged after college; a third student nearly died as a result of active alcoholism. Such severe problems were the exception rather than the rule among valedictorians at age twenty-five, however. For most, typical relationship problems and normal career establishment struggles posed the greatest difficulties seven years after high school. And as usual, valedictorians overwhelmingly continued to cope effectively with challenges and to succeed at personal and achievement tasks.

High School Plus Thirteen

Fortunately, the latest I think I've ever had to stay at work is midnight; I've been pretty lucky. I haven't had to stay here all night. I know people who have.
MAUREEN (1990)

It's like this is my fantasy. I've come to graduate school, I've met this great professor; it's like everything I dreamed it would be.
DALE (1992)

I thought I was destined for more than being an engineer for a phone company.
MICHELLE (1990)

I don't really want to be a department manager, just because they have to put up with too much grief, work too many hours for too long before it turns into anything.
PHIL (1991)

I knew I'd enjoy being a mom, but I didn't know it would be as wonderful as it is!
LISA (1994)

In the first year of residency, I was overwhelmed by the physical demands and by the feeling of uncertainty/fear while making hundreds of health care decisions.
SOPHIE (1994)

I started out as a counter person, and just got promoted and promoted and promoted.
MICHAEL (1990)

It is stimulating researching an area in which you are actively involved, particularly finding out why things work the way they do. It's been exhausting and a complete high.
EMILY (1994)

We need to have children—getting old, old, old.
THERESA (1994)

Whenever I feel sorry for myself because of the hours, stress,
I try to remember that most people like their jobs no better
than I do (if as well) but also have to worry about money
all the time.
DAVID (1994)

In 1994, Illinois Valedictorian Project participants again reflected on the highs and lows of the past few years. As compared to six years earlier, when two-thirds listed personal areas solely, in 1994, half of the thirty-one-year-olds identified only personal bests. Approximately one in three spotlighted both professional and personal joys, and the remaining 15 percent reported their greatest satisfactions solely in terms of work and educational attainment.

Thirteen years beyond the valedictory address, marriage and children topped the "best" list. Friends continued to provide one of life's major joys; over time, more and more valedictorians listed friendships as one of the best parts of their lives. Career success was an important source of satisfaction among the group. Project members were happily moving up in their jobs, completing graduate school, and implementing plans to change jobs and occupations. More men and women gratefully reached the point of financial security many of their peers had achieved in their middle twenties; many were thrilled to buy their first home. With the onset of the "full plate stage" of major adult work and family responsibilities, only a few valedictorians found the best of life in outdoor activities, recreational athletics, travel, and other leisure pursuits.

In keeping with the age-thirty transition, valedictorians had entered a period of self-assessment during their late twenties that was both difficult and rewarding. Often involving psychological counseling, their evaluation of achievement needs and relationships also often accompanied a reworking of relationships with parents, lovers, and friends. Some study members pointed to personal growth as a highlight of their late twenties and early thirties. The second project student to identify himself as homosexual came out as he approached thirty. A few valedictorians continued to stress their Christianity as the most important part of their lives.

In their early thirties, few valedictorians said the primary troubles in their lives came from work or education. Instead, over 60 percent said personal problems were the worst trials of the past few years. (The remaining men and women were split evenly between those indicating work only and those reporting both professional and personal issues.) Although romantic and parental relationships were the source of greatest delight for many valedictorians in 1994, others were struggling to find and maintain satisfying intimate relationships. Looking for a mate, enduring difficult relationships, and breaking up with partners dominated the "worst" lists of many. Some men and women weathered difficult times in their marriages; two more valedictorians divorced between 1988 and 1994. The physical health of their families became a major concern for a significant group of study participants during this period. Several lost parents, including a man and a woman whose mothers and fathers both died. One woman lost a sister to cancer, and other valedictorians became embroiled in family problems. Health issues of their own, including problems conceiving, difficult pregnancies, and depression, affected a handful.

Work did show up on the valedictorians' 1994 worst lists. As they completed graduate school and postdoctoral training, several would-be professors were deeply frustrated by the tight academic job market and the bleak funding climate for science and engineering research. A few valedictorians had been laid off during hard economic times; more were frustrated by the long hours of their own or their partner's job. Some continued in jobs they disliked, suffering from stress or feeling that they were trapped in a rut. Finally, three students were deeply disturbed by what they described (in different ways) as the worsening state of American society.

The Big Picture

Snapshots of the valedictorians' highs and lows four, seven, and thirteen years after high school reveal several central themes. First and foremost, superior academic achievers travel normal routes of development. Like their larger college-educated peer group, the valedictorians found their achievement concerns making way for a mixture of personal and work preoccupations as they moved out of their early twenties. High school valedictorians are just as involved as average students in friendships and intimate relationships; friends, lovers, and family are vital sources of happiness and support. The preoccupations of top academic achievers match their life stages. As college-age students, they care about exploring identity, clarifying vocational purpose, and developing social relationships. As young graduates, they concentrate on establishing themselves professionally and finding romantic partners. By the time they are thirty, valedictorians are starting families, and beginning to face the declining health of parents. They are also advancing professionally, coming to terms with unfulfilling work or making changes in their vocational lives.

Second, high school valedictorians continue to be well-rounded individuals. Public achievements continue to make up just one facet of what they consider vital in life. This is true regardless of the level of their adult achievement, although it is those men and women who continue to travel top-career paths who find the highest highs and the lowest lows in work. Other academically talented individuals gradually deemphasize their work selves within their core identity, locating life's joys and sorrows almost exclusively in relationships.

Third, the role of work in valedictorians' lives changes over time. Through complex configurations of career success, adjustment to unfulfilling work, or decreased vocational emphasis, valedictorians in their early thirties are more likely than they were in their middle twenties to list professional achievement among the best parts of their lives and less likely to say work is a major source of unhappiness.

Fourth and finally, the volume and severity of life problems among former high school valedictorians presents a profile of well-adjusted, effective adults. Most have faced only the normal trials of life. Valedictorians are generally successful and satisfied in work and love. Severe problems are rare among high school stars, but they do occur. Academic achievers generally solve their problems effectively, however, rarely getting trapped in addiction or despair. As in their climb to the top of the class, valedictorians bring exceptional intelligence, effort, responsibility, and optimism to their postschool lives.

Ann: Growing Joys, Growing Pains

As a senior art major, Ann spent September preparing for her one-woman painting exhibition in the spring. All fall, she explored new techniques in the, to her, less familiar medium of photography. "Everything was an experiment. . . . and that was really nerve wracking. I'm glad I took the risk, but I think it made it harder." The first semester was exhilarating, tearful, and exhausting. Her best friend and roommate spent spring break on campus to help with technical tasks as Ann worked long days and nights to finish art pieces.

One of Ann's brothers—a skilled carpenter like all the males in her family—helped her hang the show: a series of life-size, nude self-portraits. "A lot [of the show] has to do with just searching for what that 'me' is, or if there is a me at all. A specific me. What the whole show had to deal with was identity. . . . Things you saw led you to a point that they weren't really resolved, so it is a question. There's no answer." Ann carefully prepared her other brothers, her sisters, her mother, and her father for what they would see. "I didn't know how they were going to react. And I did it anyway— whether they would have liked it or not. But I did still want them to give it a chance. And they did. That was important."

The bachelor of fine arts show was the culmination for Ann of a four-year struggle to know herself apart from her prescribed roles: baby of the family, rural, Christian, good girl, valedictorian. Finally becoming comfortable and happy with herself had been the best part of college, she said. As for the future: "I don't have any real set things that I want to be or I want to do. I just want to keep growing, keep learning, keep searching. And keep finding things. Because you need to find or you get tired of searching."

The struggles and joys of becoming an adult dominated Illinois Valedictorian Project interviews during the college years. Valedictorians fretted about academic achievement in college only until the first sets of grades rolled in. Few worried again about academics until graduate school, where issues of competence and being the best again surfaced for some. Feeling competent and purposeful depended only partly on achieving academically, clarifying intellectual interests, and starting down specific career paths. The search for identity incorporated far more than classroom and career. Careerists and many strivers generally kept academic and personal realms strictly separated. School was a job, but their passion was self-exploration through friendships, extracurricular activities, and intimate relationships. Not all students separated schoolwork and self-work. Ann, an intellectual, explicitly combined her academic and personal development: "They get to be really mixed up and really related. Which is fine; it makes it easier to understand it all." Her interviews offer a particularly articulate expression of the difficulties and delights of late adolescent life.

Ann grew up as the youngest of seven children in a working-class, rural, deeply Christian family. It was difficult for her family to let go of their baby. It was also difficult for Ann. "It's hard to leave home. Boy, is it hard." Without much guidance, Ann chose to enroll at Central University, the regional university near her home where she had been awarded an art scholarship. The bustling college town and unfamiliar feeling of anonymity made the transition a challenge. Ann did not meet new people easily, she said. At the same time, going to college was an opportunity for a new adventure, an exhilarating fresh start without her high school "goody two-shoes, brain" reputation.

Her first year of college, Ann was preoccupied with making friends, remaining in close contact with her family, and ensuring her academic success. She participated actively in her classes, earning straight A's and a new reputation as a brain. Competitive and perfectionist, Ann never felt good about herself "unless I'm doing my best. If I know I can make an A or if I know I can do something to a certain degree of perfection, I have to do it. I can't cut myself short, sell myself short. I have to give what I've got." Art would definitely be her major, Ann told us, but that is all she knew. She had always enjoyed working with children at church, so perhaps art therapy would be a good path. Or maybe she could become an illustrator of Christian magazines. In any case, religion was very important to Ann and the cause of some of her growing dissatisfaction at college. "I believe in God. I believe in Jesus Christ, the plan of salvation. I try to lead my life as I feel He would want me to lead it. I find personal satisfaction in having a personal relationship with God and Christ. I'm a Christian. This isn't a Christian atmosphere at all. And that hurts. It's something really important to me. I grew up in a Christian home. I had Christian friends, went to my church, [lived with] Christian . . . people around me."

By her second semester, Ann was sure she had made a mistake in choosing Central University. She could move further from home now, she thought, to find a better art department and more challenging academics. She was beginning to consider Central a "middle point," a transition to the right university. After many discussions with her parents and a good deal of worry and soul searching, Ann transferred to a public university in a neighboring state. A good high school friend there would ease the transition, Ann thought. It was again refreshing to look forward to a new start.

Ann never regretted transferring. She stood out less among the students in the more selective university, although partly because she spoke less in classes. She continued to earn straight A's while implementing deliberate attempts to be more socially outgoing and to pinpoint a career area within art. Over her sophomore year, Ann began pulling away from her family. "Coming up here was in a way stating: 'I am now going to be independent. I still need your help, I still need your love, and I still am a part of the family . . . but basically I'm starting now to live my own life.' And that's been a big difference. Feels good!"

Ann deeply enjoyed her studio art classes where she began receiving recognition as a promising painter. Over the next three years, Ann's personal and artistic development became intertwined. Her first breakthrough occurred when she deliberately disregarded teachers and convention by working only in black and white.

> It kind of started when I threw out color. That's a big no no. . . .
> That was the first thing I did, and that was probably the best thing
> I've ever done, because it went against everything. That told me I
> didn't have to do what they told me to do. And then after that it got
> so much easier to do what I wanted to do. There were times when I
> basically quit talking to a lot of teachers and worked on what I had
> to do. And my art gradually became more me and more internal,
> and that's what I needed to do.

Ann literally put herself into her art, which shows distinct periods associated with her stages of development. She began by painting herself in boxes. The carpenter's daughter even built boxes, which she physically entered.

> I put myself in an actual box. And worked with that box. I worked
> with a frame for a while, and I worked with dealing with pushing
> out against the edges of canvasses and the edge of a frame. The
> title of this one is "The World Is a Box Which I Have Made."
> Because I made my own world. I made that box around me. And I
> didn't want it. I got to a point where I didn't want it any more. I
> wanted to take the risk. I wanted people in my life. I wanted new
> things. I wanted—I didn't want to be what I was. I didn't want the
> restrictions any more. And they were restrictions I had laid on
> myself and were somewhat restrictions that others had laid on me,
> too.

At the end of her sophomore year, Ann "shocked" her family by remaining on campus for summer classes instead of returning home. Not only did she want to continue her painting and spend the summer with college friends, Ann had come to dislike the way she slipped into a childish little sister role whenever she visited her family. She was still a practicing Christian, she said, but was actively questioning the tenets of her "Hell-fire and Brimstone" home church. "I'm trying to work things out in my mind about the beliefs that I was brought up with. I'm still trying to really think, 'Is this a sin, or is this just wrong, or is this just wrong for them?' What do I feel is right and wrong for me?"

Her junior year, Ann's continued self-exploration took her art in a new direction. She started producing what she called "hidden pictures," self-portraits without faces. "I present the hiding of the true inner self that you never show anyone else. Or that you rarely show. The vulnerable side. The insecurities and the fears. It can be the loving side. It can be a lot of things. But it's the side that you rarely show to other people. And I present the hiding of that side."

Ann had moved out of boxes and pushed against her assigned family role. Her portraits still lacked faces, however, and her struggle to understand and represent herself was frequently a painful one. The "jump from doing everything on blind instinct" to comprehending and using technical and conceptual tools in her art was a difficult transition. "It was really hard. I did a lot of crying; a lot of my friends really helped a lot. Really held me up." At times, Ann would travel blind alleys, losing weeks or months to trials that led nowhere. Although she had successfully made close friendships that she prized, Ann was still trying to shed her high school image of perfection and invulnerability. She was trying to reveal her hidden self in more than her art.

> I had other people who were just laying all their problems on top of me. Because everybody just says, "Oh, you're strong, you're the strong one, you can always handle things." And I found out I couldn't. I was going under. . . . It's really hard for me to accept the fact that I can be vulnerable. Because I don't know if I want to be or not. That is hard. Because it's risky. And I'm still accepting that. I'm still accepting the fact that I am vulnerable, I am insecure, I am not perfect, I'm not wonderful. And I'm working on letting others see that I know that.

Ann's delights during this emotional time came from a variety of sources. Peer relationships were vital, especially a friendship with a fellow artist who "helped give me the courage to go ahead and say something about myself in my art." Faculty recognition was also important. Ann was pleased to have two art pieces accepted for a competitive student show and thrilled to win an award for the best undergraduate painting. Most rewarding, however, was the excitement of growing personally and artistically.

> I work out personal problems through painting and for a long time I've been really concerned with finding myself and with dealing with things inside myself and with accepting things inside myself and with accepting ways that I am. Things about me. And so part of my acceptance is that I paint myself and I see these things. So that's what I'm working with in my paintings. . . . I'm so excited about this. This has been one of the best years that I've had. And this last semester was just tremendous for me. So many things happened, it was just amazing. And my art really jumped.

She was beginning to realize what it meant to be an adult, Ann said in 1984, starting to make her own decisions and accepting responsibility for what she did.

By her last year of college, Ann was able to come out of hiding, ready to take risks and prepared to follow her visions. Having been admitted into a prestigious bachelor of fine arts program, she held a one-woman show consisting totally of those life-size, nude self-portraits. Her family was uneasy, bewildered, and proud of her show, Ann reported. She had rejected many of the traditional roles her family represented and much of the fundamentalist religion they practiced. Yet she still considered herself a very spiritual person, Ann said, and had never considered that her own selfhood required rejecting her family. "I had a lot of role models, my mother as a housewife and raising children, just a lot of models like that where I came from. It's hard to question a lot of things, but once you start, you can question everything, and that's what makes it fun. Because you don't necessarily find that they're wrong and disagree, you just find your own versions." Comfortable with herself, her art, and her relationships, Ann was hard put to name the worst of college. "I don't know. I mean, there has been a lot of hurt and frustration through the whole thing, but ultimately that turns out good. Because you have to hit the lows to find the mediums and highs, I guess. Because you've got to know what they're like."

Ann's college story is uniquely hers, but the joys and sorrows of development ring true for all of the valedictorians. The pain and exhilaration of physically leaving home gave way to psychological separation as Ann differentiated her beliefs and actions from those of her working-class, conservative parents. Worries about competence, achievement, and social belonging faded after the first year of college to be replaced with an increasingly internalized sense of self in which she could be imperfect, vulnerable, and nonconforming. Her competitiveness declined, but her drive to do her best remained. Friends, classmates, and faculty all played a part in Ann's development. So did achievement, setbacks, and painful personal experiences. By the time she left college, Ann had achieved a deep, internalized sense of self, an identity that incorporated reworked elements from her past and new understandings from life after high school. And Ann was ready to continue growing: "I'm getting more comfortable with the risk taking, because I'm aware that that's what I'm going to have to do to be satisfied. I mean, I've got to keep taking risks or I'm not going to get anywhere."

Postcollege Life

Ann met new delights and fresh sorrows after college. The year after her senior show, she fell in love with a fellow artist, and they began living together. Jointly, they opened a cooperative art gallery in a small Midwestern city and made plans for graduate school. "Together, we make a dynamic team. We've been able to accomplish so much that neither of us would ever have tried on our own." Ann realized in college that she would probably need to earn money outside of painting, although she later wished she had prepared herself for commercial art employment. A foray into the business world, while lucrative, "wasted two years" of her life. After working in retail stores as a manager and administrative coordinator, Ann incorporated her art background in her work as a visual manager responsible for overseeing the presentation of stores' merchandise. She has been both successful and dissatisfied with this work. Perfectionism led to grief as well as satisfaction in the workplace. "I could let things go with a certain level of, 'Well, this meets their standards,' or 'My manager thinks this is good, so this is fine.' Whereas it doesn't satisfy me, so I'll push and push and push until I get it. Sometimes, you know, that can really wear you down, or it can drive you crazy because you can't just quite get it there."

Ann's unplanned pregnancy changed the couple's lives. They married, and Ann postponed her plans for graduate school. She gave up her studio, although continuing to delight in the success of the artist-supported gallery she had helped establish. Even though both partners worked full time, money was a major headache.

We were very involved in the Gallery. We had a studio downtown, you know. Our careers as artists were moving together. I mean everything moving together. And then when I got pregnant with [my daughter], we had to take a major step back and do a lot of rethinking, a lot of replanning. I'm sure we're learning. But just having her has been the biggest change. And as far as I'm concerned, I haven't been able to do really any kind of art since she's been born [a year and a half]. There's just no time and there's no mental energy—it's creative just keeping up with her.

Ann entered the age-thirty transition no longer able to accept a precarious living in which her own needs and career as an artist came first. "I'm not as willing to take as many risks. Because there's more at stake. It's not just my life; it's not just his life; it's our lives as parents. We have a responsibility to her. . . . We have to take care of her and provide for her. We can't just say, 'Oh, we'll go try this; we'll try that.' And get ourselves left penniless somewhere or do something really stupid. We have to make sure that she is taken care of. . . . So we're not as free spirits as maybe we once thought about being." Money has continued to be a major problem for Ann and her family. In 1994, she wrote that she looked forward "to being financially secure enough to not have to work at something I don't believe in."

Ann still lived with strong frustrations, deep-felt joys, and steadfast trust in herself and the future. She would get back to art, she knew, after spending "most of my time in this personality of being a mother." And she deeply loved her daughter: "Little things like taking her to the zoo and stuff like that. Those are life's good moments. Those are the things that you enjoy and that you're satisfied with. A good day! I had a good day today. That's an accomplishment. That feels good." Ann was never one to repine. "There [are] no 'should be's' really. I mean, those are a waste of time. 'I should have been,' 'I would have been,' 'I could have been,' things like that. That's a waste of time. You just do what you do, and you say, 'Well, this is what we have to do now. This is what we are going to do.'"

Ann hit some rough waters after college. Like all the stories, hers is both unique and characteristic of valedictorians. These academic achievers almost always approached life problems positively. They kept moving forward, continued finding the best even in flawed situations, and met challenges as they always had, with responsible, consistent, hard work. "I'll just put my head down and I'll get it done," Ann said of a stressful job. "I'll work twice as fast and twice as hard as anyone; I'll do it."

Like everything but their grades, valedictorians' troubles varied. While Ann reveled in risk taking, more academic achievers struggled into adulthood to shed their "shoulds." Family relationships were often more turbulent than Ann's. Having ceased being the perfect son when he refused to follow his father's footsteps into medicine, Bill spent part of his late twenties concentrating on this troubled relationship in therapy. He eventually reconciled with his father. Hope was forced to support herself through graduate school when her wealthy father refused to countenance her change from science to humanities. Unlike Bill, Hope remains estranged from her father.

Ann found intense pleasure in her college friendships but began her first intimate relationship only after graduation. Other undergraduates experienced their most absorbing joys and frustrations in romantic ties. As the years continued, valedictorians began and ended relationships, usually coping successfully with the inevitable rough times with partners, spouses, and children. Some single valedictorians in their early thirties are desperate to find mates; most have put this concern in perspective among positive friendships and accomplishments. Valedictorians with children appear to be highly capable parents.

Her art work was a source of the highest and lowest peaks of Ann's life, but jobs for survival were stressful and unfulfilling. Valedictorians vary in their attachment to work, but close identification with a high-level profession is not proof against frustration and setbacks. There have been few setbacks and fewer failures in the valedictorians' work lives, but many men and women have faced professional obstacles or found themselves working in jobs they dislike. Many have changed professions or returned to school. Not all have solved the dilemma, however. First-generation college students, including minorities, have been particularly apt to be deflected from their dreams. While continuing to perform highly at work, they have turned their identity away from professional achievement to relationships and personal interests under their control.

Big Troubles

I worry a lot. I have problems getting to sleep. Since
January, I've been having headaches almost every day

*. . . and they finally decided that it was tension
headaches.*
COLLEEN (1982)

*It was so confusing when the depression hit because I
didn't think I had anything to be depressed about.*
RORY (1994)

*It is Keith's child, and as might be expected, we are no
longer together.*
MELISSA (1986)

*I mean, there were so many times that I was just so
down, and without God, I would have killed myself
probably if I had the guts. Quite frankly, I don't have
the guts, but you know there were times that I just felt
like dying. Without God, I never would have kept
going.*
CHARLOTTE (1990)

*I was living out of my car for a week or two after trying to
live above my means. Lost my car (repossessed) and my
apartment.*
HARRY (1988)

*My car accident was a little more than two years ago.
Guess it still kind of haunts me.*
ALLIE (1988)

*Last winter quarter I felt I came very close to a nervous
breakdown. Got so bad at one point I would, you know,
talk to God about it. Where I would sit on the bathroom
floor crying. . . . I had a hard time discussing it with
anyone, because I didn't know what was happening.*
DIANE (1983)

*How hard it is to carve a life all alone. I've come to
understand my parents' fears a lot more—and why my
father drank.*
CLARE (1994)

Although sometimes severe, most of the valedictorians' troubles were the normal fare of growing up. For a handful, matters were more serious than that.

Melissa's high school love begged her to return home and get married. She left college before the end of the first semester only to be dumped by her boyfriend. They never married, but the unsteady relationship endured five more years. Melissa became pregnant three times, choosing two abortions and finally bearing a son. Seven years after high school, she married another man, a small business owner with whom she has had two more children. Melissa never returned to college; she works full time as a non-professional for a local company.

Harry's dream of becoming a scientist was forever changed by becoming a husband at age nineteen and a parent at age twenty. Supporting his wife and son meant jobs in retail sales and fast-food and a long drive to campus. Unable to find the time to work, commute, attend labs, and study, Harry switched his major to management, graduating but with mediocre grades. Harry's marriage ended in divorce, and his financial problems grew so acute he was evicted from his apartment and his car was repossessed. By 1994, however, he had earned teaching certification and won an award for his first year of high school science teaching. He is happily remarried and maintains a close relationship with his son.

Charlotte was a high school golden girl—pretty, popular, a talented dancer, and high school salutatorian. By junior year of college, she had a serious drinking problem and an eating disorder that was increasingly out of control. Despite the formal intervention of her family and at least one near-fatal car accident, Charlotte denied her dual addiction until 1988, when she finally checked herself into a hospital for treatment. More difficult times followed as Charlotte began recovering from alcoholism and bulimia. By 1994, Charlotte had been sober and physically healthy for some time. She had earned a master's degree in social work and become a professional drug and alcohol counselor. She is once again active in her church, where she was married to a fellow church leader in 1994.

The most significant event in Laura's college years was her boyfriend's suicide. This emotional heartache gave way to others when Laura was diagnosed with a mental illness: bipolar disorder (manic-depression). Highly creative and humorous, Laura had excelled in her undergraduate journalism major and assembled a competitive portfolio that earned her a position at a top newspaper. She lost the job, though, because of behavior related to her illness and has since worked only sporadically, in nonprofessional jobs. She has also struggled with chemical dependency, working with a therapist and joining Alcoholics Anonymous. Laura is married to an engineer—"the best thing since lithium!" Together, they are rehabilitating an old house and caring for their assortment of household pets.

Rory became severely depressed after graduating from college at the top of his class. He was hospitalized at one point and has attempted suicide. Helped through these trials by his family and therapist, Rory believes his problems relate both to childhood abuse by a family friend and to his compulsive approach to achievement. As he attempts to conquer periodic deep depressions, he has returned to school for a graduate degree in biochemistry and taken a job as a university laboratory technician. He derives deep pleasure from outdoor activities like hiking, mountain biking, and rock climbing.

These five students have endured the deepest trouble of any valedictorians. Others have suffered periods of depression or great stress, but such episodes have been short-lived or clearly connected to traumatic external events such as the death of both parents, a serious automobile accident, or a premature birth. One other student that we know of made a suicide attempt during a depression caused by a now-corrected health problem.

The lives of Harry, Melissa, and Rory portray extreme versions of milder problems among valedictorians: money troubles, bad relationships, and struggles with externally motivated achievement. The vast majority of top students escaped the darkest sides of perfectionism and drive. A very few, though, struggled mightily to define themselves away from academic achievement. As Rory said about being college valedictorian, "It's like I can accomplish one thing, and once I accomplish it, it just meant absolutely nothing because I needed to go on and accomplish something else. . . . I was thinking I'd have to go to a really good medical school, I'd have to graduate number one, probably get a Ph.D. at the same time, go into research. Win the Nobel prize. You know, I had my life planned out like that. I just couldn't take it. And I think that's what led to a lot of depression."

The general project pattern of optimal adjustment obviously falls short for this small group of troubled valedictorians. Even so, their stories demonstrate strong resilience in the face of trouble. Between them, the five have established successful relationships, overcome addiction, and held responsible jobs. Amid the ruins of his marriage and science ambition, Harry built a new family and a different career. Melissa found the personal strength to leave her boyfriend and commit to a successful adult marriage. Charlotte used both her strong will and her deep religious faith to recover from chemical dependency and establish a solid marriage and career. Rory and Laura still actively struggle with their conditions. Rory is doing extremely well in work and graduate school, dating actively, and working hard with a therapist to balance personal and public achievements. Laura is in a stable marriage. She is under the treatment of a psychiatrist and active in twelve-step recovery programs. The catalogue of valedictorians' severe troubles reinforces the theme that valedictorians become effective adults. The complete list of deep problems is short. Overall, the incidence of alcoholism among the valedictorians is far lower than the usual estimate of one in ten adults; the rate of mental illness approximates national averages (DSM-IV, 1994). Most importantly, even exceptionally troubled valedictorians face directly the challenges of work and love. Even they succeed.

The Latest Word

> Once I graduated from college, I just felt lost. Because until that time, there was kind of a little checklist that told you how to live your life. You go to high school; you do well; you participate in activities. You go to college; you do well; and you just get a job and get married and live happily ever after. That was like the scariest part because there was nobody around to tell you how to do it.
> RORY (1991)

No one is told how to become an adult. Rory's words represent an active struggle to forge his own life course. Most of his fellow academic achievers found smoother personal transitions. Like Ann, most valedictorians used the college years (and beyond) to explore themselves as they continued achieving. Like her, they pushed the parameters of their high school selves, admitted vulnerability, and revealed themselves as more than dutiful achievers. By their thirties, virtually all have achieved lives of productive work and satisfying relationships.

Valedictorians live in the world as they did in school, as psychologically healthy, well-rounded, socially able achievers. Top students found their greatest delights and troubles in the process of discovering themselves. With infinite permutations, problems arose in project members' lives. As they have for over two decades, the valedictorians rose to the challenges that faced them. Their lives since high school have once again shown these top students succeeding notably in the mainstream activities of American life.

Chapter Nine

The Full Plate Stage
Entering the Thirties

*It doesn't take long to find out what real living is like. A
lot of work, with some time for play.*
KEVIN

Even the rest room had spectacular views of the city and Lake
Michigan, literal window dressing for clients of the prestigious law
firm. In her office on the twenty-seventh floor, Maureen seemed
tense, tired. The firm required a minimum of 210 billable hours
of work a month, she said, and her physician husband was also
putting in long hours. Another attorney poked his head in the
room to find out how Maureen was proceeding toward an afternoon deadline. Their exchange was quick, impersonal. My request
for a résumé drew an anxious request to lower my voice and a worried look at the open door.

Bruce met me at a restaurant while he was in town visiting
friends. After a postdoctoral fellowship abroad, he was on his way
to the only academic job he had been offered. The position was
temporary, a one-year sabbatical replacement on the West Coast.
As he worked his way through a vegetarian meal, Bruce talked and
talked about life in Asia, the bleak academic job market, and his
stalled research. He really wanted to be in a relationship, Bruce
said, to keep up his languages and folk dancing, to have children
someday. How could he have these things as an academic gypsy or
even as a tenure-track mathematician?

Robin was sitting on her next-door neighbor's front porch

watching a surging mass of small children. As I got out of the car, she cut her three-year-old and one-year-old out of the pack for their naps. She also took in two neighborhood children during the school year, Robin told me, so she could afford to stay home full time. She drove her husband back and forth from work to save the expense of a second car. Summer was the busy season in his small business, so he saw the children only during the commute and the half hour before they went to bed. The new house had taken every-thing they had, but it was in a family neighborhood with parks and good public schools nearby. Besides money headaches, the ex-jock who had once considered going into sports medicine regretted only the lack of time to exercise. She would have at least one more child, Robin planned, and stay home until the youngest was in ele-mentary school.

Change Continues

In 1981, we naïvely believed that following high school valedicto-rians for ten years would show what they become. Instead the thirty-something men and women of the Illinois Valedictorian Pro-ject defy static categories. By 1994, two-thirds of the valedictorians were married and more than a third were parents. The years of col-lecting credentials, planning careers, and anticipating family con-tingencies are not yet over for many. Nor are the years of establishing relationships and bearing children.

Transitions predominate even among men and women who have finished graduate degrees, found stable jobs, or begun fam-ilies. The lives of Maureen, Bruce, and Robin have changed since the scenes just described, which occurred between 1991 and 1993. Maureen has joined another, less high-powered law firm. She has become the mother of two daughters. Although a full-time attorney, she now works considerably less than her previous sixty to seventy hours a week. Bruce's temporary professorship was extended another year. Pessimistically, he continues to seek faculty jobs in mathematics: "The number of places that I'm will-ing to live is limited, and I might well chuck the academic career path in favor of living somewhere I enjoyed." Robin has given birth to a third son and is in the midst of "the toughest decision I will ever make" about whether to have one more child. Problems in her brother's marriage and her mother's failing health also preoccupy Robin.

It is the number, extent, and intensity of an individual's roles that shape a life. Never are the roles more numerous—and rarely more intense—than in the thirties, when career establishment is not yet over and when parents of young children are trying to do it all. All eighty-one valedictorians live among simultaneous roles: friend, worker, lover, partner, spouse, parent, son or daughter, community member, graduate student, even, sometimes, person of leisure (Crosby, 1987; Super, 1980). Maureen is a full-time worker, a wife, and a mother. Bruce is single, a full-time worker, and an active folk performer. Robin is married, a mother, and a full-time worker in the home. Their busy lives are full to bursting. The designation *full plate stage* well characterizes these years, when adult commitments swell and leisure diminishes.

Satisfying adult work and love were always the aim of the high school valedictorians. Visions of someday combining the two dictated the career choices of most of the academically talented women. Men also expected to marry and have children but seemed unconcerned about future role juggling. How does it actually look, this adult life toward which the valedictorians have been aiming since 1981? Have their expectations for marriage, children, and work panned out? Anticipating reduced labor force employment decidedly inhibited undergraduate women's career aspirations. Have gifted women actually entered the labor force less intensively than men? What has lessened employment meant for women's professional achievement? How do women and men juggle children and career now that these roles are reality, not contingency?

Partners and Parents

Any definitive family profile of the valedictorians suffers from a rapidly moving target. People move in together, have children, separate, and divorce between every information collection point. The sons and daughters of the valedictorians are a swiftly expanding band. Most parents of one child expect to have others, and in 1994, all but four single valedictorians definitely or at least possibly see children in their future.

The following picture freezes the film of valedictorians' lives thirteen years after high school. By the late summer of 1994, the valedictorians were thirty-one or thirty-two years old. Just about two in three men and women were married (see Table 7). At least a half dozen others lived with an intimate partner. The same year, half of the women and a third of the men were parents. A dozen single valedictorians had lived with their parents for at least part of their twenties; two or three were at home in their early thirties, like Nick, who reported: "I am still living at Hotel Mom and Dad. After three years I decided this might not be as temporary as I once thought, so I set up an office and decorated my room."

Three valedictorians—Becky, Dale, and Harry—had been divorced. By 1994, Harry had remarried, Becky was living with a man she expected to become her second husband, and Dale was a single gay man. Jonas and his wife had separated and then reconciled. Christopher's wife was deciding whether to leave her family and job to join him as he struggled to establish a legal practice in another city. In all, fifty-two valedictorians were married and thirty-two had children. Fifteen had more than one child. Although two project mothers gave birth to first children out of wedlock, in 1994 every parent was married.

Ten years earlier, at age twenty-one, nearly all of the eighty-one valedictorians someday expected to marry or to be in a committed heterosexual or homosexual relationship. With the exception of William and one woman, Bridget, all the valedictorians reported at some point in the study they would probably or certainly have children. In 1984, both men and women planned to have the first of two to three children at age twenty-eight, and both sexes valued marriage as relatively more important than career. Women, however, saw marriage occurring earlier—at age twenty-five as compared to the male average of twenty-six. As Chapter Five outlines, expectations for early marriage and childbearing deflated the career aspirations of many female undergraduates.

Did the valedictorians carry out these plans in the ensuing decade? Certainly fewer are married than thought they would be. Five now expect never to marry, including William and the man and woman who identify themselves as gay and lesbian. For those who have married, women did indeed marry at a mean age of twenty-five and men at twenty-six. Compared to their national age cohort, valedictorian men married at the same age and rates.

Female valedictorians, however, married on average a year later than women overall, and by age thirty-one, had remained single (and never married) more often. The divorce rate among the valedictorians was substantially lower than that of their national age peers (*Current Population Reports,* 1992, p. VII; *Statistical Abstract of the United States, 1993,* Tables 60, 61).

Among the 40 percent of valedictorians who are parents, first childbirth happened about when expected for women (just before age twenty-eight) and earlier than anticipated for men (at age twenty-six). The large group of currently unmarried and child-free valedictorians, however, will in time undoubtedly raise these averages considerably. Although the highest-aspiring female valedictorians expected to marry later than the less ambitious ones, both groups actually married at the same rates and ages (Arnold, 1993c). The most professionally successful women have postponed childbearing, however. A third are mothers, as compared to a half of all female valedictorians. Women with doctoral, medical, or law degrees began their families almost two years later, on average, than the entire female group. Male Ph.D.'s and attorneys are slightly less likely than other men to be married by age thirty-one and significantly less likely to be fathers.

Early Marriage

Career limitations accompanied every early marriage. The three men and two women who married before they were twenty-one are some of the lowest occupational achievers in the Illinois Valedictorian Project. Two of the three project divorces occurred among this group. Kate (described in most detail in Chapter Two) saw marriage as an alternative to the crushing pressure of public achievement. She expected to leave the labor force forever once she became a mother. Although Kate eventually increased her work aspirations, her early views inhibited her choices and accomplishments. Like Jonas, she dropped out of college when she became a parent. Harry, as described in Chapter Eight, married at nineteen and a father at twenty, stayed in school. Working day and night to support his family, facing the disapproval of his furious parents, Harry was forced to give up his dream of becoming a research scientist. He was also on his way to divorce, as was another young spouse, Becky. Becky's marriage began in 1984 and lasted seven years. She married too early, Becky knew by 1990.

> I think we just got married because we were kind of scared—I mean, to grow up. All of a sudden you're supposed to go out in this big world, and your family is kind of pushing you. Because you got good grades, you're supposed to go out and get this job, and then you get scared, and you just jump into these things and not realize. And then once you become un-scared, once you get more stable and more confident in your job, you start looking around and [you think], "Maybe I shouldn't have made that decision." I think we both felt that way. . . . I think I would have grown up a lot faster if I hadn't gotten married.

Even with a master's degree in computer science, Becky thought marriage held back her early career development. "I don't think I worked as hard at my job as I should have the first couple of years [because I was married]. I think I could have done a lot more. Single people [at my office] work all the time. I think they really get a lot more into the work, and they learn a lot more the first couple of years."

One other valedictorian married during college. The defining experience of Alan's life was becoming a born-again Christian and joining a tiny, fervent congregation in his college town. With the counsel of his church leaders, Alan married a fellow church member the summer before his senior year. The first of their four children was born the next fall. His beliefs, not his marriage, led Alan from a spectacular academic path to a life of farming. Alan remains a fundamentalist Christian. He has no regrets about turning away from worldly success.

Finally, there is Melissa. As described in the last chapter, eighteen-year-old Melissa returned home to her boyfriend only to begin an emotionally devastating relationship that lasted six more years but never resulted in marriage. Poorly paid jobs and a son born out of wedlock left her no possibility of returning to college. Although Melissa married another man in 1988, she has no plans to resume her education.

Marrying or becoming a parent before twenty-one for this group of academic achievers was a strongly negative influence on professional attainment. Incompletely defined identity was one problem, but equally damaging was having to take on the juggling of time, money, and adult responsibilities prematurely.

The Dual-Career Life

Most of the valedictorians married after college. For these men and women, marriage is a defining factor of their lives but not a central determinant of their postcollege achievement. As a group, the valedictorians have established solid, enduring relationships with their partners. Strains within marriage have affected many, however, particularly in the full plate stage when finances and time are both in short supply. "We've had some financial problems," Robin told me, "and I can see why couples get divorced over those."

Meg began dating Steven in college and they married when Meg was twenty-seven. She followed Steven to the East Coast for his graduate school. Unable to find a teaching job, she spent a lonely year of unemployment. The next year, she landed a public school berth, where she taught until he graduated. Returning with Steven to the Midwest for his first job, she quickly found employment, and they happily bought their first house two years later. By the third year of marriage, Meg described the normal challenges of a long-term relationship.

> As we are married for a longer period of time and take on more responsibilities, we've been noticing that it seems to be more and more of a partnership, kind of a business relationship. It seems like we have to work to maintain fun sometimes, just to do fun things and not always say, "Well, this is what we have to do to close on the house, this is the problem with the car, this is what's going on with parents," that kind of thing. And although it's nice to have a companion in that sense, it's nice to have a partner that you trust and can bounce ideas off of, I don't want that to be the basis of our relationship. I would say we are first and foremost friends, talking and sharing and having fun. When we have time.

By 1992, Meg had experienced a major upheaval in her marriage. Steven had been laid off from his high-tech job, leaving the couple financially strapped and Meg frantic about their unsettled state.

As an intensely motivated, strongly risk-aversive person, Meg objected to Steven's casual approach to his job search. She was in the midst of a career crisis herself, wanting to leave classroom teaching but unable to see a clear, secure alternative. Some therapy and their strongly founded friendship saw Meg and Steven through. By 1994, Steven had long been reemployed, and Meg had left teaching to retrain as a physical therapist.

Meg followed her husband's geographic career moves. The most striking example of this common pattern among the female valedictorians is Sally. Sally earned her master's degree in agronomy with distinction. Her thesis was published, and her professors assumed she would continue to the Ph.D. and a research career. Instead, she married a military officer and began traveling to his short-term assignments. "Ten weeks," she reported, "you're not going to [be able to get] a job for ten weeks. There was a group of wives; we just did fun things." When Sally and her husband settled in a town for a year, she bought an exercise franchise and worked as an aerobics instructor. She poured herself into her business and into community and church activities. Unlike Meg, who has always been ambivalent about what she sees as gender-related career obstacles, Sally has no regrets about her abandoned science path. "Right now, I'm just thrilled that we've been able to do all the travel and meet all kinds of people. I think that's why I'm not so hurt that I've had to leave it behind." Sally finds she is happier without pressure to achieve professionally: "When I left [graduate school], I was kind of glad that I had an excuse not to work in a research lab trying to make beaucoup bucks a year. It was kind of my excuse to say I can kind of take life easy and nobody's going to look at me [and say], 'Well, you should be doing this and that.'. . . I think even if I didn't have any kind of job at all, I'd be involved in something [such as] volunteer work. . . . I'm just not the type that would be sitting around."

Meg followed her husband but managed to work full time. Sally completely abandoned her professional career in favor of an enjoyable part-time job and heavy community involvement. A few women have taken turns with their partners. Charlotte's two jobs supported the household while her husband built a new business. Jane postponed graduate school for her husband's training. A superb student at a Christian college and prepared to graduate early in premed after three years of straight A's, Jane became engaged to a fellow student, an aspiring minister. She gave up her medical school plan, instead remaining in college an extra year to become certified as a high school science teacher. She then followed her husband to the West Coast for his graduate work. During this period, she taught high school and competed on a Hollywood game show. Unmotivated students and constant discipline problems tempered Jane's enthusiasm for teaching teenagers, however. When she and her husband moved back to the Midwest, it was Jane's turn for graduate school. She earned a doctorate in science education and became a college faculty member. Now, Jane is the mother of two small children and teaches part time at a two-year college.

As in the rest of their lives, women who followed partners frequently turned challenge into opportunity. Jane, for instance, tried a new career path and thoroughly enjoyed appearing on television and winning cash prizes and a car. Meredith was accepted at graduate schools around the country in developmental psychology. She turned down more prestigious programs in favor of the university where her fiancé, Phil, worked. Not only did she find a research mentor at Phil's institution, the department she joined strongly influenced her change of concentration within the social sciences: "I often wonder how my life course would have been different if I had not followed Phil to [the university] and thus ended up in an interdisciplinary department."

Valedictorians' strong motivation, work ethic, and educational credentials equipped the women to make the most of where they found themselves. But married women have been far less likely than men to make geographic moves for their own career advancement.

Meredith is one of only three married women whose careers may take precedence over those of their husbands. All three—Meredith, Theresa, and Hope—have chosen doctoral-level research careers requiring geographic mobility. Meredith's husband has a master's degree, but the other two spouses hold no graduate degrees and are not strongly career identified. As she worked on her doctorate in theology, Hope began living with Dan, who owned a seasonal landscaping business. The two years before they married were sometimes rocky, as the couple dealt with what Hope characterized as "mostly my issues."

What does it mean for me as an intellectual to go out with somebody who's not? Will he hold me back in my career? At that point, I
had to work out the fact that I could advance my own career on my
own. When I first met him . . . I hadn't come to the realization that
my professional life wasn't depending on him directly other than
the part of his personality that needed to socialize at professional
functions. What did it mean for him as a businessperson to be married to a teacher? Would our careers conflict? . . . And if I ended up
making more money, would that bother him?

Hope finally concluded, "I was creating more conflict in my
head than we had in life." In fact, Dan was unconcerned about
making less money than Hope, willing to follow her career moves,
and open to staying home part time for childrearing. (Lisa broke
off an engagement because her fiancé, in contrast, was deeply
threatened by her professional success.) Having addressed these
questions and married, Hope took a prestigious position in the
Midwest. She began working ten- and eleven-hour days and half
days on weekends. Separated for most of the first year while Dan
worked for another season at his landscaping business, the couple
flew back and forth for occasional weekends together. Dan moved
to Hope's city the next year, but his difficulty in choosing a new
career path was still a hard part of their life two years later.

Hope's story is about the demands of high-level work and the
assumptions of traditional gender roles. It is also about class and
educational differences. For the most part, valedictorians chose
partners of the same social class and approximately equal education. The two married female physicians wed fellow M.D.s, for
example, and many engineers and business people found partners
in their professions. For working-class valedictorians, two full-time
jobs are a financial necessity, not a choice. Carol, an emergency
room RN, met her police officer husband at the hospital. Unlike
upper-middle-class professional women, Carol has found that her
significant dual-career issue has been working opposite schedules
from her husband. In 1994, she wrote: "Last month my husband
had a surprise for me—he got to go to day shift! That was terrific
news. He's been on nights for 16 years." Three men and six women
have spouses without college degrees. This group includes the valedictorians with the least postsecondary education.

Have male valedictorians struggled with dual-career issues? Like the entire project group, the majority of men adhere to traditional gender roles. Wives have followed husbands' geographic moves in almost every case. Christopher tried living in his wife's preferred city, but now stakes the outcome of his marriage on her joining him in his new location. A few men have expressed their willingness to consider career compromises for their spouses. Like the nontraditional married women in the study, these few men are high achievers and notable intellectuals. Jeff, for instance, married a fellow graduate student and said, "We're desperate to live in the same state. I think, since I'll be finishing first, things will probably be determined on where I'm going at the time." He had seen commuter marriages among academic couples, Jeff said in 1991. "I would never do something like that. I think my relationship with Roberta is much more important than a career, so if it was a choice of having to do that, I would not accept anything like that." By 1994, Jeff was completing a postdoctoral teaching fellowship in science while his wife finished her own graduate degree nearly two hundred miles away. He was also conducting a national job search for a faculty position. Roberta's job opportunities would play a large role in his job choice, Jeff planned. Kevin was also willing theoretically to move for his wife's career. "Jennifer's promotions will be geographically all over, so she's really making a sacrifice, but also a choice, because she went into an industry that is male-dominated. . . . The right city and the right place. The right choice. We're going to go for it [and relocate]." Kevin spoke these words in 1990, but the couple has never moved.

Academically talented women have been far more affected than men by their spouse's careers. Only Sally left her career track completely when she married, however. For the most part, married women remained on their paths and accommodated themselves to what they saw as mild compromises by waiting their turn and by taking advantage of circumstances. For their part, married men pursued professional advancement with occasional talk but little action regarding dual-career sacrifices. Geographic mobility never became an issue for many men and women. And compared with parenthood, marriage by itself played a minor role in the career development of high school valedictorians.

The Prechildren Full Plate

Whether single or married, valedictorians without children juggle heavy commitments. Many work far more than forty hours a week. "When I traveled, I would tend to average easily sixty hours a week," said Kevin, a fast-track engineer. "Almost every weekend," he spent "two to four hours just to clean up and prepare." Hope works every weekend at her research job in medical ethics. David strongly dislikes his heavy schedule as a corporate attorney: "I lack control over my life, not all year-round, but for months at a time." Jonas says his forty-five to fifty hours of supervisory work are "too much!" Yet all would agree with Jake's assessment that "working only eight hours a day, or eight-and-a half hours is just not a way to get ahead." Being on call as a physician, working holidays and weekends as a nurse or physical therapist, or traveling for business all make heavy claims on valedictorians' time.

Graduate and professional students are just as busy. Besides studying and working as a research assistant, Scott heads his graduate chapter of the Society of Mechanical Engineers, plays the violin at church, ushers at a theater, captains a softball team, and flies his co-owned airplane. Medical students as well as interns and residents maintained grueling schedules. Several graduate students were obliged to seek employment beyond their university assistantships. Hope, for instance, was a full-time graduate student and teaching assistant while she also held several "marvelous, stimulating jobs. . . . I was a waitress, I reviewed books, and I was a receptionist at a mortgage company. I worked at a temporary agency that sends people out. For about a year and half I was the secretary at a real estate company. In the meantime, I worked as a runner at a law firm." Hope attributes her ability to manage all this to "being in my twenties," but the year she went to school full time and worked at three different jobs, "I didn't really learn much, got mono in December, and lost about thirty pounds."

Beyond work and study, adult men and women maintain full personal lives. Valedictorians spend much of their free time with friends, partners, and parents. They play and coach sports, work on homes, gardens, and cars, and participate in church, arts, and community activities. Two-thirds of the valedictorians participate in organized volunteer services through their communities or churches. Among other roles, valedictorians are church deacons, chamber of commerce officers, youth sports coaches, pregnancy crisis counselors, and volunteer AIDS workers. They are responsible, as Darren put it, for "grown-up areas of taxes, real estate, financial planning, and office politics."

When she was single, Robin's social and athletic activities filled her afterwork hours: "We would go out all the time. Thursday, Friday, Saturday nights. Part of it was I was looking for a man." Despite his long work hours, David spends time with friends, holds professional baseball season tickets, sponsors a fantasy league baseball team, reads avidly, and skis. Becky and her live-in partner lead hikes in the Rocky Mountains, ride horses, and occasionally join work crews picking up litter along the mountain roads. In addition to her active memberships in the Illinois Society of Electrical Engineers and the National Black MBA Association, Michelle heads a Junior Achievement business project for teenagers and performs in her city's black repertory theater. Sally teaches aerobics ten hours a week but never feels as though she has enough time. Between them, Sally and her husband run a church youth group, teach an adult religious education class, perform in musical groups, and belong to the Christian Women's Club, the Officers' Wives' Club, and the Knights of Columbus. Sally's remark that she is "not the type" to be "sitting around," fits most of the men and women in the Illinois Valedictorian Project. As Jake again sums it up for the group: "Trying to juggle time is a big factor."

Considering Children

Recall that at age twenty-one, nearly all of eighty-one valedictorians expected that they would become parents. That year, 43 percent of women said that finding a career they could combine with childrearing was one of the top three criteria for choosing their occupation. Only six twenty-one-year-old men listed combining family and work as one of their top career criteria, and three of these had in mind finding professions lucrative enough to support a family. It was clear that most men considered childrearing a female task. "I assume this question is for women," wrote John in the margin beside a 1986 survey question asking about planned work continuity. In 1991, Derrick recounted his frustration with his wife's ambivalence about combining career and family. "We talk about it all the time but we never seem to get anywhere. I don't want to blame it on Mary Ann, but I think it is more because she's unsure about what she wants to do." I asked Derrick directly whether he thought this was Mary Ann's problem. "Well, I think it's both of our problems, but I think that right now the deciding part is more on her than on me."

Obviously, Derrick had not considered modifying his own fast-track accounting path to work in the home. His response was typical. No male valedictorian expected to reduce his labor force participation for childrearing. A few did express concern after their marriages about the effects of fatherhood on either career advancement or free time. Jeff, who made the highly unusual statement that he expected to share child care with his scientist wife, wondered in 1991: "How much does your life really change? I know it will change a tremendous amount, and I'm not sure I want to give up all those things that I do. . . . They expect so much of you doing research that it would mean I'd give up everything else that I do if I had kids." Several women made almost identical statements, but Jeff was a rare man in questioning parenthood because of the trade-offs he perceived between family and career. Jeff is still unsure whether he and his wife will choose to have children. As Kevin prepared to marry at twenty-seven, he, too, worried about the career effects of future fatherhood.

> A lot of choices about how hard will I want to work to advance [are] going to come about soon. You don't get anywhere working eight hours a day. You can be super proficient, but you have to show that you want to put that extra effort in. That's a choice that I've already personally made in three-and-half years; it's been easy because I've been single and can put the extra time in. But it gets harder later; it's a choice of how much work. I've kind of made that choice right now. I'm going to work hard at it. We'll see.

The few men who worried in advance about juggling kids and work waited until they were married or already established in demanding career tracks. Most fretted about paring their work to forty-hour weeks. Female valedictorians, in sharp contrast, had been discussing the balance between childrearing and paid work since they were nineteen. They were considering part-time work or no paid employment at all. Even women on elite career tracks continued to factor family into their future work visions.

By age thirty-one, four men and seven women were unsure whether they would have children. They were not a random group. Seven of the eleven held terminal degrees and all worked at top track professions. Three only were married: Jeff, Hope, and Bridget. Jeff and Hope, of course, were already unusual in their families' dual-career paths. Jeff holds far more egalitarian views of sex roles than nearly all the other male valedictorians, and Hope is one of the few women whose work as a scholar takes precedence over her husband's career. Accountant Bridget has always denied interest in having children. Her husband wants kids, though, and she was struggling with her decision. "I am leaning toward not having children more so than he. I feel that decision will affect me a lot— will I still work? If so, will it be part time or full time?" Absorbing professional work appears to be the primary reason these talented men and women are seriously considering a child-free life. As Ann said the year she gave her senior art show, "That was the first time I had really questioned not having [children]. Because I was really into myself and my work. . . . Right now my art is very important."

The demands and pleasures of high-level careers have caused some valedictorians to question, but not rule out, future parenthood. A still different story characterizes the only four valedictorians who said in 1994 that they expected never to be parents. The group includes Barry and William, who have chosen nonmainstream life-styles and subsistence-level work and Dale, who is gay. Cheryl, the only woman in this small group, wishes to retain her current full life of work and satisfying leisure activities. In short the handful of determinedly child-free valedictorians are unusual project members with individual reasons for their life-style preferences.

Among valedictorians who definitely or possibly want children are some single women who already feel the pressure of biological time. None, as far as we know, is currently considering rearing a child as a single person. Many are professional women who have devoted long years to postgraduate training. In her twenties, Yvonne consistently said her ideal life would include a marriage, childrearing, and part-time practice as a physician. By her early thirties, Yvonne's ultimate still included "spending time with someone

I love," enjoying nature and music, growing spiritually, and helping others through her profession. For the first time, however, children did not appear in her vision of the ultimate. "*Hopefully*
someday!" was her written response to the question of whether she
expected to have children. Theresa, a married mathematician, now
thinks she should have started her family in graduate school. Only
now beginning the tenure track years of a faculty career, she hopes
to find a college where she can lengthen her probationary period
to accommodate childrearing.

In summary, anticipating children led half of the undergraduate women to choose careers they perceived as accommodating
motherhood. Future motherhood has continued to factor into the
professional considerations of nearly all the female nonparents.
Undergraduate males, on the other hand, separated family expectations from occupational aspirations. Most nonfathers continue
to see childrearing as a woman's problem. Only a few have been
concerned before the fact about juggling work and family. Even
these men frame the compromise in terms of limiting their work-
week to forty hours, not working part time or leaving paid employment altogether. It is nonparent men and women in elite
occupations who are most aware of the potential career costs of
rearing children. And single woman are beginning to eye the biological clock. In these ways, gender differences related to expected
family contingencies continue to appear among former high
school valedictorians in their prechildren years.

Adding Children: Partner, Worker, and Parent

By the time the valedictorians reach their early thirties, their work
and personal slates are already full. For the 40 percent of valedictorians who are mothers or fathers, the juggling act intensifies and
new activities crowd center stage. (My label "partner, parent,
worker" is a slight variation on Faye Crosby's 1987 characterization
of the full plate stage as centered on these three roles.) Having
children changes marriages and revolutionizes the personal lives
of both men and women. Parenthood also throws into relief differences among the valedictorians about what it means to lead a
successful life. It is at this stage that gender differences have again
emerged strongly in the Illinois Valedictorian Project. Fourteen

years after high school, the lives of academically talented males—with and without children—match their college expectations for continuous, full-time work outside the home. ("Work" refers here to labor force employment and graduate study.) Not one male valedictorian has taken part-time employment or interrupted paid work for childrearing. Far less exact is the fit between women's expectations and the realities of their work and family lives.

Women have so far worked much more continuously than they expected. In 1984, at age twenty-one, two-thirds of female valedictorians planned to leave paid work completely or to work part time while rearing preschool children. Contrary to these plans, three-quarters of thirty-one-year-old women have worked continuously and full time in the labor force or graduate school. They worked more intensively than they envisioned mostly because they remained single or child-free longer than they had anticipated a decade earlier. But even those who were mothers worked outside the home more than they expected. In their early thirties, mothers' life roles vary considerably, spanning full-time labor force participation (eleven women), part-time employment (five women), and full-time work in the home (six women). The result is that a third of valedictorian women with children have found themselves working more continuously than they expected. Most of this group would prefer to work less outside the home, however. Among those who have carried out their expectations for "doing it all," half would now like to reduce or interrupt their full-time career involvement. Such signals point to more and more work reductions among female valedictorians as the group reaches the peak years for rearing young children. There are no such hints that males will leave full-time employment. These findings are also in keeping with the research finding that increased levels of education are associated with greater labor force participation for women (Blau and Winkler, 1989; Spitze, 1988). Women valedictorians have so far been more likely than their general female age cohort to work outside of the home and to hold full-time employment, a pattern that holds true even for women with young children (unpublished 1991 U.S. Department of Labor figures, cited in Kemp, 1994, pp. 185, 189).

During the valedictorians' college years, gender differences in career expectations became the Illinois Valedictorian Project's lead story. More than a decade after their high school honors, gender differences in actual work lives are far less pronounced than the valedictorians themselves expected. Nevertheless, childrearing has already taken one in four female valedictorians away from a full-time career. Another quarter of the women plan to follow. So far, the women who consider themselves deeply career invested are single, postponing children, or working as full-time professionals and mothers. Although highly successful in their work, none of the six women who work full time in the home had consistently enjoyed her professional life. "No more lab work!" Rachel listed as a highlight of her early thirties. Colleen, who also left paid work completely, had been a highly successful business executive. A sketch of her story helps make sense of her decision to rear her child full time. Colleen's mother had a Ph.D. in nursing but always wished she could have been a doctor. She knew her valedictorian daughter could go where women of her era could not. Colleen enrolled in a fine liberal arts college to prepare for medical school. Her first-year science class was an ordeal, and her chemistry grade sub par. Clearly, Colleen told her mother, she was not cut out to be a doctor. Being an accountant, Colleen's mother then thought, would be prestigious and lucrative. And Colleen was so talented in mathematics. (This first year of college, Colleen also started getting terrible headaches. The college doctor was stymied. Colleen's parents began searching for a doctor who could diagnose their daughter's condition. One doctor finally diagnosed the pain as tension headaches. Colleen started a regimen of biofeedback and meditation. The headaches lessened but did not go away.) In 1986, Colleen was a fast-track certified public accountant for one of the Big Six accounting firms. Asked what work she expected to be doing in her thirties, she wrote, "Anything but public accounting!" Colleen got out of the career she had never wanted. She earned an M.B.A. at the most prestigious business school in the United States, specializing in finance. With the new M.B.A. and her sterling accounting credentials, Colleen quickly became a fast-track business executive. She enjoyed her work until the situation changed around her. "My new boss was impossible to work for. I went from loving my job to hating it in a very short time." Colleen, married a few years ago, is now a mother and works full time rearing her small son. Possibly having more children and working part time from her home is now Colleen's ideal. Colleen was as successful in work as in school. Her vision of rearing children and her less-than-perfect job together led her out of her stellar career path. So did her realistic appraisal of what it takes to stay on the corporate fast track.

Women's extra stage of career development—the "whether" as opposed to the "what"—continues beyond occupational choice and professional establishment. For the majority of women with professional husbands, reducing paid work is a real option, but having a choice whether or not to work can be a recipe for dissonance. Not every valedictorian found a fulfilling career path or personally meaningful work. The heavy demands of elite occupations can be deeply frustrating. Maureen changed law firms to reduce frustrations, and she remains firmly committed to her profession. Still, the lure of letting down beckons. "I enjoy what I do, and I really get a kick out of just about everything that I do. It gives me a lot of satisfaction. . . . Sometimes after a seventy-hour week, I want to stay home and not come back, but I think everybody says that."

Working-class mothers like Carol or Monica see no financial alternative to full-time employment. Carol hopes someday to cut down her nursing shifts to thirty-two hours a week and to stop working holidays and weekends. "At this point, we can't afford for me to work less and buy a new home." Monica longs to stay home with her child but considers herself lucky to work only six days a week. Even these women, however, see reduced employment as desirable and acceptable. In their early twenties, both foresaw themselves working continuously and full time in the labor force, but both also listed combining career and family among their top occupational values.

We have been able to document the negative effects on career aspirations of expecting discontinuous labor force participation (see Chapter Five). The impact of actual career reductions on final professional attainments must await the next decade of the project. The story is far from over. Among them, the six women working full time in the home hold an M.B.A., a master's of public policy, a Ph.D. in chemistry, and a Ph.D. in engineering. The sole bachelor's degree holder of the six, Robin, articulated the likely future of the currently child-centered women: "I'll work a lot of years, I'm sure."

What of the lowered expectations of many college women? Knowing their likely future included full-time work at least through their early thirties, would more female valedictorians have increased their professional aspirations? No definitive answer is possible, but it appears likely in light of the close correspondence between women's family plans, labor force expectations, and career aspirations. The highest-aspiring women, like virtually all men, made career plans that never revolved around future family contingencies. They expected to fit marriage and family into their lives as they occurred, and this is precisely what these women have done. Bearing children later has been one important strategy—and result—of high-level professional training. When parenthood becomes a reality, not a contingency, women and many men have made changes in their work and personal lives.

Workers, Fathers, and Husbands

Ann's husband worked long hours when their daughter was born, "so she naturally drifted closer to me from the beginning. Which means the demands on me later on were more, even though he's always been involved in the whole thing . . . it's still 'Mommy' when [she's] sick and 'Mommy' when—you know. 'Daddy' means play and 'Mommy' means security." Both fathers' involvement and their secondary role in childrearing hold true across Illinois Valedictorian Project parents. Although valedictorian fathers continue to work full time in the labor force, their children are a central focus of these men's lives. Many spend less time at work after becoming fathers. All center their nonwork hours around family activities. Even the most traditional work around the house, change diapers, and spend individual time with children. Monica's traditional Latino husband promised in the delivery room that his laboring wife would never have to get up in the night for feedings. She never has. Robby, an advertising executive, takes his two sons on errands or grocery shopping: "I'll usually take one of them, you know, alternate." Robby also takes his children swimming, joins Legos games, and reads to them. He says he is sometimes torn about the long hours he puts in at work. "It's hard. Nan is terrific, I mean, Nan just never puts any pressure. But I feel a lot of internal guilt. I try and remind myself of the long-term perspective, that

I'm building something for them as well as myself, but yeah, it's hard sometimes." Over his company's protests, Robby insists on flying home every weekend when his job takes him out of town for three-week commercial shoots.

Robby has rearranged his life so his children are the focus of all his leisure time, but he has not stepped down from his intensive work schedule, seeing his efforts as benefiting his family as well as his own strong ambition. Robby and Nan had some trouble in their seven-year marriage after the children were born. They "sort of got scared" into entering a year of couples counseling. "We were having a hard time coming to terms with where we were going to come out in parenting style, and that was a source of a lot of tension between us. We had to then kind of work through our old feelings about the pluses and minuses of the way we had been brought up to then get to a point where we could decide together how we wanted to bring up our kids." He and his wife learned how to communicate better, Robby said, and how to address their feelings. "I think we had a real good marriage before. I think we have an outstanding marriage now." Robby's adulthood has been traditional. He works long hours in the paid work force, and his wife works full time in the home. His children are very important to Robby though, and he participates far more in their daily lives than his own executive father ever did in Robby's life.

Jake has followed a different path as a father. Like Robby, Jake was an outstanding college student, graduating after three years with his university's top academic prize. In college, Jake expected Robby's life. He saw only difficulties in marrying someone as career centered as he, Jake said. All in all, he would prefer a traditional wife who genuinely wanted to concentrate on childrearing. When Jake fell in love with a fellow engineer at his church young-adult group, it was clear he had linked his life with another ambitious professional. "I think I was always pretty open . . . that if I married someone that would want to work, we could kind of figure out what we were going to do about that." Jake and his wife never considered maintaining two fast-track jobs: "Why do you have children if you're just going to send them to day care for someone else to raise them?" Jake would have considered staying home, he said, although he was relieved that Sandra decided on part-time work. "It was actually very tough for my wife because she was on a fast track to become a manager. They were trying to groom her. . . . So she really sacrificed a lot more than I did." Jake, too, deliberately stepped off the management track, arranging a schedule as a project engineer that would allow him to take care of his son while Sandra worked part time. "What we do is I work from six in the morning until two-thirty and then she works from about three to six. So that way I can stay home and spend time with Jonathan and take care of him. And her company's pretty flexible, so they let her work pretty much any hours she wants right now. So far it's working out pretty well." When a special meeting or deadline keeps Jake in the office, Jake's parents watch Jonathan for a few hours.

Jake has no regrets about his decision to give up management in order to care for his son part time, but he does understand its consequences. Working only eight hours a day will definitely curb his career, he said, but he is less ambitious now than in college. "I think I'll still be able to produce results, but it won't be as much as working ten hours a day." His family life and Christian faith are by far the most important parts of Jake's life. His leisure hours are spent in church-related family activities. Working twelve-hour days just isn't worth it, Jake said. "I don't think it's a sustaining happiness."

Parents' Lives

I hate to say, "God, I can't wait until they're older." I know when they are older I'm going to say, "What happened?"
ROBIN

I hate people with young kids and new babies saying, "Slept through the night first thing when we brought them home from the hospital." I hear that all the time, and it just makes me want to slap them.
ANN

As we met for carefully scheduled nap-time interviews in rooms strewn with toys and baby equipment, valedictorian parents of very small children described exhilarating, exhausting, rewarding, and trying times. Robin used to take her oldest son, R.J., to one of her two weekly softball games: "I bring up a stroller, a playpen, toys, bottles, pacifiers. I have to be there a half hour early to set up!" Robin's parents watched R.J. during her other weekly game, but she stopped playing when his first brother was born. Managing young siblings is frequently a challenge: "[R.J.'s] very patient for quite a while, and that's how I am—patient, patient, patient, and then I lose it. He's pretty good and he's good with his brother. He'll let his brother knock down his toys, knock down his toys, and then all of a sudden he'll turn around and whack him." Darren has been keeping a frantic pace establishing himself at work, working on his first house, and spending all his free hours with his two young children. "The awesome responsibility of marriage and having children is definitely the best (and sometimes the worst) part of my life over the past five years. . . . I would like to spend the next five doing good work, getting my house finished, and raising my kids from happy toddlers to successful school-children. Hopefully this will make my life a little more 'coastable' than the last five."

Toy-strewn rooms, child-oriented activities, ear infections, and the ever-present diaper bag are some of the more visible mani-festations of a parent's full plate stage. Less obvious are changes in valedictorians' relationships with their partners. Too little sleep, scant time, and differences over discipline can fray tem-pers and impede communication. "Basically, the only time for me to talk to my husband is between nine and ten at night," Robin told me. Relationships change to reflect new priorities, as Ann describes.

Whereas I would like to say that your marriage is the absolute most important thing—and it is—there are times when you just say, "Well, they'll understand." You take each other for granted, because when things start going on at work or the kids get sick or whatever, you just don't talk to the other person because you don't see them for a couple of days, basically. . . . Because a child demands the attention. They always get the priority. And at work if you don't give [your employers] what they ask for, you're fired. I mean, [those are] your choices. So what it is, mostly, is you bal-ance—the juggling act. And then when you can catch up on your personal relationship, you do. And then you go back to the whole juggling act.

Parents vary greatly in the amount of time they spend with their small children and the arrangements they make for their care. The impact of childrearing on adult lives is far more dramatic for women than men. Both values and necessity drive women's choices. Strong career orientation and the need for two salaries press women toward employment. Weaker professional attachment and ample partner salaries lead away from full-time work. Surrounding the twin factors of work orientation and material circumstances are valedictorians' values—about the good life, about motherhood, and about day care.

For years, Robin cast about for a profession. Finally training as a teacher after college graduation, she worked only a year before her first child was born. There is nothing Robin would rather do than spend time with her children. Certainly, teaching can wait—she is not even sure she will choose to return to the classroom when her youngest reaches elementary school. Her husband's small business barely supports the family. Robin has been willing to make considerable financial sacrifices to remain home with her three sons because of her bedrock belief that parents should care for their own children. "If you don't have to work, I can't imagine it. Not that your life is wonderful, not that staying home fulfills every need you have, but I don't think going to work does either. Going to work makes you more tired and more difficult with your children and makes them more of a pain in the neck."

Valerie had always expected to be an employed mother. She and her husband deliberately began their family when Valerie was in graduate school. "We planned down to the minute practically to get pregnant in either September or October to try to deliver as early into the beginning of the summer as possible, because I'd have my summer off. Then to go back to school for the second year with a sitter for the ten to twelve hours per week that I'm in class." The plan worked perfectly, but when the couple moved for Patrick's medical residency, Valerie found no one with whom she was willing to leave her infant daughter. "If I had an aunt who was ready with open arms to take care of Andrea, I would probably be working today. I'd be fulfilled professionally, and Andrea would be fine." But no close relatives live nearby, and Valerie's physician husband works long hours. Even more important to Valerie is the discovery that "given the way I want to be as a mother, I cannot work and raise her. . . . They're such formative weeks, months, and years, and [children are] really vulnerable to whoever it is that's teaching them how to live." High-strung Valerie cannot realistically envision giving less than her best to either family or career. "Given how conscientious I am and even was just in college, I realize that I would have gone crazy and been a dysfunctional mother and wife if I did work. Because I would still have to be the one who was the primary planner and provider for the care."

Monica's extended Latina family understands her financial obligation to work. After all, Monica's own mother had to work full time while her five children were small. Fortunately, Monica's sister can look after Luis along with her own children. No other valedictorians can rely on family to take care of their children. A few men and women have nearby parents who can pinch-hit when a child is ill, an unusual work situation comes up, or parents need some time alone. For the most part, however, parents are on their own to juggle roles and time and finances.

When women want to work full time, have to work full time, or lack family support, day care is their answer. Searching for child care can be a time-consuming, discouraging task, and perceptions of the acceptability of day care ranged widely among both male and female valedictorians. But many women found care providers they perceive as excellent. They are skeptical that children require their full-time presence. Some believe they would be so unhappy sacrificing their deeply held achievement values that they would be ineffective stay-at-home mothers. Others know that reducing work in fields like laboratory science research might well mean giving up their career paths forever. Even the least conflicted feel the pull, however. As Ann said: "Every morning that I leave [my daughter] at my sitter's, I have a sick feeling in my stomach. Even though I feel I have one of the best sitters I could possibly have. And I know she's fine the minute I'm out the door. I mean, I totally trust my sitter. But I still have that ball in the pit of my stomach every morning that someone else is raising my child."

Robin remembers her own mother's being home during her childhood. Only four valedictorian women, including two African American women, had mothers who worked continuously and full time in the labor force. As the first generation to choose their configurations of work and family, female valedictorians' models are few. Just as importantly, the constraints women perceive are real. Part-time professional work, flexible advancement ladders, or even forty-hour full-time jobs become less and less attainable as women pass into elite occupational ranks (Rothman and Marks, 1987). She would find more part-time opportunities at the bachelor's level, says Ph.D. engineer Emma.

For women like Emma, who have devoted years to postgraduate training, career establishment demands peak in the late twenties and early thirties. So do the needs of infants and very small children. Emma decided to rear her family full time knowing she will never reenter engineering research. Emma's decision is in keeping with what she thinks is important in life and also rests on her husband's concurrence and his sufficient salary. Other women deeply wish to continue exercising their talents in the high-level professions for which they have trained. These valedictorians hope that by establishing themselves professionally now, they can juggle their roles more easily when children arrive. Of the female aspiring college professors, for example, only Meredith is a mother. And Meredith became pregnant as a thirty-one-year-old doctoral student.

In their late twenties and early thirties, academically talented women find themselves facing difficult choices. On the one hand are realistic obstacles to simultaneous fast-track achievement and full participation in the lives of children. Work pressures are real. So are pressures to fulfill the role of mother. Monica told us, "It's so funny. Ten years later you figure you [will] go to your high school reunion, and everybody is going to talk about what they accomplished in their life. No one. Everybody brought out the baby pictures." However, there are also societal attitudes that devalue the career of childrearing. "I felt like a second-class citizen—'Well, she's not doing all kinds of things that look nice on our survey from the class of 1985,'" said Sally about an alumni questionnaire that included no "homemaker" box for her to check. Valerie concurs: "The problem is that society doesn't place a price on raising kids, but Patrick does, and he keeps on assuring me of that. So I guess I do too." Such personal and collective values about what makes a successful life continue to shape valedictorians' goals and choices.

The decade of their thirties finds virtually all valedictorians juggling full configurations of adult roles. They continue to wade straight into the challenges of life, continue to do their responsible best in every task they encounter. "I'm sort of on the brink," Valerie said of balancing the needs of a colicky infant and an active three-year old with the work of typing college students' papers at night. "But I'm not going to have a mental breakdown, because then nobody would take care of them. I have this safeguard."

Nearly a decade and a half after graduating as the best high school students in Illinois, the valedictorians have made diverse choices about family and career. For this group at least, being a high academic achiever appears to make relatively little difference in the constellation of life roles and preoccupations of the age-thirty transition phase. Male valedictorians' patterns of labor force participation and marriage closely resemble those of their larger generation. For academically talented women, the picture differs slightly from the national profile—female valedictorians marry a little later and participate somewhat more heavily in paid work than women in their age group nationally. The pressures of their generation—intimate relationships, intensive childrearing, heavy professional demands, and economic concerns—preoccupy both former valedictorians and their age peers. An examination of valedictorians' current lives tells more about reaching thirty in the 1990s than it reveals about exceptional achievement.

Still very much in the process of working out their adult roles, the valedictorians are clearly part of a generation in transition in terms of gender roles. Unquestionably, many men have made some accommodations to childrearing. It is only women, however, whose achievement lives continue to be defined by their choices about family.

Chapter Ten

Values and Vocations
The Mission of Achievement

> *No values are effective, in a person or a society, except as*
> *there exists in the person the prior capacity to do the*
> *valuing, that is, the capacity actively to choose and affirm*
> *the values by which [one] lives.*
> ROLLO MAY, *MAN'S SEARCH FOR HIMSELF* (1953, P. 79)

> *All rising to great place is by a winding stair.*
> FRANCIS BACON, "OF GREAT PLACE," IN *ESSAYS* (1625)

Rory climbed the academic mountain to the first two summits.
High school valedictorian, he was also first in his university class.
As he anticipated the next step of medical school or a doctoral pro-
gram in science, Rory became seriously depressed. With the help
of a therapist, he began a difficult period of self-examination.
Much of his ongoing struggle concerns what it means to achieve.

> I've been thinking quite a bit about success and have decided it's
> not anything near what it's cracked up to be. To be sure, achieving
> some goal is quite a thrill, especially if it's a difficult one. Family
> and friends are proud, and people respect you for what you've
> done. But the thrill doesn't last. You wake up a day or week or a
> month later and realize the thrill is gone. So you have to achieve
> something else to get the thrill back. Sooner or later you realize
> that achieving difficult things just for the thrill of accomplishment
> is about the worst reason you can have for doing anything.

Success and happiness are not the same thing at all, Rory wrote. He knew from his own experience that "you can be incredibly successful and be miserable." Achievement for its own sake had become deeply oppressive to him. Rory now sees genuinely meaningful achievement as making a difference in *another* person's life. He no longer aims for the top professional ranks or the most prestigious graduate degree.

The decision to cease scaling the heights does not mean abandoning the trail altogether. After five years away from formal education, Rory is pursuing a master's degree and working in his field of biochemistry for the first time. He will consider a Ph.D. if he continues to enjoy school, Rory says. Enjoyment of nature and a hoped-for family will take equal place with work in his life.

Like so many of the Illinois Valedictorian Project men and women, Rory chose to step off an elite achievement path. He stopped aspiring to the highest professional level for two distinct reasons. First, he never found deep personal meaning in his achievement tasks. Second, he valued a balanced life of relationships, work, and leisure more highly than intense commitment to professional attainment. One or both of these reasons caused most of the eighty-one project members to turn away from the roads to eminence.

Adult valedictorians are successful in work and relationships. Their vocational attainments are high level and significant but only occasionally extraordinary. Fourteen years after high school, at least three-quarters of top students do not appear headed for the pinnacles of the postschool achievement world. Most backed off, like Rory, because they were not overwhelmingly committed to their work and because they valued balance over optimal achievement. Some aimed low because of limited visions of what they could become or poor understanding of how to reach high-level goals. A very, very few were not successful enough to face decisions about top-level paths. Whatever the reasons, valedictorians on solid but unspectacular career trajectories have incorporated their choices into their self-view. They are quite content to classify work as one among several important adult roles.

Some of the academically talented students are still on pathways potentially leading to eminence. The membership of this group is, of course, debatable. None of the Illinois Valedictorian

Project members has so far reached the very top of a profession, become famous, or made revolutionary contributions to a domain of endeavor. It is possible, however, to identify those twelve to fifteen men and women who still place public sphere attainment at the center of their lives. Between 15 and 19 percent of the valedictorians appear eligible to become recognized as among the top practitioners in their professions or to transform understandings or practices in their field. Unlike Rory and most of the other valedictorians, individuals on extraordinary achievement tracks have found deep personal meaning in their occupations. For them, "work" is inseparable from identity; personal and professional are conjoined. These are the students who have come to see work as vocation. No more than in high school are these top adult achievers one-sided workaholics. Like all valedictorians, they prize relationships and personal interests. They differ from their peers in the intensity of their professional involvement, their presence at the top levels of early occupational paths, and their personal connection to careers. It is because of their powerful commitment to their work that these men and women have continued to identify themselves in terms of professional achievement and to make sacrifices for vocation. It is this group that appears to have the potential for professional accomplishment as spectacular as their academic achievement.

As always, the valedictorians themselves illustrate best what conditions nurture the development of talent. In very different ways and in very different domains, the two students featured here express their deepest values through careers. Each is still attempting to use her full potential in professional achievement. Each remains on a path that promises exceptional adult attainment.

Beth: Sharing Ideas

> The world of ideas is the most powerful world to me. Ideas are important. The most powerful are those that can be shared with everyone.

When Terry Denny and I met Beth before she turned twenty, we independently wrote that Beth had the air of a graduate student. Her plain clothes, straight hair, and unmade-up face stood out in a public university where "girls" were preoccupied with sororities, football, and bar-hopping weekends that began on Wednesday night. Besides departing from the regulation look and social interests, Beth was clearly an intellectual. From the beginning of college, she described personal engagement in both science and humanities courses, developed friendships and romances among graduate students, and interacted with professors and teaching assistants outside the classroom. Over the years of the valedictorian project, Beth has followed a sometimes meandering path with utterly consistent motivations. Connecting with other people and connecting with the world of ideas have always been Beth's passions; putting the two together led her to a deep vocation for teaching. On the journey to expressing her values through career, Beth met the best and the worst of educational conditions for talent development. When Beth was twenty-seven, Denny wrote of her, "I think she represents a searching, exploring, risk-taking style of educational and career development that is quite unusual for our women in the study, and I think that she also appears to be one who is going to end up on her feet and be successful in achieving her career goals, which are not easy ones and away from which she could very easily have strayed." Beth reached her goal by means of her exceptional ability, intellectual confidence, and self-sufficiency. The goal itself, however, was a matter of values.

Beth graduated as valedictorian of a public high school in her urban university neighborhood. The second of four children in a highly educated family, eighteen-year-old Beth described herself as "quiet and studious." Her mother was a dominating force in the household. Increasingly conscious of her mother's controlling, manipulative style and its effect on her, Beth distanced herself from the relationship over the years of the project. Her father, Beth said, was "calm . . . cooperative . . . but not a very forceful presence."

Early in her high school years, Beth felt pressured by her parents to earn high grades, but she increasingly focused on learning for its own sake as high school progressed. Nine years after being named valedictorian, she said of these early years: "I think that doing well in high school was tied into a lot of ways that I was starting to discover to derive intellectual pleasure from my surroundings. That has stayed with me." Although Beth earned top college entrance examination scores and enough advanced placement credits to skip a semester of undergraduate work, she worried that university would be much, much more difficult than high school. "I was intimidated about going to college. Big scary place that I thought it was going to be."

Beth was as much put out as relieved to find that college academics were not nearly as challenging as she had imagined. The most rigorous of her first-year courses, chemistry, was her favorite. She was impressed with the enthusiasm of her chemistry teacher and teaching assistant (TA), "so then I got really gung ho about chemistry." It was her TA who told her about the chemistry fraternity on campus. "I first joined it for social reasons. I really liked the people there, and I didn't like a lot of the people that I found in my dorm. And that was why I joined. And now it's really exciting to see, 'Oh my God, there's that professor, and he's over there, just this far away from me, and I can go up and talk to him.'" Ten years later, Beth still identified the fraternity as a central factor in her intellectual and social development.

> I remember the weekend that I first encountered the chemistry fraternity in college. I remember I was talking to my parents over that weekend, and I said, "The most amazing thing happened. . . . I met some cool people down here." There's something about sharing a certain kind of perspective so that a lot of jokes click and a lot of hobbies click and other things click other than just sitting around talking about molecular orbitals, which I also enjoy. . . . I think the first stage [in my identity as a chemist] definitely happened when I was a freshman. I realized that I felt comfortable with these kinds of people who were leading these kinds of lives.

Besides getting to know chemistry graduate students and professors through the fraternity, Beth sought a job with a chemistry professor. With the encouragement of her course professor, Beth applied and was hired to work ten hours a week ("I won't have to work for food service any more!").

Her first year, Beth felt little pressure to pin down her major and career. After college, she said, "I might be working; I might be in graduate school; I might be married and a housewife." As college progressed, Beth expressed less and less interest in marrying soon after graduation. She would probably marry, she said at age nineteen, "but not for a long time." Future children also seemed likely, but family concerns were absent from Beth's career planning.

Her remaining undergraduate years saw a deepening of Beth's first-year interests. She increased her connection to the chemistry fraternity, dating older graduate students she met there, living in the fraternity house for two years and becoming president her junior year. At the same time, Beth participated in a series of experiences that molded her as a scientist. Besides her ongoing work in a professor's laboratory, she was able to teach, conduct independent research, and work in an industrial laboratory during her last two years of college. It was her acquaintance with a young teaching assistant and the encouragement of a professor who urged her to apply that led Beth to seek the undergraduate teaching assistantship. The first semester of teaching introductory chemistry to nonmajors was not always smooth: "I think I took a risk in deciding to teach. That was not a great success my first semester. It was a lot of work. I felt very inadequate a lot of the time." Second semester was more successful, and Beth was invited to teach the chemistry major introductory sequence during her senior year. "You get people who are bright and who don't buy bogus answers from you and who are willing to work hard and who want to challenge themselves and learn some chemistry. And it's really exciting to teach them." In 1992, Beth reflected on teaching courses she had so recently taken herself. "There are so many things that I had to go back and learn when I was teaching. . . . When I was encountering these ideas a second time around two years later, they fit so beautifully in a way that they never had for me [before], and I was sold by that point—that this was a good way to spend one's time, thinking about these ideas. I hadn't quite made the connection that teaching these ideas was going to be the best life for me at that point."

The most rewarding part of teaching, Beth said, was affecting students. "It's again the touching [of] lives. You feel that you personally have helped these people to learn something. It's rewarding in that way . . . to explain things to people who are thinking about them and also accept different ways." Along with making a difference in students' lives, accepting divergent ways of thinking and solving problems became central themes in Beth's vocation.

Beth worked over the summer between her junior and senior

years at an industrial research laboratory. She found out about the job because she "knew somebody who knew somebody who worked there." Although mildly worried initially that people in the laboratory would expect her to know everything about chemistry, Beth found she was well able to perform the work, and she enjoyed the job: "I was in a lab. There was a lot of interaction with other people. It was really good."

Returning to college for her final year, Beth began an independent senior research project and continued to teach. Her research advisor, a chemistry professor, was helpful and supportive. "I'm on my own on a day-to-day basis. But when it comes to figuring out what I'm going to do, I have a lot of guidance." The research project and summer job convinced Beth that she enjoyed chemistry research. "I really like working in the lab. I like thinking. I have a substance that is in front of me, and I'm figuring out something that hasn't been figured out before. It's kind of neat. I feel creative." The project itself was unsuccessful ("I basically had negative results"), but Beth enjoyed the work and advising relationship.

Deeply involved in her studies and career choice, Beth also prized relationships. "Being able to socialize in a group and fit in," had been the best part of college, she said as a senior. Asked how she had changed since high school, Beth spoke of increasing confidence, academic accomplishment, and personal connections. "I feel that I have created a good record for myself here academically, that I can feel proud of myself. I feel that I have touched people's lives here. That people are perhaps happier because they knew me. Who knows? But that's a nice feeling. I just feel that I can do a lot more things than I thought I could do before."

At the time of her senior-year interview, Beth was still considering either medical school or a Ph.D. in chemistry. Her research advisor suggested she begin doctoral study with a particular professor at an Ivy League research institution. This suggestion fit Beth's steadily increasing identity as a chemist. The prestigious program promised to be rigorous and demanding. "I really want to get into a good program because I feel that it would challenge me more." The choice also fit her personal life, because her current boyfriend lived in the same city as the graduate school. Beth moved to the East, disappointing her mother by deciding against medicine. However, the relationship with her boyfriend had ended before the move. "He was looking for a wife, and I wasn't looking for a husband," she explained later.

Up to this point, Beth's was a model of a straight career road. Like Allie (Chapter Five) or Darren (Chapter Seven), she had a series of classroom and nonacademic experiences that allowed her to explore her interests and develop tacit knowledge about the career of a scientist. Membership in a professional peer group and close interaction with practicing scientists were vital in connecting Beth to opportunities and socializing her into chemistry. By the time she left college, she was capable, confident, and directed as a scientist.

That path suddenly forked in graduate school. After the required year and a half of doctoral coursework, teaching assistantships, and urban living, Beth began her research. A terrible laboratory experience ensued. Beth and her research advisor clashed repeatedly over what the advisor saw as Beth's unnecessary perfectionism and what Beth perceived as the advisor's "intellectual sloppiness." Beth felt her ideas were stifled, that the advisor was saying, "No, abandon your thought and take my thought." Other students and professors urged Beth to change to a new research group and advisor, but Beth wanted out. "I felt that I had traveled a very straight-arrow path. No sense of personal freedom and conscious decisions and trying things out. . . . It really felt important to me to get out of school and find something else to do with myself, something productive, something stimulating that isn't just sort of having a bunch of inertia and walking down the academic track because that's the direction you happened to have started in."

Beth found a job as a chemistry teacher at a private school. During the second of her two years there, she taught advanced placement chemistry. "There will never be another class like teaching that advanced placement chemistry course. I was happy. Those kids were smart. There were eight of them, and I could talk about a lot of the stuff that I thought was really neat in freshman chemistry that I hadn't been able to talk about in other courses. We got along so great. I think they loved me as much as I loved them." Beth particularly enjoyed working with girls who saw themselves as incapable in science. "I think that a lot of female students came into chemistry being really afraid that it was something that they would not be able to understand, and it gave me a lot of pleasure to show them that, in fact, it is something they can understand. . . . They'd end up acing it. It was fun, a lot of fun."

Living in the city on a private school teacher's wage was hard and Beth knew if she stayed she would inevitably return to teaching eighth-grade introductory courses. She moved to the South for a one-year teaching position at a small college. In addition to classroom teaching, she began tutoring informally while supervising the night computer laboratory. "I got to know a lot of students that way, and I got a reputation for being helpful. People from my chemistry classes, other people's chemistry classes, and everyone's calculus classes would come and ask me questions. I was like a little tutoring machine, and I really enjoyed that. And sometimes I would have review sessions, too—while I was on duty, I'd step into the other room and help a bunch of students." The year was wonderful for Beth. "I really felt like I had a lot of energy that needed to be used constructively: exercise and intellectual stuff—intellectual, professional, personal, social—I really felt on the ball."

College teaching also cemented Beth's resolution to return to graduate school for her Ph.D. This time, she deliberately chose a less prestigious institution where she perceived there was more emphasis on educating graduate students, where her ideas would be respected, and where professors "are more thoughtful, whole human beings." Now she approached graduate school knowing what she wanted and committed to getting the degree. "I think of myself now as not all that achievement driven. I don't think I want a Ph.D. because I want people to call me doctor or because it's something that, just in the abstract, I decided I wanted to achieve. I think I want to finish my Ph.D. because not having it is keeping me from having the kind of job I want."

Beth was one of the stars of her doctoral cohort. As she had everywhere else she had been, she made close friends among her peers. She performed her dissertation research at a national laboratory and did some teaching. As she approached her defense, however, her relationship with her research advisor "absolutely fell apart." In the summer of 1994, soon after the thesis defense, she wrote:

Finishing my dissertation was an exercise in idiocy. Communication between myself and my advisor had broken down to the point where I couldn't come out of a meeting with him without crying all the way home in the car (NOT crying in front of him, though!). When he doesn't understand something, he attacks. His natural, everyday diffuse air of condescension becomes focused, insulting and downright mean! He was only mean in private, though. In public, I was his shining star, his wunderkind, his golden grad-student puppet-toy. He gave me no trouble at all during the defense; he only played games during all the little one-on-one negotiations I had to do leading up to the defense. Fortunately I had made this decision to finish. I would consciously give in on everything, do it his way, getthehellout and then lead the REST of my life according to how I say. It paid off.

Beth's advisor was irritated at modifications she had introduced to his pet technique and suggestions. He was also deeply disapproving of her steadfast adherence to a teaching career path, even though she had entered the program with that expressed intention. His implorings to choose a prestigious research position having failed, her advisor called in reinforcements.

He had one of his buddies on the faculty pull me aside after my research seminar and [have] this whole long talk with me. Old-school German guy, real near retirement, right? "I'm not going to tell you what to do with your life or anything, but I think it's important that you be encouraged along a more research-oriented career path and blah, blah, blah." And . . . then I [started] to give my feedback: "Well, thank you for your input and I really appreciate all your encouragement." Because basically he's telling me I'm talented and I shouldn't waste my talent. "I'm looking for a job where I think I can be happy." And he goes, "Pfft! Happiness! We have no control over happiness whatsoever, so we might as well not even consider it when you're planning a job. You could go to a teaching job and be really unhappy. You could go to a research job and be really happy. You don't have any control over it, you can't predict it, and therefore it's not a valid criterion for making a decision." I [said something] like, "Okay, you're right. I'm being really stupid. But I'm going to do it anyway." And then it got really bad when he said, "Don't think that I'm telling you what to do with your life. I couldn't care less what you do with your life!" So I tell this to people afterwards, and they think I'm exaggerating. He *said,* "I couldn't care less what you do with your life!"

How did Beth resist the pressure of powerful authorities to change her path? First, she continued to insist on a personal connection with her work. "Whenever I talk about my work, it's very clear that it's not just something I do to get through and get out. If it doesn't have a stamp of me on it, then I'm not satisfied. . . . It's a really personal creative expression."

Second, through a difficult distancing from a controlling mother, her initial graduate school experience, and unsatisfactory romantic relationships, Beth had learned to trust her own values. Helped by "hearing a whole chorus of women's voices get mad at the same professor for the same unacceptable consistent behavior to all of us," Beth was not convinced by faculty pressure to change into a research track. "It actually clarifies it for me. You know, once you're willing to really get mad and realize that people are trying to manipulate you who don't have your best interests at heart, whether it is my graduate school professors or my mother, the process of getting mad makes clear a lot of things that were really murky before and let me be more pushed around."

In sharp contrast to her undergraduate years, both of Beth's graduate experiences were personally difficult and intellectually disappointing. As Beth herself wrote, in reaction to a draft of this chapter: "My experience illustrates what's terribly wrong with graduate education. Yes, I got through it, but I very easily might not have, and how many Beth's don't get through it and aren't able to make their particular, value-based contributions?"

Beth turned down a faculty job with strong research and graduate supervision expectations. Instead, she chose a teaching position as one of the basic sciences faculty at a nursing school. Beth is delighted with the predominantly female undergraduate population, her colleagues, and her new city. She is expected to remain active in science but has clearly been hired to teach and guide undergraduates. Her program has enjoyed a remarkably stable faculty, who connect in such ways as having lunch together every day, "so I am being welcomed into a family, in a very tangible sense, as well as being hired to do a job." Beth arrived precisely where she aimed, ready to exercise her vocation, develop her interests, and enjoy personal relationships.

In addition to the two emotionally grueling graduate experiences and her estrangement from her mother, Beth suffered from the early deaths of her younger sister and her mother during her last year of graduate school. These experiences have all marked Beth, but none has come close to breaking her. She trusts deeply in her own resources. "Self-sufficiency is so important to me. . . . Just feeling like I have all kinds of levels of myself inside me and all kinds of resources. I've had a lot of various experiences and I like myself. I'm an excellent companion, you know. And I spend a fair amount of time alone. I like being alone." As for marriage and children, Beth is consistent in her belief that she could have a satisfactory life with or without a partner and children.

> I think I'm very open and aware of opportunities for somebody to be a lifetime partner and/or a father to children. Those are things that I would like in my life. And I see them as sort of an and/or thing. . . . I can have the children without the long-term partner, and I can have the long-term partner without the children. Or I can have both! . . . And I could have a satisfying life with neither. I can see myself at eighty years old, you know, sort of looking back over my life having been single the whole period of time and saying to myself, "this was a life worth living." And that's really important to me to keep clear.

Happy with who she is, Beth does not aim for recognition or prestige. "I'm trying to achieve happiness. And that changes day to day." She has resisted the pulls of research science, even though remaining at the national laboratory would have been "such a natural path." "Wouldn't it just be nice to live out the rest of your life here?. . . . Snap out of it. 'Hey no, you're a teacher. Get out of here. Run like hell!'"

Beth did run, in her own direction, toward her own values. "I think of myself as having traveled a meandering path at this point, and I like it." Eleven years after her high school graduation, I asked Beth if she had a career mission. Her unhesitating answer had to do with teaching.

> Oh, I have so many missions! It's definitely not to provide a weed-out challenge, that's for sure. I don't know how to word this right. I think that it is to help students to trust their own instincts when it comes to understanding science. It is to cultivate an environment in which I am not presenting one road to get from A to B as the

only possible path—when students dart off on another path to say, "Oh no, remember I taught you this." [Instead] I say, "Oh, let's see where that takes us," and even if it's a totally wrong path, [I prefer] that we get to the point where the student realizes that, instead of my saying "no, no, no." There are a lot of gender issues caught up in that desire, from the three years I spent doing just teaching as part of my professional life. There were a lot more intelligent young women than intelligent young men who were scared to death of taking chemistry. It's not exclusive, of course. There are gender issues, there are minority issues, there are all kinds of non-traditional wonderfully talented people who aren't succeeding in science and should be.

As we sat in her brand-new faculty office three years later, I asked Beth if she felt an obligation to her talent to develop fully her ability for research. Her response was swift and emphatic. "I feel an obligation to my *talents* to nurture more of them."

Deborah: Life as Vocation

It's hard for me to imagine a life where you go to work and you come home and a whole different set of values is operating or a whole different way of relating and being.

Deborah's get-acquainted talk with the project occurred seven months after she graduated from a public high school in an afflu-ent suburb. After fifty-nine interviews with first-year college stu-dents, we had almost given up on questions about the system of schooling, personal fears, and anger. As mentioned in Chapter Two, Deborah alone had plenty to say about these matters, and her answers were extraordinary. She had "played along" with a giant educational machine that put in people and spit out products, Deborah said. The whole process of grades and grading "is hurt-ing more than it's helping. The attitudes it creates in people—it's the grade that somebody wants. It's not knowledge that they're spending the time with. It's a rank or it's a certificate, a piece of paper, and that becomes all that's important. And it's the same with a lot of the leadership positions." Deborah herself had tried "to see the value in [education] for its own sake." By senior year, however,

"I had those feelings of the educational system and the role that I was playing in it and how it was influencing other people." She regretted and resented being "controlled by the school system" that had rewarded her with top grades.

At her high school, Deborah helped begin a peer help network and a school relations project. She campaigned for a liberal political candidate, was active in a service organization, played two musical instruments, and spent time with friends and family. "I definitely care about relationships that I have. Close relationships. I [also] have a generalized caring about the people around me, the college community or the high school community that I'm in at the time." Deborah's deep religious beliefs were far from the fundamentalist tradition of so many valedictorian project members. Her church activities centered around social justice concerns. She had been passionately interested in such issues since junior high school, Deborah said. "I guess my involvement in church has exposed me to a lot of situations with people in need, and the youth minister . . . was someone who inspired that. I guess it's rooted in the church and in the family to some degree, too. It had a lot to do with some teachers that I had in high school, and the church. I guess I was able to look at things differently."

After fifty-odd valedictorian descriptions of anger at inconsiderateness and fear of accidents, Terry Denny and I heard eighteen-year-old Deborah take a larger perspective. "What angers me is seeing systems and the way they affect people and use people. Whether it be the educational system. Whether it be the political system of this country or any other country. Whether it affects [people] to their direct disadvantage or whether they don't realize. Just seeing that, how it's molding people's lives." She saw few people willing to put themselves on the line to make a difference. What scared Deborah? "I guess wanting to do so much and knowing that there's only so much that I'm going to be able to do. Just not knowing exactly what to do, I guess. Just hoping that doesn't overwhelm me and hoping that it doesn't just disillusion me so totally that I don't ever become involved in things."

Deborah describes her parents as "good people" and her upbringing with two siblings as "nurturing." Although her college-educated parents were churchgoers and her mother was involved in community activities, Deborah was the only family member with an overwhelming commitment to social and political issues. She was similarly distinctive among eighty-one valedictorians: "I definitely want to see myself making some kind of impact," she told us in 1982. Terry Denny reacted strongly to meeting Deborah.

> Well, it's confession time. This is my sixtieth interview, and if I do have a favorite of all the young women that I've interviewed, this is the one. This is the kind of person that you wish you had as a daughter. She's good. She's a good person. She's caring about the right things. Social justice. Wants to do something important with her life. She's bright. She's studying. She's thinking. She's feeling. She's purposeful. She's very unusual too, because I don't believe that there is more than a handful of all of these students that are committed to making a positive difference in the world that won't benefit them necessarily. . . . Doesn't have a particularly distinctive countenance, but she has a human warmth that makes her absolutely beautiful and I look forward to our next conversation with high hopes.

Deborah chose to attend a small liberal arts college with a reputation for excellent academics and a progressive student body. College was different from high school, she said as a first-year student: "I guess I feel a lot more freedom academically and a lot more freedom to question." She continued her church affiliation at college and continued to rely on the youth minister in her home town. "I've talked with him when I'd come back for breaks and kind of threw questions at him, trying to work it out." She considered a political science major as a route to addressing such issues as nuclear disarmament, civil rights, poverty and welfare, and competence in government.

Particularly in her first two years of college, Deborah struggled with issues of faith, relationships, and achievement. "I had to wrestle out some doubts I had about the Church and about my belief in God," she said at nineteen. Going to college had deepened her high school questions and fed her struggle with challenging input from her courses and peers. Socially, freshman year was a rough time. Actively struggling with her faith, Deborah was equally an outsider to the campus Christian fundamentalist group and to the aggressively secular student population. Feeling misunderstood and lonely made for a rocky start to college. "It's easy to say that you have a generalized caring about people that make up your community. But it's very difficult when that becomes tested in specific relationships. Especially now, I guess, when conflicts do arise, or differences, I think they're much more intense in college than in high school. People are much more heterogeneous and the differences are much greater and larger. So [that caring has] been tested." A first-year professor influenced her to remain at the college when she was seriously considering transferring. "I just felt like I wasn't fitting in, and I just didn't feel it was the right place for me. And he said, 'I know that you are not the type of person to run away from things, and do you think that that is what you are doing now?' And I had to think about that one for a long time and just the whole idea of giving things a chance."

As Deborah questioned her beliefs and felt out of place in an antireligious student community, she was also considering her academic path. She sought a field of study that would connect to her deepest values and prepare her for a career of social activism. A future in pastoral counseling or the ministry was a possibility, as was secular work in political institutions. After two years of college, Deborah was still torn. She declared a major in psychology, deciding for the moment that she would participate in the political process but not make it her career. "Am I really going to be happy knowing the things that go on and the kinds of compromises you have to make? . . . You try to be realistic, but there's still so much optimism in my realism, and I just don't think that I could survive." Deborah continued to perform superbly in her academic work but remained ambivalent about her top grades. "I know definitely that it certainly doesn't come down to a letter on a paper or just making the dean's list. But I also still feel the drive to do well, and I question that a lot. I mean exactly what is it I'm trying to do here? And that I still haven't resolved. I still feel very strange about it."

Such intensity on so many fronts was wearing. "I have a tendency just to want to do everything and to spread myself really thin emotionally as well as academically. . . . It's quite a struggle." Her central goal, Deborah said sophomore year, was "having some center, some peace, something that I know is right or something that I can work out and go back to and use as a kind of center in my life, which I don't think I have right now. And possibly that might be my religious beliefs, but that again is something I'm going to have to work on. I'm still not sure." Her 1983 interviewer was deeply concerned about Deborah. "Deborah is going through really dire straits at this time; society, school, the stuff of life is really getting her down."

A third interview with Deborah was reassuring. A college junior, she had formed strong, satisfying friendships. She had reaffirmed her commitment to her religious faith and church and felt less intimidated by the campus environment. "I feel as though now I can extract the things I like, and I can change according to the way I like. Those things that are not attractive to me or that go against what I believe in, I feel free [to reject] and not threatened by them anymore." Her nonreligious friends had come to understand that Deborah was "not out to convert the world and that I'm struggling with my faith and it's not an absolute thing for me either, which caught a lot of them by surprise."

By junior year, Deborah had culminated "a very natural and gradual progression" by "coming out" as lesbian. "I always had a consciousness of being different, but [before college] I didn't have the language for it, and I never had the occasion for it. . . . And then in college it was really the first time I met women who identified as lesbians and learned that this was something that you could be. You could really be one and live your life that way." "Freedom," "mutual respect," "affirming," and "shared experience" were some of Deborah's descriptions of the campus climate for her friendships with both lesbian and straight women. "I appreciate it more and more as time goes by," she said in 1994. "I think women were just empowered there."

As she made close friendships, feeling part of the college community made a tremendous difference to Deborah. "After I felt I had established those relationships, I felt a lot more confident, and at that point, I guess, I had kind of a group of people I felt comfortable enough with that I could move on from there."

"Moving on from there" meant deepened commitment to her church's strong social justice agenda. Although she considered spending a year away from campus, Deborah chose instead an intensive internship sponsored by a local church. Visiting hospitals and nursing homes was a highly rewarding learning experience, in which Deborah learned more about herself and about the realistic obstacles and joys of helping people in need. She had also moved on in the area of academics. Academic work was meaningful to her when she expressed her own ideas and produced something creative, something different. Much of the time, however, she did not find a way to make coursework relevant and personal. "There's a lot more involved than just raw intellect in getting a good grade and achieving a high grade point average. I do wonder whether I'm wasting my energy, playing that kind of a game. And it bothers me. It bothers me a lot."

Deborah had become more comfortable on the career front, deciding to give herself a few years after college to make decisions about the ministry or government service. Without defining the specifics, she anticipated a future as a gay woman, with meaningful relationships and challenging work that contributed to people's lives. She accepted the risks of leaving defined graduate school and career paths: "I know that it would be the wrong thing for me to go right on to grad school just because it's familiar and safe."

By the time she graduated from college, Deborah had found her center of religious faith. "I have wrestled with it. I have thought about it a lot. And there was a period of time when I didn't really believe there was a God. But there's just something that leads me back and makes me feel as though it's the right thing. It's not always a strong feeling, but it's always there somehow, and somehow I get back to that and plug into that."

As a senior, Deborah reflected back on her college experience, noting the diversity of her experiences. "I think I put a lot into it. I kind of rushed headlong and exposed myself to a lot of things and questioned myself and opened myself up to good and bad." Nine years later, she again returned to the theme of growing through sometimes painful experiences. "[College] wasn't the easiest place, but I think the easiest place isn't always the place you want to be, as hard as that is to feel. I'm really glad that I went there."

As a high school senior, Deborah was already strongly committed to the religious, political, and relational values that would continue to guide her life. As a college senior, she had deepened her openness to experience and embraced difficult struggles. In a sermon she wrote and delivered as part of her internship, Deborah described six aspects of inauthentic living. "The first is being both in the world and of the world; the second is viewing life as a possession to be defended; the third is being obsessed with product, outcome, results—success; the fourth is relating to others in a guarded, inauthentic, protective way; the fifth is clinging blindly to group affiliations; and the sixth is objectifying other people." Aiming for prestigious jobs and top grades, Deborah went on, is to "play the game by the world's rules," becoming "separated from other people and from the deepest parts of ourselves." Her own statement of purpose in the senior year of college continues to describe Deborah's fundamental approach to her life: "There are things that guide my life, but I'm always questioning those along the way. I try to be real, to constantly examine things and say, 'do I feel like this is authentic and genuine and I'm living that way?'"

In the period immediately after college, Deborah worked to establish her independence, gain confidence, and "get started on my own life." She worked in human services programs, first as a youth advisor in a church outreach project with inner-city low-income families. "It was an interesting and important experience for me to get a sense of what a community-based ministry is all about. And also to understand what I now see as liberation education, how that happens with people." When the project ended, Deborah lived with her parents and worked in a battered women's shelter while looking for jobs. Living at home was particularly difficult because Deborah had not come out to her parents as lesbian and felt lonely and isolated from her campus community. Though short, that period was a difficult time of relocating her identity away from her college environment and relationships.

Deborah's next job was on the West Coast, leading religious activities at a care facility for senior citizens. Becoming acquainted with institutional politics and seeking ways to communicate with people living with physical disabilities stretched Deborah in ways she found valuable. "It was really painful, but it was helpful, really good learning. . . . I was constantly racking my brain trying to think of what is it I'm trying to say and what is it that they're trying to say to me. What are we talking about when we're talking about these scripture passages? What do they mean for this person right now in [his or her] point of life?"

Another positive aspect of this period was Deborah's friendship with an older staff person who connected her to the city's lesbian community. "I really grew that year in terms of understanding that this is a community and that I was a part of it."

Confirmed in her desire to work within a religious framework, Deborah acted on her long-standing plan to attend divinity school. She chose an interdenominational program where "many people that I really respected in my life and had nurtured me spiritually and in the Church had gone." Once enrolled, Deborah continued her deep personal exploration of spirituality and social change. Butting up against the theological canon distressed her, as she attempted to fit her own experience into traditions she often found intolerant and dogmatic. "Sometimes it was worth struggling against, and sometimes it wasn't. Sometimes I felt like I learned a lot from the struggle, and sometimes I felt like it wasn't worth it. It just made me less, it took from me."

As she had in college, Deborah threw herself into her school-work with her mind and heart. And, also like college, graduate school was an important time of coming to know herself and committing to her values. "It was just a constant struggle from day one for me to be there. . . . I have a friend who talks about me, describes me as being in the process of being born, not in the sense of being a born-again Christian but in the process of being born, which makes a lot of sense for me. . . . I guess I was making choices about how I was going to be in life, and I was making choices about how I related to institutions, who I choose as my friends and who I choose to be aligned with politically and spiritually. And so I always felt like I was fighting."

Deborah became a leader in speaking out against institutional policies and practices she found objectionable, working partly through her active role with a gay and lesbian student group. She found her home not in divinity school but at a social action theological institute. Her year at the institute was spent in the company of diverse women struggling together to transform social institutions without replicating unjust structures and relationships.

I learned ways to ask questions. I got even more challenged in terms of relating to institutions and institutional identity. My best friend, who [later became] my roommate, I met there, an African American woman. And two of my intimate friends really challenged me on racism and understanding what it means for me to make choices about what I do with my privilege. . . . I really learned how tempting it is to want to be a good person who is acceptable and gets in and gets things. . . . The [institute] made me feel stronger in my different identities that comprise who I am, and I came back not feeling so much that I have to apologize for who I am. Taking more control of my own faith and spirituality, my own education, which is something I wish I had [done] in the beginning. Being able to confirm my suspicions as being true—that I'm not a crazy marginalized weirdo, but that there was a truth to what I was saying and feeling and other women, or other people, could corroborate that. Because it's so important, and it's a struggle. People say you're not crazy, and there's a reason why [other people] want to make you feel crazy, but you're not.

Deborah blossomed at the institute, which supported her personal identity growth along with her intellectual, spiritual, and activist development. A close friendship with her African American classmate grew into Deborah's first long-term primary relationship. When Deborah completed divinity school, she moved to a new city and became involved in the family and community life of her partner and former classmate. She found a job as a secretary at a church-sponsored social action office, spending much of her time off the job assisting people with AIDS. She continued to confront practices she saw as wrong

One of the things that I've come to understand is that there isn't anywhere you can be that you can't make significant choices. I'm a secretary, but every day just about, I can add to the dynamics, or I can see about changing them. . . . I found that I've had to put myself on the line and speak about things. I've had to make a choice. Here I am, and I've had this opportunity to be educated, and now I have to say something. And it could mean that I lose a respected recommendation, and that's what it's going to have to mean.

After several years as a secretary, Deborah began work as a member of the professional program staff. Her job involves linking the advocacy agenda of her office with the efforts of local congregations. In addition to providing supporting resources to church groups, she helps congregants become advocates and does some legislative lobbying. In dealing with such social problems as discrimination, access to health care, and violence, she finds her work both rewarding and difficult.

Deborah's relationships continue to be central in her life. She seeks out people who will "hold her accountable" and tries constantly to reach outside the valuable but limited perspectives with which she was raised. "I never quite believed everything that I heard, and I never quite believed all the images. . . . Also, just knowing the different ways that I don't fit in, and when I understand that, take that in, I can see other ways that other people fit in and where their reality is. . . . I can listen and hear stories that are different from mine—be committed to being a responsible person." Trying to change the world is not the greatest challenge according to Deborah. "The harder thing to do is not getting out there with your life on the line but doing those little things—like how you deal with the person right next to you. That can really say a lot about your commitment."

The ending of Deborah's primary relationship after several years was a very painful time for her. She maintains a friendship with her former partner and tries to avoid defining herself in terms of a central relationship. Still, "there are a lot of sides of me that are not being nurtured or expressed right now . . . and I would like to share that with someone special."

Deborah's career path remains flexible. In 1994, she was pursuing the steps toward ordination but unsure where her commitments will lead her. The political arena is still a possibility. Deborah has already faced dilemmas about compromising for career advancement.

> There are times when the things that I value force me to make a choice about "getting ahead" in terms of the career markers or vocational markers. And there have been several times when I've had to really weigh that, and where I've decided that the way I choose to be in the world—vocationally and just generally personally—[is] more important than getting up that next step on the ladder. . . . I guess what works for me is the connections, the people who are important to me and the communities that are important to me, so that I see that our well-being, our corporate well-being, is improved by something I can do. I consider that a victory.

From the early days of childhood, Deborah said, she had felt "an affinity to people on the margin." Having made connections with what other people were feeling, she could not remove herself from the pain of the bullied or less-valued children: "I never really felt like I could distance myself. I think there were times maybe when I wanted to. But it just wasn't a possibility. I just couldn't do it." Along with her personal sensibilities, Deborah credits important people for her chosen path. "I feel really blessed by a lot of the adults who were in my life. I feel like there are all these people who encouraged me. . . . A lot of them were teachers . . . and people who helped me not to be afraid of myself and what I could do. And helped me not to feel alienated or isolated. . . . And a lot of [them were] people in the Church also, and that was very important to me."

Deborah sees herself as a warrior, seeking out information and connections that do not come intuitively, putting herself on the line by speaking out, and pushing herself to live with integrity. "Battling is not something that's unfamiliar to me in the least. That doesn't mean to say that I embrace it all the time. But I think there are some people who just immediately run the other direction. And I don't. I expect it. And in some ways I do embrace it." Ten years after high school, Deborah identified her greatest delight: "I guess living on a deeper level. I'm very aware of being alive. It sounds really corny, but I feel real. I feel like life is real. It's real, and even though there's a certain kind of pain that comes with not believing a lot of the myths and the images, beyond that is another very powerful reality, and for me it happens to be a spiritual one as well as a political one. . . . So things hurt more, but the blessings mean more too."

Deborah cherishes her multiple lenses on life. Her story is not only about being gay, but this identity is inseparable from her life as vocation. "If someone were to say that you could be straight tomorrow, I would never do it. I would love for homophobia and heterosexism not to exist anymore, but I really like who I am. I can't separate out that part of me from the rest. It's integral; it has so much to do with who I am." Certainly, Deborah says, identifying as lesbian has helped nurture her sense of empathy and being on the margin.

But more fundamentally than that, in a more positive way, it has a lot to do with my vision and imagination and creativity, in the sense that gay people always know that there is always more than one level of reality. . . . Just to be able to blow categories apart and to deal with ambiguity, you are forced to integrate ideas and emotions and social context in a very different way. Life is just constantly a creative exercise. . . . It's not just about reacting, but it is about shaping your own response and asking your own questions and not always reacting to the questions imposed upon you. . . . So I think that it has a lot to do with being not just willing and able, but joyfully embracing other possibilities than the standard paths, rewards, and sanctions.

Deborah's lifework of living with integrity and making positive contributions to people's lives occurs in her employment and personal life, in large things and small. The themes of struggle and openness to experience weave through her life and result in an extraordinary story of dedication to the highest human goals. For Deborah, as I quoted her saying earlier, values and vocation are inseparable.

It's hard for me to imagine a life where you go to work and you come home and a whole different set of values are operating. Or a whole different way of relating and being. . . . I guess I'm more willing to see the ways in which benefits are handed out differentially by institutions and that has been a long struggle. I mean, the more privileges you have, the more allegiance you're encouraged or reinforced to have for the institution that you're a part of. . . . But [that seeing is] what we're called to do, I think, if we're really about solidarity and justice and transformation.

The Core of Commitment

Fame, wealth, and power do not motivate Beth or Deborah, yet these two women are among the few valedictorians still in contention to make sweeping contributions to their talent domains. Beth and Deborah use their gifts in very different contexts and for different ends. In important ways, however, they are similar to each other and different from the larger valedictorian group.

Both women sought personal meaning in academics before the end of high school. Each attempted to arrange her college study in terms of interests and relevance rather than defined career ends. Intellectuals both, the women deliberately sought out cognitive and personal challenges in college. Their academic studies reflected their deepest values and connected directly to student life outside the classroom. Beth's college employment and social life centered around chemistry and chemists. Deborah's theology, psychology, and political science studies closely paralleled her identity development, personal commitments, and extracurricular life. Both Beth and Deborah excelled in college academics without making top grades their goal. Probably as a result of their deep engagement in undergraduate studies, the two women formed close relationships with influential faculty. For Deborah, learning also occurred through church activities, mentors, and guides. Both women participated in undergraduate testing experiences that confirmed their vocations and helped them to grow in skills and self-understanding. Beth performed research and, most importantly, was exposed to teaching. Deborah worked as a pastoral counseling intern.

As they defined their adult achievement paths, both women considered their choices tentative. Unusual among the entire valedictorian group, they made decisions after college that reflected risk and exploration. Both Beth and Deborah reached a point in their early twenties at which they decided that the mapped-out academic path that had served them so well was both overly confining and too comfortable for growth. Instead, they deliberately sought new experiences, moved away from the Midwest, and resisted cementing their career futures. It was as a result of postcollege experiences that each returned to graduate school to deepen her understanding about material that personally engaged her and to relate learning to life goals.

Both found their graduate environments far less nurturing than college. As graduate students, Beth and Deborah took personal control of their educations. Beth voluntarily left the prestigious program where she was progressing well if unhappily. After time away from school, she deliberately chose a lower-ranked doctoral department more consonant with her ideas and values. There too, she described a harsh interpersonal climate. Deborah began publicly critiquing the divinity school curriculum and practices from the basis of her own experience and her deepening understanding of alternative perspectives.

The willingness to be different has been a strong characteristic of the two women since high school. In college, Beth followed an unusually scholarly trajectory in an anti-intellectual peer culture, while Deborah's religious beliefs stood out at her elite, secular liberal arts institution. After college, the women continued to resist the stereotyped achievement routes laid out for top students. Cutting their own paths was far from easy. Deborah felt socially excluded at the beginning of college and later struggled against traditional graduate school and career advancement expectations. Opening herself deliberately to foreign voices and challenging relationships meant continuous, intense self-reflection and struggle for Deborah. Beth's refusal to compromise her intellectual standards and professional ideals led to clashes with powerful research supervisors. On another level, Beth had to confront a deeply problematic relationship with her mother in order to choose her own life path.

At the same time as they remained flexible and open to experience, these valedictorians saw themselves as having choices and an important degree of control over their lives. Neither anchored her aspirations around expected primary relationships or motherhood, for example. Both see multiple routes to fulfilling their self-chosen missions. Questioning the assumption that people and institutions have other individuals' best interests at heart has also been liberating for the two women, enabling them to reject external measures of prestige or standard professional routes.

Individuality, independence, exploration, and risk taking are cornerstones of the exceptional vocational commitment of Beth and Deborah. These traits have enabled the two women to shape as well as adapt to their academic and work environments. Equally important, however, are personal relationships. Both Beth and Deborah's achievements represent an interpersonal model of talent development. Beth's intensive interactions with chemistry professors and graduate students and her desire to touch the lives of others through her teaching lie at the heart of her achievements and commitments. Deborah similarly developed her path with strong influences from friends, teachers, and mentors in and out-

side of the church. Each woman continues to put personal connections at the very center of her life and vocation. Beth is eager
to change the way young women think about themselves, not just
about science. She disdained career advice from a professor without personal interest in her well-being. Deborah wants to help people in a broad sense but also stays closely focused on her own
personal relationships and work interactions.

Beth and Deborah are driven by mission, not achievement.
Both are ambivalent about standard achievement measures such
as grading, institutional prestige, and job status. Their considerable vocational energy and deep work commitment comes from
their fundamental values for personal growth, the communication
of ideas, authentic relationships, and social change. It is by these
values that Beth and Deborah measure success.

In their early thirties, the most career-invested women and men
in the Illinois Valedictorian Project are those who have found deep
personal meaning in vocations. The qualities and conditions that
keep students centered on work are different than those that made
them high school valedictorian. To reach the head of the class, students needed to conform to the school system and work equally
hard at all subjects. Like their age peers in the 1980s, valedictorians aimed for prestigious, secure, high-paying careers. Having been
well-rounded cooperative successes in high school, they continued
to function comfortably as college academic achievers. Fourteen
years after high school, most valedictorians were indeed working
in high-level, prestigious, secure professions. They remain comfortable in standard achievement settings. They are still well
rounded, with professional involvement taking its place among
other important life roles.

For Beth, Deborah, and perhaps a dozen other valedictorians,
the story looks somewhat different. These men and women have
moved beyond achievement goals to express their deepest values
through their vocations. As compared to the rest of the group,
these valedictorians are risk takers and nonconformists. They are
intellectuals who framed their college education around ideas,
learning, and personal values instead of career training or achievement. With the help of influential people and significant experiences during the college years, the members of this group
developed strong career identities and faith in their choices. They

do not sharply separate work and personal life, nor are they motivated primarily by security, prestige, or pay. The occupations they have chosen feature intellectual work, personal expression, and meaningful interpersonal connections.

A sense of vocation as life mission characterizes less than a quarter of the top academic achievers fifteen years after high school. The members of this small group pour their talents into work to achieve goals associated with their deepest values. It is these few valedictorians who still hold exceptional potential for transforming their talent domains—for becoming eminent.

Chapter Eleven

What Really Happens to High School Valedictorians?

We know what a masquerade all development is and what effective shapes may be disguised in helpless embryos. In fact, the world is full of hopeful analogies and handsome, dubious eggs called possibilities.
GEORGE ELIOT, *MIDDLEMARCH* ([1871–1872] 1977, P. 56)

The Illinois Valedictorian Project began at high school graduation ceremonies. As we watched, the top Illinois high school students of 1981 took center stage before their parents, teachers, administrators, and classmates to speak of promises. The forty-six women and thirty-five men had fulfilled their obligations to themselves, their parents, their teachers, and their talents. They had worked hard, done their best, and excelled. As they formally marked the exit from childhood, honored students vowed to demonstrate their gratitude and utilize their talents through continued effort. Commencement day rhetoric focused on the promise of youth for leading society and the hope that the most talented young people might one day transform that society. Implicit on the happy occasion was the promise that exceptional effort, motivation, and ability would continue to result in extraordinary attainment. The best high school students faced limitless futures.

Following these men and women from the valedictory address to the present has revealed what academically talented students become. Being valedictorian means something beyond high school. The broad story of the Illinois Valedictorian Project is one of continued success. Former high school valedictorians continue to achieve magnificently in college academics and two-thirds go on to graduate study. Although less uniformly outstanding, the occupational attainments of these top students feature high levels of professional work. Thirty or so work in the top tiers of such professions as college teaching, law, medicine, business, and science. A dozen remain in contention for exceptional careers. Valedictorians follow normal pathways of adult development to establish successful personal lives as well. They form satisfying, enduring friendships and intimate relationships. In their early thirties, two-thirds of the valedictorians are married and more than a third have children. Project men and women cope effectively with normal life difficulties and occasional serious troubles. Good kids have become contributing adults.

Even as they accepted their high school prizes and made their speeches, valedictorians knew theirs was only the opening victory of the life achievement contest. Beyond the positive general findings lie individual and group differences in valedictorians' adult outcomes. Academic attainment is no guarantee of an optimal transition between school and work. The promise of higher education to develop the talents of bright, motivated students is not always kept.

"'Success' is never merely final or terminal. Something else succeeds it. . . . The world does not stop when the successful person pulls out his plum; nor does he stop, and the kind of success he obtains and his attitude towards it, is a factor in what comes afterwards" (Dewey, [1922] 1983, p. 174). John Dewey's observation frames two of the three major issues that determined valedictorians' post–high school success: the particular kind of accomplishment measured by school grades and students' attitudes and values about what constitutes adult success. The third major lesson of the Illinois Valedictorian Project is that race, class, and gender affect the fulfillment of promise in particular ways. In short, what happened to high school valedictorians in the decade and a half after high school graduation tells important, interlocking stories of the meaning of academic achievement and the social context of talent development.

Grades Beget Grades

Academic talent is a stable quality. Findings from the Illinois Valedictorian Project establish a strong connection between top high school grades and future educational attainment. The project's eighty-one stellar high school graduates all began postsecondary education. Seventy-five received at least a four-year bachelor's degree and two completed nonbaccalaureate nursing degrees. Only four students did not finish a college degree in the fourteen years after high school. Even this small group completed an average of two years of undergraduate study; none left school for academic reasons. As compared to general and even high-ability students nationally, the valedictorians' 95 percent college graduation rate is extraordinarily high (Educational Testing Service, 1991). Although their college entrance examination (ACT) scores varied, the group continued to earn top undergraduate grades. With a mean grade point average of 3.60 on a 4-point scale, they earned mostly A's in college. Three-quarters earned college academic honors, including Phi Beta Kappa membership and other top university awards. Six valedictorians earned perfect straight A records in college, and several completed degrees after only three years of undergraduate study.

The top high school students continued their academic achievement beyond college. By 1994, just under 60 percent had received a graduate degree or were active graduate students. Almost one in three had received a terminal doctoral, law, or medical degree. An accounting of their graduate attainments is impressive: fifteen Ph.D.'s, six law degrees, three medical degrees, twenty-two master's degrees. High school valedictorians are still entering graduate school, so this strong catalog of educational accomplishment will undoubtedly expand over time.

A history of academic success, in sum, is an extraordinarily powerful predictor of further educational attainment. What high school teachers measure by top grades apparently mirrors what college professors reward. High school valedictorians and salutatorians are as close as it gets to rock-solid bets for superb undergraduate grades and college graduation.

What Grades Reward

What is it that academically talented students are doing so reliably? Once it is established that outstanding high school grades are superb indicators of top college grades, a more important question of validity comes to the fore: What does scholastic performance have to do with success beyond school? The relationship between academic and postschool achievement reveals a far more complex picture than the direct correspondence between high school grades and postsecondary academics. The story includes valedictorians' own views of what makes for school success, the patterns of their motivation and personal qualities, and the domains in which they focus their endeavors.

Dewey wrote that "the kind of success [one] obtains . . . is a factor in what comes afterwards." Earning high academic marks is a particular kind of success and therefore relates to specific sorts of outcomes. From the earliest days of the project, valedictorians themselves distinguished between intellectual ability and academic talent. Top grades, they told us, came from knowing how to succeed in classroom tasks and expending the effort to do so. "It's easy to study for the grades, I think," Dan told us (Chapter Two). "You don't really have to be born smart. I'm kind of book smart. I'm not really born smart. . . . I have an attitude for school—it's a system. If you know how to study, you'll do well at school." All the valedictorians enjoyed learning, a few passionately so. The group was clearly very capable intellectually. Still, valedictorians overwhelmingly attributed their success to hard work and school savvy.

Valedictorians were highly motivated to excel academically because of early family and school experiences. Nearly all of the group came from stable, two-parent families. Most, although not all, describe their home environments as psychologically healthy and nurturing. Parents modeled and stressed values of doing one's best and working hard. Working-class and middle-class parents touted academic success as the key to upward mobility. Early and consistent recognition from teachers reinforced students' classroom efforts and built their identities as academic achievers. Academically oriented peer groups, religious involvement, and family expectations guarded teenagers against distractions from school achievement. Valedictorians were far less likely than their national peers to use alcohol and other drugs (Bachman, Johnston, and O'Malley, 1981). They were more highly motivated to be busy and to work hard than any tested national sample (Arnold, 1987; Helmreich, Spence, and Wilhelm, 1981; Spence and Helmreich, 1978; Spence, Helmreich, and Stapp, 1974). And all were exposed to the 1980s' economic downturn, focus on individual attainment, and emphasis on business and financial wealth (Astin, Green, and Korn, 1987).

Valedictorians cooperated in school with the fervor of true believers in the American dream. These successful students were supremely comfortable with the structure, tasks, and values of formal schooling. Top grade earners possessed extensive tacit knowledge about effective studying, test taking, and classroom demeanor. They were willing to follow the written and unwritten rules of school, both when they found personal meaning in learning and when they did not. Only two valedictorians differed sharply from the profile of contented achievers-within-the-system. Deborah (Chapter Ten) was uneasy about school reward systems. "Sometimes I think about [high school] in terms of the things it taught me that I wish I didn't learn. A certain amount of obedience and law-abidingness, I guess, a lack of creativity, a real reining myself in." And William pushed the written and unwritten rules of both his high school and college. An activist and a poet, respectively, Deborah and William continue to be outliers in the occupationally conventional valedictorian cohort.

Old-fashioned virtues describe valedictorians as a group: bright, motivated, ambitious, responsible, cooperative, hard working. Having given their best effort and whole-hearted cooperation to academics, valedictorians believed that success and happiness lay in doing well what you were supposed to do. This was the pact, the unwritten promise of the meritocracy: work hard, do your best, excel, and be rewarded.

The school achievers rarely fit stereotypes of narrow study grinds or social misfits. In high school, they led exceptionally well-rounded lives. Academically, they worked hard and succeeded in everything from home economics and physical education to advanced humanities, mathematics, and science. Valedictorians took part in innumerable school-related activities, held student body leadership positions, and participated in respected social and friendship networks. Friends, music lessons, sports, church activities, and employment occupied them after school. Psychologically healthy and interpersonally capable, valedictorians were good kids leading conventional teenage lives. As a group, they were not notable intellectuals, nor were most dedicated intensively to a single talent domain.

Their superb grades rewarded a constellation of ability, hard work, academic tacit knowledge, and cooperation with institutional demands. Rewarded for being generalists, the top students were also well adjusted, well rounded, and socially involved. This profile of success relates closely to the eventual outcomes of the group. Beyond high school, project members continued to express their talents in mainstream American achievement settings. Most chose educational and career pathways leading to secure, prestigious, well-paying professions. Fewer than a dozen men and women let intellectual passions guide their postsecondary educations. Almost none chose alternative life-styles or creative occupations. As college students, most stressed vocational training or a combination of interests and career preparation. Valedictorians have continued to work hard and play by the rules. They remain well rounded as adults, effective in both relationships and occupations. Their achievement continues to take place in conventional institutional settings.

Gateway to Eminence?

Genius consist[s] neither in self-conceit nor in humility, but in a power to make or do not anything in general, but something in particular.
GEORGE ELIOT, *MIDDLEMARCH* ([1871–1872] 1977, p. 56).

Valedictorians are the people who excel at "something in general" rather than "in particular." They are highly successful career achievers. Their occupational attainments vary far more than their academic performances, however, and very few now center their lives in vocational achievement arenas. Unlike creative eminent achievers, academically talented students rarely fell in love with a single talent domain that they placed at the center of their lives

(Ochse, 1990; Feldman, 1986). They did well at everything in school, making decisions pragmatically instead of following a specialized personal interest. Coming of age in the Reagan era reinforced valedictorians' practical bent. Eight in ten valedictorians chose professions with scant possibilities for creative eminence. Fourteen years after high school, valedictorians are business people and accountants (fourteen), engineers (twelve), and nurses, physical therapists, and social workers (eight). They are lawyers (seven), physicians (three), and high school teachers and school administrators (three). Six women currently rear children full time; all plan eventually to return to professional employment. Nine valedictorians work at nonprofessional jobs not requiring college degrees. The study's two visual artists earn their living through industrial filmmaking and retail display merchandising. Applied fields such as accountancy, engineering, medical practice, and law offer progressive ladders of advancement and financial rewards, but rarely provide arenas for transforming disciplines or domains of thought and practice.

Twenty percent of the valedictorians do work in professions with exceptionally high potential for intellectual creativity. These include college mathematics and science professors (five), research scientists (five), and doctoral-level social science and humanities researchers (four). The group also includes a poet who supports himself with nonprofessional work, an innovative architect, and a community activist. Most of these valedictorians, however, have also chosen paths that do not normally lead to eminence. They hold teaching-centered faculty positions, for instance, and applied science jobs in industry. Most work comfortably within conventional systems of thought and action; only a handful aim to change them.

Outstanding academic performance is a strong general indicator of vocational accomplishment fourteen years beyond high school. Nearly nine in ten valedictorians hold professional-level positions, including 40 percent who work in the highest-level occupations. The career trajectories of high school valedictorians reflect their predilection for conventional achievement arenas. Their occupational accomplishments reflect the same qualities that enabled them to reach the head of the class: intellectual talent, interpersonal ability, responsibility, hard work, and effective functioning within standard institutional structures. Educators have traditionally viewed giftedness in terms of divergent approaches to a specific talent domain. This definition fits top grade earners imperfectly. Roads to eminence lie primarily in creative professions and nonstandard approaches. Only a few men and women remain on these tracks. In general, the members of the Illinois Valedictorian Project continue to achieve highly in standard ways and in mainstream institutions. The best academic performers are safe bets for career achievement, but most appear unlikely to end up as mold-breaking, transformative leaders.

Developing Academic Talent

No [person's] abilities are so remarkably shining as not to stand in need of a proper opportunity, a patron, and even the praises of a friend to recommend them to the notice of the world.
PLINY THE YOUNGER, *EPISTLES* (BOOK VI, EPISTLE 23)

Excellent college grades do not guarantee high career aspirations or outstanding professional success. Perhaps the most important findings of the Illinois Valedictorian Project concern the conditions for developing academic talent. Gender, race, and class deeply affect the process of transforming academic talent into professional success. The most straightforward transition between school and postschool achievement occurred for white men. All the male undergraduates expected full-time continuous employment during their adult lives. None questioned whether he would have a professional career or anticipated occupational compromises for family life. Men's view of their intelligence in relation to peers remained constant or increased slightly over the undergraduate years. Intellectual self-concept was related to men's career aspirations and professional outcomes. So were ability, the selectivity of their colleges, and their desire for prestigious, challenging careers (Arnold, 1994). Holding undergraduate jobs or internships in their chosen fields also contributed positively to men's eventual career status. Fourteen years after high school, male valedictorians are indeed working full time and continuously in the labor force. The most vocationally successful are those with the highest ACT scores, the greatest intellectual self-esteem, the most prestigious college degrees, and the greatest desire for high-level careers. The majority of the men with these characteristics grew up in families with at least one college-educated parent.

The process of translating academic skills into career achievement requires finding an appropriate vocational channel and knowing how to negotiate that channel. Professionally related work experience during college was helpful to students as a form of career socialization. Such experiences were particularly vital for students without professional family members. The unwritten, tacit knowledge of how to choose careers and negotiate high-level occupational tracks was readily accessible to male students from privileged backgrounds. They were more likely than first-generation college students to orient their undergraduate education around intellectual interests (as intellectuals) or around a combination of intellectual goals and vocational training (as strivers) (Katchadourian and Boli, 1985). Intellectual approaches to college yielded the highest-level professional outcomes; strivers were the next most successful group. Working-class students, in contrast, were predominantly careerists who managed the transition from school to career by choosing narrowly focused vocational studies in areas such as accountancy or engineering. All of the project's students of color fall into this latter group. Although careerists nearly always achieved their vocational goals, they are not the highest career achievers in the valedictorian project. Some feel trapped today in narrow channels they chose at age eighteen.

Women's achievements tell a different story. Gender differences began emerging as early as the college choice process. The overall selectivity of their undergraduate institutions was no different for men and women, but the women highest in ability were far less likely than men to choose the top-tier colleges. Men earned undergraduate degrees from Harvard, Yale, Princeton, MIT, and Stanford; the only Ivy League female attended Cornell. Once in college, women and men earned equally superb grades and academic honors and were equally likely to plan graduate study. Half of the women chose male-dominated majors such as engineering, science, mathematics, business, and agriculture. The remaining half divided evenly between fields with equal gender representation (like biology) and those that are female dominated, such as nursing, education, and physical therapy.

Despite their outstanding performance in challenging curricula, women lowered their self-estimate of their intelligence between the senior year of high school and sophomore year of college. By college graduation, no female valedictorian said she was far above average in intelligence in relation to her peers while a quarter of graduating men rated their own intelligence as far above average. This decrease in reported intelligence occurred despite women's earning outstanding academic records that equaled or even slightly surpassed men's records.

In addition to the disturbing decline in their intellectual self-estimate, female valedictorians undertook an extra career stage as undergraduates. As early as their sophomore year of college, at age nineteen, women began considering what kind of career they wanted in the constellation of adult family and paid work roles. Anticipating future role juggling and unable to imagine combining motherhood with the highest professional echelons, women began voluntarily leaving male-dominated college majors and pre-medical tracks. Their attrition from science and engineering fields began during their sophomore year of college and continued through college, graduate school, and even postdoctoral work. Even those women who remained in science, mathematics, and engineering majors struggled to envision a professional path that would accommodate their deeply held values for vocational achievement and family involvement. What kind of career? became a central question for most female valedictorians. It was a nonissue for academically talented males.

Women's planning began at a time when none of the contingencies of marriage, children, or job were known or under their control (Angrist and Almquist, 1975, 1993). Only one woman was married by 1985, the year most valedictorians graduated from college. Nevertheless, two-thirds of female college seniors expected to reduce their future labor force participation to accommodate childrearing, either by working part time or by leaving paid employment altogether. The thirty valedictorians who did not plan to work continuously and full time outside the home included half of the women in male-dominated professional fields. As they graduated from college, women articulated their vocational goals much more vaguely than men. Many had great difficulty envisioning themselves in high-level careers and were unclear about the steps needed to reach top professional positions. Few were personally acquainted with high-achieving adult women in their fields. Even fewer knew women who had successfully accomplished the role balance to which they aspired.

Their contingent approach to career planning negatively affected many women's career aspirations. By the time they left college, two distinct groups of women had emerged among the former high school valedictorians. One group resembled male valedictorians in aspiring to the highest professional levels. A second group chose significantly lower-level careers. The two groups were not separated by the factors that made a difference in men's career aspirations and outcomes. Women planning high- and average-level careers were equivalent in ability, college selectivity, and intellectual self-esteem. Members of the two female groups came from similar socioeconomic levels, were equally interested in graduate degrees, and were just as desirous of using their best talents in professional work. Work and family values, rather than talent, college quality, or family background, separated female valedictorians from males five years after high school. High-aspiring women planned more continuous labor force participation and later marriage and childbearing than their less-ambitious female peers. Plans for combining career and family explained with great accuracy variations in females' occupational aspirations. Such factors made absolutely no difference in the vocational ambitions of men.

Highly career-oriented women usually expected eventual marriage and children but made vocational plans that did not revolve around future family contingencies. Case studies and quantitative analyses showed that the high aspirers' greater career commitment related to their undergraduate experiences. Members of the top group developed solid career identities through professionally related paid and unpaid internships, research and teaching assistantships, and summer jobs. They became part of professional reference groups of peers and, often, graduate students. Outside the classroom, these women interacted with faculty and professionals in their fields, who supported, encouraged, and occasionally pushed them. Most importantly, key faculty connected young women to opportunities. Women who participated in career socialization experiences outside the classroom were more likely to aspire to high-level work. Active assistance from faculty, opportunities to test themselves in work settings, and recognition by peers and professionals led to clear visions of career goals and firm identities as career achievers. Testing experiences and occupational contacts allowed undergraduate women to envision themselves in elite achievement settings. Once they had seen what professional work was like and been convinced by sponsors and their own accomplishments that they were capable of succeeding, women aimed high.

Women's aspirations mattered. Three-quarters of female valedictorians from the top career group are high-level occupational achievers at age thirty-one to thirty-two. Anticipating continuous work and late marriage and childbearing relates closely to lofty aspirations and notable work accomplishments. Contrary to their expectations, women from both vocational groups married at the same rate and ages. Expecting delayed marriage is a more powerful predictor of career outcomes than actual marriage age. Many valedictorians who depressed their career ambition for future family roles married later than anticipated, and most have worked continuously and full time in the labor force. Without the interpersonal net of talent development that characterized the high-aspiring group, however, equally able women were unable to envision and value high-level professional roles or to accumulate the tacit knowledge to establish elite careers.

Women in top-career echelons did carry out their college plans to delay childbearing. Career-related gender differences in the valedictorian project will almost certainly intensify as more women add the role of parent to the full plate adult life stage. Five women have already changed to part-time employment and six more do not work at all outside the home. Among other project mothers, half would like to reduce their labor force participation. Consistent with their plans since college, valedictorian fathers work outside the home continuously and full time. Two or three men have slowed their professional advancement slightly to participate more fully in family life. No man has changed his career field for fatherhood, however. Childrearing—anticipated and actual—continues to define the achievement lives of women only. For them, superb college grades do not ensure high-level professional aspirations or attainment.

A talent development process occurring outside the classroom is necessary for academically talented women to understand, aspire to, and reach top-career levels. Students enter college measuring success in terms of grades and school accomplishment. Achievement identity shifts over the undergraduate years to an adult measure: future career status. With family expectations blurring career goals, women's achievement identity also becomes hazy. The complexity of the school-to-career transition for women accounts, I believe, for lowered intellectual self-esteem among academically talented female undergraduates. Women faced considerable difficulty in establishing identities as postschool achievers when talent development was restricted to the college classroom.

African American and Latina students also needed more than college academic success to make an optimal transition from school to work. The nine students of color in the Illinois Valedictorian Project took longer than the larger group to finish college. Two never completed degrees. Valedictorians of color were less likely than white students to attend graduate school. None has earned a Ph.D., law, or medical degree. As compared with white students, they have been more often underemployed and more often unhappy with their work.

Unlike white women's obstacles, undergraduate hurdles for African American and Latina valedictorians did not center on career and family role planning. Rather, women and men of color never received the untaught practical knowledge needed to translate academic talent into professional attainment. They were unskilled at choosing colleges, weighing financial aid offers, selecting majors, and navigating the university. With limited ideas of career possibilities and narrow visions of education as vocational preparation, black and Latina valedictorians approached college as careerists. Although they continued to perform well academically, students of color were unsure what steps led to their professional goals. When they discovered they disliked or were blocked from their naïvely chosen career tracks, they received no assistance in envisioning and following new paths. Faculty members did not serve as supporters, guides, or sponsors. Only the sole student who transferred to a historically black university established a personal connection with a faculty member outside the classroom. Many students were further estranged from campus intellectual and social centers by living at home and spending long hours at outside employment. Racism and active exclusion in predominantly white universities combined with students' poor tacit knowledge to push minorities to the margins of higher education.

The experience of Eric, the student who eventually attended a predominantly black college, shows how a talented African American student can bloom in a nurturing undergraduate environment. Isolated and earning poor grades at his first, predominantly white university, Eric (as described in Chapter Six) was sponsored into the core social and academic systems of his second college. Through a network of professors, fellow students, and practitioners in his field, Eric learned the academic and career management information he needed to succeed. Faculty contacts, a peer reference group, and pregraduate professional positions enabled him to translate his academic talent and motivation into a strongly positive personal and professional identity. The conditions for talent development in Eric's historically black college stand in stark contrast to the abandonment experienced by the talented students of color in predominantly white universities

First-generation college students of all ethnic groups were similarly at risk during the transition from academic to career achievement. Knowledge about career alternatives and how to reach them was not embedded in these students' backgrounds. Viewing college as vocational training for upward mobility, many men and women chose narrow channels based on incomplete information about themselves and the world of work. Escaping unsatisfying ruts meant connecting to the talent development networks of higher education. For those who did so, personal connections with faculty, testing work experiences, and professional reference groups led to increased professional identity, self-understanding, practical career knowledge, and eventual attainment. Most undergraduate careerists, however, never gained access to adult sponsors, guides, and mentors. They continued to earn top grades in college and to cling to their narrow paths. Their adult vocational accomplishments are solid but seldom outstanding. Most never came to consider career involvement as deeply, intrinsically meaningful.

The stories of women, minorities, and working-class students are variations on a theme. Female valedictorians struggle to define their future achievement selves amid a hazy future of somehow combining family and career. Students of color find themselves on the edges of higher education because of exclusion from core career socialization systems and unsophisticated practical knowledge. And first-generation college students misunderstand the routes to stellar careers. These three groups overlap, of course, and so do their achievement issues. All newcomers to elite career spheres, the members of these groups have two factors in common. First, for somewhat different reasons, all have difficulty imagining clear career goals. Women have few models for combining high-level work and motherhood. In envisioning what they might become, minority and working-class students also have few models in their immediate world. Second, the members of these groups possess scant practical knowledge of how to negotiate elite career paths. Working-class students, for instance, believe that undergraduate majors must be directly tied to career ends, when, in fact, the most successful valedictorians are those who approached college intellectually, letting intrinsic interests guide their choices and following a process of extended exploring, deepening self-knowledge, and gradual career focusing.

Valedictorians are talented and motivated, but they are also achievers within standard institutional systems. In college, they continue to perform what they believe is their task—working hard and succeeding academically. During the undergraduate years, however, the achievement arena moves beyond school. Envisioning goals and managing career exploration is an achievement project that occurs mostly outside the classroom and has relatively little to do with mastering academic content. The knowledge needed to find a personally meaningful career channel is not formally taught, nor does it automatically accompany top grades. When sophisticated families and friends cannot guide career exploration, students must look beyond the null academic environment of classes, majors, and grades to translate their academic success into life goals. Many students, male and female, found nothing in college beyond the visible curriculum and instruction in the classroom. They did their best, earned good grades, and went on to their chosen professions. The costs, however, were significant: their talents were not fully developed, their options were incompletely explored, and their eventual achievement was diminished. Many landed in jobs they dislike, even more in careers that do not engage their passions.

Academically talented students who found their way to satisfying careers and outstanding professional achievements shared a common undergraduate experience that went beyond academics. Women who manage high-level careers and families, students of color with satisfying professional work, and working-class students in top occupational positions participated as undergraduates in an interpersonal talent development process. Significant interactions with faculty outside of the classroom were vital in their transition between school and work achievement. Professors' recognition of them as talented future colleagues reinforced students' achievement identity and built their confidence. Faculty initiated promising students into the unwritten knowledge of their fields—what professionals do, how they live, and how they build careers. Most importantly, faculty connected students to opportunities. In research positions, internships, guided projects, and jobs, students saw firsthand what their professional lives could be. Envisioning themselves in the roles of supervisors and professors became possible when students saw real people performing in specific situations. Aiming high became likely when students saw they could succeed. Practicing professionals took their place alongside faculty as mentors, sponsors, and guides. Participation in a peer reference group of undergraduate and graduate students in the same field became another ongoing mechanism of professional socialization and identity in a talent domain.

By the time they graduated from college, students who had participated in this talent development process envisioned themselves clearly as professionals and possessed sophisticated knowledge of career paths. Relatively few students received this kind of higher education experience, however. Some, mostly males from privileged backgrounds, succeeded without this process, finding their family connections, background knowledge, and gendered role expectations sufficient for high-level career aspirations and attainment. Women, students of color, and first-generation college attenders, however, needed more than the null academic environment to aspire and achieve as highly as their talents allowed.

In short, nearly all valedictorians succeed in careers. Race, class, and gender affected their aspirations and attainments, however. Overall, students of color and men and women from working-class backgrounds are less occupationally successful than other valedictorians. Women's achievements rest on gendered role expectations rather than talent. Members of each of these groups are found at the highest occupational levels, however. These are men and women whose undergraduate experiences assisted the transition from college to profession. Access to mentors, interactions with sophisticated insiders, and career socialization experiences are vital elements of undergraduate talent development. Even the best students need such conditions to develop their talents for adult life.

The Meaning of Success

Your whole life you've been told, you go to high school, you go to college. And then once you get out of college, you're not given as much direction anymore. You know, there's no purpose in life anymore. What should you do after you graduate from college? You accomplished everything that everyone told you you should.
Jake (1994)

Valedictorians leave high school at the top. Most continue to stellar academic performance in college. Yet their career attainment varies considerably. And even though most are strong occupational achievers, the great majority of former high school valedictorians do not appear headed for the very top of adult achievement arenas.

Two potential explanations for these findings have already been advanced. First, valedictorians achieved their academic honors by accommodating generalist demands in an institutional setting. Both the literature on eminence and project members themselves differentiate between scholastic attainment and intellectual giftedness. Although many valedictorians are clearly intellectually gifted, the achievements of the overall group continue to occur in conventional occupations and in well-rounded lives that avoid single-minded involvement in specialized talent domains.

A second, quite different, explanation for valedictorians' superior but unspectacular career attainment lies in the talent development process of the undergraduate years that was just summarized. Women, people of color, and first-generation college students can continue to earn top grades without transferring their achievement identities to career spheres. Without an accompanying interpersonal talent development process for members of these groups, superb academic performance alone is insufficient for them to envision, aspire to, and reach the highest levels of adult career achievement.

The valedictorians themselves continually raise a third possibility. The measure of success in life, they say over and over again, is not public professional achievement. "I guess one thing you can do is to say, 'I'll accumulate as much wealth or get as high a position [as I can] or become president of a company,' and all that," Jake said in 1994 about life since high school. "That's one thing that society tells you you can have as a purpose in your life." Jake had graduated college after only three years with his university's highest undergraduate award, next earning an M.B.A. at a top business school and zooming up the career ladder of a prestigious international computer firm. In his early thirties, he deliberately stepped away from the top tier, however, preferring to devote himself to family and church activities. "I guess I realized that—from all my work at school and stuff like that—it's never ending, you have to keep going ahead. And that'll just wear you out. I just don't think it's worth it anymore . . . to have to strive for going up higher in the company, owning my own business, or something like that. . . . You never know how long you'll live or how much time you'll have to be young, to get out and hike or camp or spend time with the kids. So I just didn't think it was worth it."

Always generalists, always well rounded, most former high school valedictorians value relationships, personal interests, and balanced roles over achieving as much as their talent will possibly allow. Career attainment, while still important to most project men and women, is just one among several desirable adult roles. Values about what it means to lead a good life shape valedictorians' adult outcomes every bit as much as talent or academic success.

Self-definitions of success come partly from valedictorians' backgrounds and families. Undergraduate influences also determine the value top scholastic performers place on adult achievement domains. The most outstanding career achievers in the Illinois Valedictorian Project are those who have found deep intrinsic meaning in learning and work. Women who lacked assistance in connecting intellectual passions to vocational arenas never seriously considered themselves as top-career achievers. Newcomers to higher education rarely received the help to understand what a personally chosen path might yield. Prizing intensive career involvement is impossible without clear goals and a personal connection to vocation. Those men and women who participated in talent development networks value career highly. Intellectuals who let their curiosities and commitments guide their paths have been more likely than other valedictorians to develop a sense of vocation in which their careers connect to their deepest values. It is these women and men who still see success as using their best talents in careers. Continuing to pour themselves into achievement arenas, it is they who are most likely to reach the heights of occupational attainment.

Promises Kept, Promises Broken

That was my past, of course: I was valedictorian.
Futurewise, you have to make something new out of it.
You have to be valedictorian again.
BARRY (1982)

High school valedictorians kept their commencement day promises. They have continued to give their best effort to academic achievement and career establishment. In their early thirties, most of the men and women of the Illinois Valedictorian Project are highly educated, professionally successful adults. They are also successful friends, partners, parents, and community members. The top Illinois high school seniors of 1981 are today contributing mightily to society.

Higher education, in contrast, did not always keep its promise to develop the talents of even its best students. Left with classroom achievement alone, many students never found a negotiable path to a clearly envisioned career corresponding to their deepest interests and values. We have learned from these talented students what makes a difference in the fulfillment of promise. The Illinois Valedictorian Project shows that equating grades and adult career success is a very tricky proposition, particularly when it comes to academically talented women, students of color, and

first-generation college students. Without a web of faculty involvement and nonacademic opportunities, even the best grade earners do not acquire the needed tacit knowledge to travel
exceptional career pathways. By the time they are adults, valedictorians' motivation has largely been channeled away from
careers. Those few who remain on top tracks have found pathways that connect their values to vocation. The remainder define
success outside public achievement spheres.

Valedictory Lessons

> *Tonight we, the Class of 1981 of Township High School,*
> *must end a very special chapter in our lives and set out on*
> *a new journey. . . . We are grateful for the blessings that*
> *these past four years have held and for the chance to set*
> *new goals and dream new dreams. We must look to the*
> *future, strengthened by what we have gained here and*
> *guided by the dreams we choose to follow. My wish for each*
> *of you is that this graduation may be the start of the future*
> *shining with the promise of new adventures, new successes,*
> *and new kinds of happiness.*
> ELIZABETH, VALEDICTORY COMMENCEMENT ADDRESS
> (1981)

We all share a deep personal and societal stake in developing the
talent of young people. Our academically best students have much
to teach all of us about success, fulfillment, and becoming an adult
in late twentieth century America. Supports and obstacles to adult
achievement stand out in bold relief when they affect individuals
with optimal skills and credentials. These are students who should
succeed. Having examined what makes a difference in the realization of potential under ideal circumstances, we can apply these
lessons for the benefit of all young people.

Lessons About Individual Success

Parents, students, and teachers can learn from the valedictorians
that work, perseverance, and focus lead to academic success and
life attainment. No matter what an individual's ability level, achieve-

ment requires sustained effort and a belief in the efficacy of hard work. This contrasts with the numerous cross-national studies that have found that Americans believe innate ability, not effort, primarily determines educational achievement (Stevenson and Stigler, 1992).

It is also important for parents, teachers, and students to understand that academic achievement alone is insufficient to guarantee high career aspirations and a smooth transition between school and work. Occupational success requires experiences and relationships that enable young people to discover and implement intrinsically involving career paths.

Lessons About Higher Education

Even top students too often move through our colleges and universities without ever connecting with a faculty member who takes a personal interest in them. As U.S. professors are rewarded more and more for research activities and less and less for direct student contact, learning becomes increasingly restricted to classroom settings and academic material alone (see, among others, Astin, 1992; Boyer, 1990; Hulbert, 1994). The results for talent development are deeply troubling. In particular, capable, motivated minority youths, women, and first-generation college students are not being enabled to develop their talents fully; they continue to lack knowledge of occupational alternatives and career management processes. Intentional undergraduate experiences must go beyond academics. For all students, a network of career exploration opportunities, sponsors, and mentors is a critical accompaniment to coursework.

Lessons About Career Development

The skills, motivations, and personality traits that contribute to educational attainment are predictors of professional careers but not necessarily of top-level occupational accomplishment. Continued personal investment in high-level adult achievement requires the formation and implementation of what Levinson (1978) called the "Dream"—an individual's view of self in the adult world. Developing the vocational Dream is a largely nonacademic

endeavor occurring in early adulthood. When the transition
between education and career establishment is left to chance, a
viable, personally absorbing occupational Dream is unlikely to
form; in addition, gender and social class will overshadow ability
and interests in determining career outcomes (Gottfredson, 1981).
Even high-ability individuals will then turn to nonwork arenas for
their sense of purpose. According to the Illinois Valedictorian Project, academic achievement reduces gender and social class differences in career outcomes only when professionally related
undergraduate experiences overcome circumscribed views of the
occupational world.

Lessons About a Generation

Men and women who came of age in the 1980s and early 1990s
have struggled to make sense of an economic and occupational
world in which clear paths are few. This generation expects to
marry and have children. Both men and women take for granted
that they will work outside the home but that women will still take
the role of primary child care givers. Young adults' perceptions of
the occupational structure of opportunity guide their career aspirations and achievements. Women realistically perceive barriers to
simultaneous high-level employment and childrearing in American workplaces and family structures. Also correctly, men and
women perceive that the paths to creative occupations are chancier
and less clearly marked than those to technical professions. Students face serious pressures to avoid such risky paths. Following
the tail of the baby boom through economically turbulent times,
contemporary young adults are keenly aware of fierce competition
and job insecurity. They have not reacted as their fathers might
have by making work the center of their lives. Even approaching
young adulthood, they have questioned the meaning of achievement. For the most part, they have rejected a competitive, striving,
workaholic image of occupational success. Instead, they strive for
balance between work and family, achievement and relationships.
Whether their efforts to maintain balance will survive external pressures is one of the many questions that will be answered in the next
decade of their lives.

Lessons About Success

Are schools rewarding the right people as the highest achievers? If the goal is hard-working, productive, adaptable adults, then U.S. high schools are recognizing precisely the correct group. As we have seen, the high school valedictorians in the Illinois Valedictorian Project can be counted on to continue achieving personally and professionally. Whether this is what schools should reward is, in the end, a question of values. Measuring outcomes returns inevitably to decisions about the meaning of success, decisions faced by an entire generation. What is life success? Is it notable career attainment? A doctoral degree? Significant contributions to society? Is it eminence, happiness, close relationships, or creative expression? The valedictorians came to their own definitions about what it means to lead a good life. They have fulfilled their promise according to their own life goals. Talented men and women can choose what life success means to them. Society's and education's promise to them—and to all young people—must be to ensure they consider all the roads they can travel and find the pathways of achievement open to all.

Note to Researchers

The Illinois Valedictorian Project was designed as a longitudinal study of the background, experiences, achievements, and perceptions of top high school achievers. In the first fourteen years of the project, the eighty-one study members participated in periodic intensive semistructured interviews and completed a variety of standardized and project-designed survey instruments. Findings reported in this book draw from both qualitative and quantitative data collected between 1981 and 1994.

Sample

Following a pilot interview study of former high school valedictorians at the University of Illinois at Urbana-Champaign, all high schools in Illinois were surveyed to determine if they recognized a valedictorian and if the top student delivered the traditional valedictory address. Of the 500 (approximately half) high schools that responded, about 350 recognized a valedictorian and 270 had the top student speak at commencement. Within the population of these 270 schools, the first stage of the sampling procedure used the high school as the sampling unit. The goal of the maximum variation sampling strategy (Patton, 1980) was the inclusion of representative types of high schools. The sampling procedure, therefore, attempted to maximize the variety of high schools by community (rural, urban, suburban), by type of student body, by public versus private control, by size, and by geographic location.

High schools were stratified by type and location. The schools were then arranged by commencement date. This strategy allowed a project researcher to attend each graduation to witness the public recognition of the valedictorian and to gain firsthand a sense of the community and school context. Conflicts in graduation dates were resolved by choosing a high school in a category (such as location or student body type) that was not already represented in the sample. In this way, 33 public and private schools were identified and the sampling population turned to the valedictorians and salutatorians at these schools. Several schools recognized more than one valedictorian in cases of identical grade point averages. Salutatorians were included on the urging of pilot study valedictorians. A few nonvaledictorians and nonsalutatorians among the top graduates were also included (ten students) on the advice of school informants who identified those students as the top students in the various schools. Several of these honor students made speeches at graduation. This small group of ten have been retained in the study on the basis of analyses that show their similarity to the formally designated valedictorians and salutatorians.

The eighty valedictorians and salutatorians and ten honor students received letters asking them to participate in a ten-year study. Of these ninety students, there were seven non-respondents, one student declined, and another joined the study but died soon after the initial interview. The nonrespondents included three valedictorians and four salutatorians who failed to reply to four letters. Two of the three nonresponding valedictorians were covaledictorians with sample members and the salutatorians' high schools were each represented by the school's number one student. These considerations, as well as the very high agreement rate to undertake a major commitment, do not indicate that the 10 percent nonresponse rate is a serious problem.

In sum, the nonprobability sample features a wide diversity of high school achievement settings, rather than a proportional representation of all Illinois high school seniors. The size of the sample, the single cohort design, the lack of directly comparable national data, and the nonprobability sampling prohibit direct generalization of project findings to the national population of high school valedictorians and salutatorians. As an initial study of a unique population, however, maximizing the variety of high school settings for top academic performance is a feasible sample design. And single-cohort longitudinal studies can be justified in the case of populations that are previously unstudied and in intensive qualitative designs (Vaillant, 1977). The greatest threat to validity in longitudinal studies, subject attrition, has not been a problem in our work. Remarkably, all eighty-one surviving members of the Illinois Valedictorian Project have remained in touch with the study.

Qualitative Data Sources and Analysis

The first data source of the project comprised observational information in the form of extensive field notes from high school commencement exercises. Copies of each valedictory address were also collected and analyzed. Other data sources included student letters, résumés, writings, and art work. Six waves of interviews provided the bulk of project data. Karen Arnold or Terry Denny conducted individual interviews with each of the eighty-one valedictorians for each of the first four years of the study, from 1981–82 to 1984–85. Both of us eventually interviewed nearly every valedictorian. Interviews were conducted in person at the student's home, college room, or workplace. Occasionally, interviews took place in a researcher's office; during the sixth and most recent wave, half of the interviews were conducted as taped telephone conversations. In all interviews, we encouraged students to discuss their experiences and preoccupations in their own terms, using interview protocols as guidelines to open-ended conversations about academic, work, and personal lives.

Field notes from graduation ceremonies were used in the first set of semistructured face-to-face interviews to investigate high school experiences and students' perceptions of being named valedictorian. Interviews of one to three hours began by exploring scholastic and family experiences, perceptions of achievement, and performance motives. Subsequent interviews focused on personal, academic, and career experiences and aspirations. About a third of the group was interviewed a fifth time between 1985 and 1989, when the Illinois Valedictorian Project was without funding. A complete round of interviewing was conducted in 1990–91. Approximately half of the group was interviewed in 1992–94, with this wave still in progress.

All interviews were audiotaped and transcribed. The framework for data analysis followed a grounded theory approach involving a continuous interplay between data collection and interpretation (Strauss and Corbin, 1990). This approach aims at obtaining increasingly adequate theoretical understandings of study findings. Emerging themes from previous interviews formed the basis for subsequent interviews and questionnaire items in which issues were explored systematically and in greater depth. We asked students to respond to statements they had made in previous years and to group findings as a form of member check (Lincoln and Guba, 1985).

In order to determine patterns of responses, analyses of qualitative interview data were carried out by coding transcribed interviews by theme and sorting related pieces of text by categories. Researchers read and reread the typed interview transcripts as well as interview and commencement field notes, research memos, résumés, correspondence, and open-ended survey responses for each student. Data analysis proceeded inductively, beginning with open coding in which transcripts were examined line by line for meanings and issues and continuing with the development of larger conceptual categories from clusters of descriptive codes (Strauss, 1987). The most salient themes in individual cases and the most frequently recurring issues across cases formed the basis for the organization of the data report (Spradley, 1979).

Quantitative Data Sources

In addition to the interviews, questionnaire data were collected at multiple points in the study. In 1981–82, soon after high school graduation, the project participants responded to a section from the University of Michigan Social Research Institute national survey of 16,000 1981 high school seniors (Bachman, Johnston, and O'Malley, 1981). The annual survey included items on values and attitudes, educational aspirations, high school activities, and alcohol and other drug use. The Michigan survey also included an item asking respondents to rate their intelligence in relation to their age peers. The study group responded to the self-estimate of intelligence item at five points over fourteen years. The entire survey was replicated in 1991.

In 1984, the valedictorians completed two standardized instruments measuring gender roles and achievement motivation. The Personal Attributes Questionnaire (PAQ) is a self-administered personality inventory that measures gender-related personality traits (Spence, Helmreich, and Stapp, 1974). The instrument includes a "masculinity" scale, representing instrumental, agentic traits and a "femininity" scale, reflecting expressive, communal characteristics. (Reliability coefficients for the M and F scales range from .61 to .76.) The Work and Family Orientation Questionnaire (WOFO) is a measure of achievement motivation and attitudes toward family and career (Spence and Helmreich, 1978). WOFO scales include: "mastery," the desire for intellectual challenge; "work," the desire to work hard and be busy; "competitiveness," the desire to succeed in competitive interpersonal situations; and "personal unconcern," the desire to avoid negative interpersonal consequences of achievement. (Alpha coefficients for the scales range from .50 to .76.)

A project-designed questionnaire eliciting labor force participation plans and work values was administered in 1985. Work values items were drawn from a longitudinal study by Angrist and Almquist (1975), who had themselves modified an earlier scale from Rosenberg (1957). Items were chosen which appear consistently in the research literature on scholastic and career outcomes. Variables such as socioeconomic status, family role expectations, ability, achievement motivation, and gender-related personality differences are examples of factors commonly associated with achievement outcomes. In addition, measures such as intellectual self-esteem and labor force participation plans were chosen in response to themes drawn from the valedictorian interview data.

Short questionnaires were distributed in 1988 and early 1994. These updates collected current information about career and educational experiences, marriage, and childrearing. The self-report questionnaire also asked project members to state the "ultimate" for them, a question repeated in each interview over the fourteen-year study period.

Quantitative Analyses

Measures of central tendency, frequencies, and other standard descriptive statistics were computed for questionnaire items such as work values, undergraduate work experience, parental education, and so on. Reported findings also draw from correlations, t-tests, and other bivariate analyses. All differences on quantitative measures reported in the text are statistically significant at the .05 level.

In Chapter Five, results were presented that draw on multivariate analyses. Discriminant function analyses were first conducted in the fifth year of the study to determine the career-related differences among the study women (Arnold, 1993c). Analyses relied on both qualitative and quantitative data. Each valedictorian's current career status was first ranked according to the Hollingshead (1957) Two Factor Index of Social Prestige, a measure of vocational level that incorporates education, occupational prestige, and income. Raters additionally considered professional aspiration level, the extent of planned labor force participation, and the importance ascribed to future career roles, in order to classify women into two vocational groups. This classification was initially carried out independently by three raters who had worked with the study group for a minimum of three years. Interrater reliability ranged from .83 to .89. The few discrepancies in raters' classifications of the forty-six women were resolved by discussion after reviewing interview transcripts. Quantitative measures of the classification criteria were then used in discriminant function analysis to determine the appropriateness of the group assignments and to understand more about the combination of variables that maximally differentiated the groups. In addition to drawing from interview data to assign women to groups, raters used a set of specified achievement criteria. These criteria included level of highest planned degree or professional position, clarity of career goals, choice of a male-dominated profession, degree of anticipated labor force participation, relative importance of future work and family roles, and degree to which occupation is chosen to maximize childrearing manageability. Two vocational groups resulted: an A group of twenty-two high career achievers and a B group of twenty-four women who planned to design their work lives around family considerations. The analysis method follows Terman's comparisons of two vocational groups, representing the one hundred most and the one hundred least successful men in his longitudinal sample (Oden, 1968).

Discriminant function analyses were performed to obtain the linear combination of variables that maximally separated the vocational groups. The variables that were included in the discriminant function analysis were those that were theoretically important and those that had contributed to important bivariate relationships in the data set. ACT scores and socioeconomic ratings were included to investigate differences involving ability and socioeconomic background. The function accounted for 69 percent of the variability due to groups and correctly predicted group membership of 94 percent of the study women. When men were included in a discriminant analysis with the same variables, only 68 percent were correctly classified into high and low vocational groups, a finding that indicates that the variables that separated women so accurately fail to explain men's patterns.

A similar discriminant function analysis was conducted with the males in the Illinois Valedictorian Project based on the 1988 questionnaire information (Arnold, 1994). Three raters placed male valedictorians into two vocational groups based on their career and educational attainments and aspirations. The resulting discriminant function analysis correctly classified 94 percent of the twenty A group and fourteen B group men. The men, however, were separated by a different set of variables than were A and B group women.

In 1991, two independent raters again placed the women into two vocational groups, this time according to actual career level at age twenty-eight. Interrater reliability was .89. Women's scores on the 1985 discriminant function were examined to see how well they predicted 1991 group membership. A discriminant analysis using the same variables as the senior-year function was conducted for the 1991 vocational groups in order to examine the patterns associated with career status of female valedictorians ten years after high school (Arnold, 1993c).

Tables

Table 1. Valedictorian Profiles: Guide to Case Material.

Name	Chapter	High School; Community	Current Activity (1994)	Highest Degree Earned
Jonas	1	Public high school; inner city	Personnel supervisor	Two years college

Significant Experiences:
Lost both parents by 1978; transferred colleges; left college and married in 1984; two children; religious conversion in late twenties.

Name	Chapter	High School; Community	Current Activity (1994)	Highest Degree Earned
Marilyn	1	Public high school; rural	Postdoctoral scientist	Ph.D.

Significant Experiences:
Grew up on farm; transferred from comprehensive state university to research university; difficulty finding permanent research position; single.

Name	Chapter	High School; Community	Current Activity (1994)	Highest Degree Earned
Kate	2	Catholic single-sex school; small city	Homemaker	Associate's degree in nursing

Significant Experiences:
Left college in 1982 and community college in 1984; married in 1984; two children; homemaker and medical office worker before returning to school for 1994 degree.

Table 1. Continued

Name	Chapter	High School; Community	Current Activity (1994)	Highest Degree Earned
Matthew	3	Public high school; suburban	Graduate student	Ph.D. in progress

Significant Experiences:
Ivy League degree in philosophy; self-employment as commodities trader before returning to graduate school in psychology; single.

Name	Chapter	High School; Community	Current Activity (1994)	Highest Degree Earned
Martin	4	Catholic single-sex school; urban	CPA, internal auditor	Master's of accounting

Significant Experiences:
Worked in public accounting firm after graduation; left in 1990 to work for single firm; married in 1993.

Name	Chapter	High School; Community	Current Activity (1994)	Highest Degree Earned
Meredith	4	Public high school; suburban	Graduate student	Ph.D. in progress

Significant Experiences:
Double major in mathematics and music; worked as computer research analyst before returning to graduate school in developmental psychology; married in 1992; child 1995.

Name	Chapter	High School; Community	Current Activity (1994)	Highest Degree Earned
Kevin	4	Catholic single-sex school; urban	Engineer, manager	M.B.A.

Significant Experiences:
Broad college extracurricular involvement; co-op program in engineering; moved from technical to management track; married 1990, child 1994.

Table 1. Continued

Name	Chapter	High School; Community	Current Activity (1994)	Highest Degree Earned
Gail	4	Public high school; mid-sized town	Accounts manager	B.A.

Significant Experiences:
Difficulty choosing college major; returned to hometown for work in general business; married 1988; child 1992.

Allie	5	Catholic single-sex school; small city	Postdoctoral scientist	Ph.D.

Significant Experiences:
First-generation college student; moved from engineering to graduate work in science; significant undergraduate research experience; difficulty finding permanent research position; single.

Monica	6	Catholic single-sex school; urban	Bookkeeper	Three years college

Significant Experiences:
Immigrated to United States from Mexico in childhood; bilingual; first-generation college student; left college due to financial and time constraints; married 1987; child 1990.

Michelle	6	Public high school; inner city	Engineer	M.B.A.

Significant Experiences:
Highly successful, involved college student; channeled into engineering but more attracted to business; dissatisfied with engineering position; single.

Table 1. Continued

Name	Chapter	High School; Community	Current Activity (1994)	Highest Degree Earned
Eric	6	Public high school; inner city	Engineer	B.S.

Significant Experiences:
First-generation college student; left first college when family problems affected grades; transferred to historically black college; engineering co-op program; degree and marriage 1990; adopted children 1991.

Name	Chapter	High School; Community	Current Activity (1994)	Highest Degree Earned
Darren	7	Public high school; rural	Industrial filmmaker	B.A.

Significant Experiences:
Grew up on farm; guided into broadcasting by high school mentor; worked in television station during college; married 1988; first of two children, 1990.

Name	Chapter	High School; Community	Current Activity (1994)	Highest Degree Earned
Rachel	7	Public high school; suburban	Homemaker	Ph.D.

Significant Experiences:
Straight A student and award winner at religiously affiliated college, studying chemistry and English; after 1991 Ph.D. in chemistry, left laboratory science to work as technical writer; married 1989; child 1993.

Name	Chapter	High School; Community	Current Activity (1994)	Highest Degree Earned
Nick	7	Catholic single-sex school; mid-sized city	High school teacher and coach	B.S.

Significant Experiences:
From working-class family; attended Catholic university majoring in accountancy; worked as certified public accountant, 1985–1991; returned to school for teacher certification while teaching at Catholic high school; single.

Table 1. Continued

Name	Chapter	High School; Community	Current Activity (1994)	Highest Degree Earned
Ann	8	Public high school; rural	Visual merchandising manager	Bachelor of fine arts

Significant Experiences:
Youngest of large, religious family; transferred between public universities; honors and awards as undergraduate painter; began cooperative artists' gallery after graduation; married 1988; child 1989.

| Beth | 10 | Public high school; urban | Chemistry professor | Ph.D. |

Significant Experiences:
Undergraduate research and teaching in chemistry; left first doctoral program; taught science at independent school and small college three years before entering new graduate school; teaching-oriented faculty position, 1994; single.

| Deborah | 10 | Public high school; suburban | Activist in church-sponsored organization | Master's of divinity |

Significant Experiences:
Active involvement in social justice issues since high school; liberal arts college degree; attended women's theological institute in addition to divinity school; worked as secretary, then staff person in church organization; considering ordination; single, lesbian woman.

Note: All names are pseudonyms. Jonas, Michelle, and Eric are African American; Monica is Latina; remainder are white European Americans.

Table 2. Undergraduate Majors of Valedictorians.

Undergraduate Major	Women	Men	Total (n)	Total (percent)
Science (agronomy, animal science, biology, chemistry)	10	4	14	(17)
Engineering and computer science	8	9	17	(21)
Business (finance, marketing, business administration, accountancy)	7	10	17	(21)
Applied health (physical therapy, nursing, applied life sciences)	7	0	7	(9)
Mathematics and economics	3	3	6	(7)
Communications and journalism	3	2	5	(6)
Social science (political science and government, psychology)	4	2	6	(7)
Humanities and art (English, philosophy)	1	3	4	(5)
Education	2	1	3	(4)
Art and architecture	1	1	2	(2)
Total	46	35	81	(100)

Note: Eight students who completed double majors are listed under the field pursued professionally. Double majors, with primary major listed first, were chemistry/English; communications/Afro-American studies; biology/theology; engineering/German; education/political science; mathematics/music; journalism/history; mathematics/classics.

Table 3. Highest Degree Earned by 1994.

Degree	Women	Men	Total (n)	(percent)
Ph.D. (completed or in progress)	10	5	15	(19)
M.D.	3	0	3	(4)
J.D.	1	5	6	(7)
M.B.A.	3	7	10	(12)
Other master's degree	9	3	12	(15)
Bachelor's degree	16	13	29	(36)
Nonbachelor's nursing degree	2	0	2	(2)
Some college, no degree	2	2	4	(5)
Total	46	35	81	

Note: Total undergraduate degrees, 77 (95%); total graduate degrees, 46 (57%); total women with graduate degrees, 26 (57.5%); total men with graduate degrees, 20 (57%); total terminal degrees (Ph.D., M.D., J.D.), 24 (30%.)

Table 4. Occupations of Valedictorians in 1994.

Occupation	Women	Men	Total
Accountant	2	2	4
Other business	3	7	10
Childrearing full time	6	0	6
Engineer/computer scientist	6	6	12
Lawyer	1	6	7
Nonprofessionals	7	2	9
Ph.D. research or study in humanities/ social sciences	3	1	4
Physical therapist, nurse, social worker	8	0	8
Physician (includes one medical school professor)	3	0	3
Professor (college-level science, mathematics)	3	2	5
Scientist (nonfaculty)	2	3	5
Teacher, educational administrator (precollege)	1	2	3
Other	1	4	5
Total	46	35	81

Note: Nonprofessionals work in jobs not requiring a college degree. Valedictorians listed in "other" category include one woman working with a religious organization as a social justice activist, and four men: an architect, a farmer, an industrial filmmaker, and a poet/substitute teacher.

Table 5. Comparisons of Valedictorians and Stanford Cohort Study Undergraduate Typology.

| | Student Type | | | |
Study	Careerist (percent)	Striver (percent)	Intellectual (percent)	Unconnected (percent)
Valedictorians[a]	46	28	12	14
Stanford Cohort[a]	23	24	25	28
Valedictorian women[a]	41	28	11	20
Stanford cohort women[a]	16	26	34	24
Valedictorian men[a]	51	29	14	6
Stanford cohort men[a]	29	25	15	31
Valedictorians changing fields in college (33 percent of total)[b]	16	17	30	55
Stanford cohort changing fields in college (49 percent of total)[b]	38	41	58	66
Valedictorians changing fields after college (15 percent of total)[b]	5	17	10	45
Valedictorians changing fields during and after college (38 percent of total)[b]	21	34	40	100

Note: Comparisons based on Stanford Cohort Study class of 1981 (Katchadourian and Boli, 1985). Katchadourian and Boli conducted annual interviews with 320 members of the Stanford class of 1981 from their first year to graduation. The study explored the degree to which students identified with career or intellectual aims of higher education and the factors associated with these patterns. The resulting typology classified students according to vocational and intellectual motivations for college study (careerist: high vocational, low intellectual focus; striver: high vocational, high intellectual focus; intellectual: low vocational, high intellectual focus). Ten years after the study cohort graduated, Katchadourian and Boli (1994) conducted a follow-up study in which they investigated the lasting effects of elite college attendance and undergraduate careerism and intellectualism.

[a]Percentage of each type in entire study group: for example, 46 percent of valedictorians are careerists.

[b]Percentage of each type that changes: for example, 16 percent of valedictorian careerists changed fields in college.

Table 6. Self-Report of Intelligence Compared to Peers.

Intelligence Self-Estimate	1981 High School Seniors (n = 81)		1983 College Sophomores (n = 81)		1985 College Seniors (n = 80)		1991 Age 28 (n = 73)	
	Male (percent)	Female (percent)	Male (percent)	Female (percent)	Male (percent)	Female (percent)	Male (percent)	Female (percent)
Average	7	7	9	27	3	7	14	14
Slightly above average	23	28	19	27	16	23	14	21
Above average	47	44	50	42	56	70	58	57
Far above average	23	21	22	4	25	0	14	8

Note: The question asked was taken from the 1980 national study of high school seniors reported in Bachman, Johnston, and O'Malley (1981): "How intelligent do you think you are compared to others your age?" It was repeated at intervals throughout the Illinois Valedictorian Project. Responses were made on a 7-point scale ranging from "far below average" to "far above average."

Table 7. Marital and Parental Status in 1994.

Marital Status	Women (n)	(percent)	Men (n)	(percent)	Total (n)	(percent)
Ever married	31	(67)	21	(60)	52	(64)
Divorced	1	(2)	2	(6)	3	(4)
Never married	14	(30)	13	(37)	27	(33)
Parents	21	(46)	11	(31)	32	(40)

Note: At least six valedictorians were living with significant others in 1994. One valedictorian self-identifies as lesbian, another as gay. One man has divorced and remarried, appearing in both the married and divorced categories. Percentages in male and total categories therefore add to more than 100%.

References

Albert, R. S. "Family Positions and the Attainment of Eminence: A Study of Special Family Positions and Special Family Experiences." *Gifted Child Quarterly*, 1980, *24*, 87–95.

Almquist, E. M., Angrist, S. S., and Mickelson, R. "Women's Career Aspirations and Achievements: College and Seven Years After." *Sociology of Work and Occupations*, 1980, *7*(3), 367–384.

Angrist, S. S., and Almquist, E. M. *Careers and Contingencies*. New York: Dunellen, 1975.

Angrist, S. S., and Almquist, E. M. "The Carnegie Mellon Class of 1968: Families, Careers, and Contingencies." In K. D. Hulbert and D. T. Schuster (eds.), *Women's Lives Through Time: Educated American Women of the Twentieth Century*. San Francisco: Jossey-Bass, 1993.

Arnold, K. D. "The Illinois Valedictorian Project: Top Academic Achievers Five Years After High School Graduation." Paper presented at the annual meeting of the American Educational Research Association, Washington, D.C., Apr. 1987.

Arnold, K. D. "Academically Talented Women in the 1980s: The Illinois Valedictorian Project." In K. D. Hulbert and D. T. Schuster (eds.), *Women's Lives Through Time: Educated American Women of the Twentieth Century*. San Francisco: Jossey-Bass, 1993a.

Arnold, K. D. "The Fulfillment of Promise: Minority High School Valedictorians." *The Review of Higher Education*, 1993b, *16*(3), 257–283.

Arnold, K. D. "Undergraduate Aspirations and Career Outcomes of Academically Talented Women: A Discriminant Analysis." *Roeper Review*, 1993c, *15*(3), 169–175.

Arnold, K. D. "The Illinois Valedictorian Project: Early Adult Careers of Academically Talented Male High School Students." In R. F. Subotnik and K. D. Arnold (eds.), *Beyond Terman: Contemporary Longitudinal Studies of Giftedness and Talent*. Norwood, N.J.: Ablex, 1994.

Arnold, K. D., and Denny, T. "Academic Achievement: A View from the Top." Paper presented at the annual meeting of the American Educational Research Association, New Orleans, Apr. 1984.

Astin, A. W. *What Matters in College? Four Critical Years Revisited.* San Francisco, Calif.: Jossey-Bass, 1992.

Astin, A. W., Green, K. D., and Korn, W. S. *The American Freshman: Twenty-Year Trends.* Los Angeles: Cooperative Institutional Research Program, University of California, 1987.

Astin, H. S. "The Meaning of Work in Women's Lives: A Sociopsychological Model of Career Choice and Work Behavior." *Counseling Psychologist,* 1984, *12*(4), 117–126.

Bachman, J. G., Johnston, L. D., and O'Malley, P. M. *Monitoring the Future: Questionnaire Responses from the Nation's High School Seniors.* Ann Arbor: Institute for Social Research, University of Michigan, 1981.

Betz, N. E., and Fitzgerald, L. F. *The Career Psychology of Women.* San Diego, Calif.: Academic Press, 1987.

Bierce, A. *The Devil's Dictionary.* New York: World Publishing, 1941. (Originally published 1911).

Blau, F. D., and Winkler, A. E. "Women in the Labor Force: An Overview." In J. Freeman (ed.), *Women: A Feminist Perspective.* Mountain View, Calif.: Mayfield, 1989.

Bloom, B. S. (ed.). *Developing Talent in Young People.* New York: Ballantine, 1985.

Bloom, B. S., and Sosniak, L. A. "Talent Development vs. Schooling." *Educational Leadership,* 1981, *38,* 86–94.

Boyer, E. L. *Scholarship Revisited: Priorities of the Professoriate.* Princeton, N.J.: Carnegie Foundation for the Advancement of Teaching, 1990.

"Carnegie Survey of Undergraduates." *Chronicle of Higher Education,* Feb. 5, 1984, pp. 27–30.

Chase, S. E. *Ambiguous Empowerment: The Work Narratives of Women School Superintendents.* Amherst, Mass.: University of Massachusetts Press, 1995.

Chickering, A. W., and Reisser, L. *Education and Identity.* (2nd ed.) San Francisco, Calif.: Jossey-Bass, 1993.

Crosby, F. J. *Spouse, Parent, Worker: On Gender and Multiple Roles.* New Haven, Conn.: Yale University Press, 1987.

Current Population Reports: Marital Status and Living Arrangements. (PO20–468). Washington, D.C.: U.S. Department of Commerce, March 1992.

Dewey, J. "Human Nature and Conduct." In J. A. Boydston (ed.), *John Dewey: The Middle Works, 1899–1924.* Carbondale: Southern Illinois University Press, 1983. (Originally published 1922.)

DSM-IV. (*Diagnostic and Statistical Manual of Mental Disorders,* 4th ed.) Washington, D.C.: American Psychiatric Association, 1994.

Educational Testing Service. *Performance at the Top: From Elementary Through*

Graduate School. Princeton, N.J.: Educational Testing Service Policy Information Center, 1991.

Eliot, G. *Middlemarch: Norton Critical Edition.* New York: W. W. Norton, 1977. (Originally published 1871–1872)

Erikson, E. *Identity and the Life Cycle.* Madison, Conn.: International Universities Press, 1959.

Erikson, E. H. *Identity, Youth, and Crisis.* New York: W.W. Norton, 1968.

Feldman, D. H. *Nature's Gambit.* New York: Basic Books, 1986.

Freeman, J. "How to Discriminate Against Women Without Really Trying." In J. Freeman (ed.), *Women: A Feminist Perspective.* Mountain View, Calif.: Mayfield, 1975.

Gardner, H. *Frames of Mind: The Theory of Multiple Intelligences.* New York: Basic Books, 1983.

Goertzel, M. G., Goertzel, V., and Goertzel, T. G. *Three Hundred Eminent Personalities: A Psychosocial Analysis of the Famous.* San Francisco, Calif.: Jossey-Bass, 1978.

Gottfredson, L. S. "Circumscription and Compromise: A Developmental Theory of Occupational Aspirations." *Journal of Counseling Psychology Monograph,* 1981, *28*(5), 545–579.

Hafner, A. L. "Gender Differences in College Students' Educational and Occupational Aspirations: 1971–1983." Paper presented at the annual meeting of the American Educational Research Association, Chicago, Apr. 1985.

Hastings, P. K., and Hoge, D. R. "Religious Trends Among College Students, 1948–1979." *Social Forces,* 1981, *60*(2), 517–531.

Helmreich, R. L., Spence, J. T., and Wilhelm, J. A. "A Psychometric Analysis of the Personal Attributes Questionnaire." *Sex Roles,* 1981, *20*(4), 1097–1107.

Holland, J. L. *Making Vocational Choices: A Theory of Vocational Personalities and Work Environments.* (2nd ed.) Englewood Cliffs, N.J.: Prentice Hall, 1985.

Hollingshead, A. B. *Two Factor Index of Social Position.* New Haven, Conn.: Author, 1957.

Hulbert, K. D. "Gender Patterns in Faculty-Student Mentoring Relationships." In S. M. Deats and L. T. Lenker (eds.), *Gender and Academe: Feminist Pedagogy and Politics.* Lanham, Md.: Rowman & Littlefield, 1994.

Katchadourian, H. A., and Boli, J. *Careerism and Intellectualism Among College Students: Patterns of Academic and Career Choice in the Undergraduate Years.* San Francisco, Calif.: Jossey-Bass, 1985.

Katchadourian, H. A., and Boli, J. *Cream of the Crop: The Impact of Elite Education in the Decade After College.* New York: Basic Books, 1994.

Kemp, A. A. *Women's Work*. Englewood Cliffs, N.J.: Prentice Hall, 1994.

Kobasa, S. C. "Stressful Events, Personality, and Health: An Inquiry into Hardiness." *Journal of Personal and Social Psychology*, 1979, *37*, 1–11.

Lazarus, R. S., and Folkman, S. "The Concept of Coping." In A. Monat and R. S. Lazarus (eds.), *Stress and Coping: An Anthology*. (3rd ed.) New York: Columbia University Press, 1991.

Levine, A. *When Dreams and Heroes Died: A Portrait of Today's College Student*. San Francisco, Calif.: Jossey-Bass, 1980.

Levinson, D. J. *The Seasons of a Man's Life*. New York: Knopf, 1978.

Lincoln, Y. S., and Guba, E. G. *Naturalistic Inquiry*. Newbury Park, Calif.: Sage, 1985.

Lubinski, D., and Benbow, C. P. "The Study of Mathematically Precocious Youth: The First Three Decades of a Planned 50-Year Study of Intellectual Talent." In R. F. Subotnik and K. D. Arnold (eds.), *Beyond Terman: Contemporary Longitudinal Studies of Giftedness and Talent*. Norwood, N.J.: Ablex, 1994.

Maddi, S. R., and Kobasa, S. D. *The Hardy Executive: Health Under Stress*. Homewood, Ill.: Business One Irwin, 1984.

Marcia, J. "Development and Validation of Ego-Identity Status." *Journal of Personality and Social Psychology*, 1966, *3*, 551–559.

Markus, H., and Nurius. P. "Possible Selves." *American Psychologist*, 1986, *41*, 954–968.

May, R. *Man's Search for Himself*. New York: Dell, 1953.

Ochse, R. *Before the Gates of Excellence: The Determinants of Creative Genius*. New York: Cambridge University Press, 1990.

Oden, M. S. "The Fulfillment of Promise: 40-Year Follow-up of the Terman Gifted Group." *Genetic Psychology Monographs*, 1968, *77*, 3–93.

Osipow, S. H. *Theories of Career Development*. (2nd ed.) Englewood Cliffs, N.J.: Prentice Hall, 1973.

Patton, M. Q. *Qualitative Evaluation Methods*. Newbury Park, Calif.: Sage, 1980.

Perleth, C., and Heller, K. A. "The Munich Longitudinal Study of Giftedness." In R. F. Subotnik and K. D. Arnold (eds.), *Beyond Terman: Contemporary Longitudinal Studies of Giftedness and Talent*. Norwood, N.J.: Ablex, 1994.

Perry, W. G., Jr. "Sharing in the Costs of Growth." In C. A. Parker (eds.), *Encouraging Development in College Students*. Minneapolis, Minn.: University of Minnesota Press, 1978.

Polanyi, M. *Personal Knowledge: Towards a Post-critical Philosophy*. New York: HarperCollins, 1966.

Renzulli, J. S. "The Three-Ring Conception of Giftedness: A Developmental Model for Creative Productivity." In R. J. Sternberg and J. E. Davidson (eds.), *Conceptions of Giftedness*. New York: Cambridge University Press, 1986.

Rosenberg, M. *Occupations and Values*. New York: Free Press, 1957.

Rosser, P. *Sex Bias in College Admissions Tests: Why Women Lose Out*. Cambridge, Mass.: National Center for Fair and Open Testing, 1989.

Rothman, S. M., and Marks, E. M. "Adjusting Work and Family Life: Flexible Work Schedules and Family Policy." In N. Gerstel and H. E. Gross (eds.), *Families and Work*. Philadelphia: Temple University Press, 1987.

"The Secrets of Success." *The Black Collegian*, 1988, *18*, 100–102.

Spence, J. T., and Helmreich, R. L. *Masculinity and Femininity: Their Psychological Dimensions, Correlates, and Antecedents*. Austin: University of Texas Press, 1978.

Spence, J. T., Helmreich, R. L., and Stapp, J. "The Personal Attributes Questionnaire: A Measure of Sex-Role Stereotypes and Masculinity-Femininity." *JSAS Catalog of Selected Documents in Psychology*, 1974, *4*(43).

Spitze, G. "The Data on Women's Labor Force Participation." In A. Stromberg and S. Harkess (eds.), *Women Working*. Mountain View, Calif.: Mayfield, 1988.

Spradley, J. *The Ethnographic Interview*. Troy, Mo.: Holt, Rinehart & Winston, 1979.

Statistical Abstract of the United States: 1993. Washington, D.C.: U.S. Department of Commerce, 1993.

Steinem, G. *Revolution from Within: A Book of Self-Esteem*. Boston: Little, Brown, 1992.

Sternberg, R. J. *Beyond IQ: A Triarchic Theory of Human Intelligence*. New York: Cambridge University Press, 1985.

Stevenson, H. W., and Stigler, J. W. *The Learning Gap*. New York: Basic Books, 1992.

Strauss, A. *Qualitative Analysis for Social Scientists*. New York: Cambridge University Press, 1987.

Strauss, A., and Corbin, J. *Basics of Grounded Theory Methods*. Newbury Park, Calif.: Sage, 1990.

Subotnik, R. F., and Arnold, K. D. (eds.). *Beyond Terman: Contemporary Longitudinal Studies of Giftedness and Talent*. Norwood, N.J.: Ablex, 1994.

Super, D. E. "A Life-Span, Life-Space Approach to Career Development." *Journal of Vocational Behavior*, 1980, *16*, 282–298.

Terman, L. M. *Genetic Studies of Genius*. Vol. 1: *Mental and Physical Traits of a Thousand Gifted Children*. Stanford, Calif.: Stanford University Press, 1925.

Terman, L. M., and Oden, M. H. *Genetic Studies of Genius*. Vol. 4: *The Gifted Child Grows Up: 25 Years' Follow-up of a Superior Group*. Stanford, Calif.: Stanford University Press, 1947.

Terman, L. M., and Oden, M. H. *Genetic Studies of Genius*. Vol. 5: *The Gifted Group at Mid-Life: 35 Years' Follow-up of the Superior Child*. Stanford, Calif.: Stanford University Press, 1959.

Tinto, V. *Leaving College: Rethinking the Causes and Cures of Student Attrition*. (2nd ed.) Chicago: University of Chicago Press, 1993.

Vaillant, G. E. *Adaptation to Life*. Boston: Little, Brown, 1977.

Wagner, R. K., and Sternberg, R. J. "Tacit Knowledge and Intelligence in the Everyday World." In R. J. Sternberg and R. K. Wagner (eds.), *Practical Intelligence: Nature and Origins of Competence in the Everyday World*. New York: Cambridge University Press, 1986.

Warnath, C. "Vocational Theories: Direction to Nowhere." *Personnel and Guidance Journal*, 1975, *53*(6), 422–428.

Weiner, B. "History of Motivational Research in Education." *Journal of Educational Psychology*, 1990, *82*, 616–622.

Index